THE SCOTTISH DOG

Also published by AUP

THE SCOTTISH CAT
edited by Hamish Whyte

GLIMMER OF COLD BRINE
a Scottish Sea Anthology
eds Alistair Lawrie, Hellen Matthews and Douglas Ritchie

HAMISH BROWN'S SCOTLAND
Hamish Brown

MIDGES IN SCOTLAND
George Hendry

SCOTLAND'S GOLF COURSES
Robert Price

THE WATERFALLS OF SCOTLAND
Louis Stott

THE SCOTTISH DOG

edited by

Joyce and Maurice Lindsay

ABERDEEN UNIVERSITY PRESS
Member of Maxwell Macmillan Pergamon Corporation

First published in 1989
Aberdeen University Press

© Joyce and Maurice Lindsay

British Library Cataloguing in Publication Data
The Scottish Dog: an anthology.
  1. English literature. Scottish writers. Special subjects:
Dogs—Anthologies
I. Lindsay, Joyce II. Lindsay, Maurice, *1918–*
8208'036

ISBN 0–08–037738–6
ISBN 0–08–037739–4 pbk

PRINTED IN GREAT BRITAIN
THE ABERDEEN UNIVERSITY PRESS
ABERDEEN

CONTENTS

WORKING DOGS   **43**

DOMESTIC DOGS   **74**

ILLUSTRATIONS

ACKNOWLEDGEMENTS

To Alan Bold and Richard Price for providing us with new poems, our thanks. To Iain Crichton Smith, for so readily agreeing to produce an English version of a Gaelic poem by Duncan Ban Macintyre. To Dr George Bruce, our thanks not only for a new poem, but for his prose reminiscences of Spicey, his fine photograph of Fraserburgh harbour *circa* 1905, and for drawing our attention to the R L Stevenson contributions. To Dr Douglas Mack for bringing the contributions of James Hogg to our notice and Frances Walker for numerous suggestions from the literature of childhood. To Fred Urquhart, for providing an abridged version of an incident from his novel *The Palace of Green Days*. To W Simpson of the National Library of Scotland, for suggestions, and to the staff of the Mitchell Library, Glasgow (in particular, Mr Joe Fisher of the Glasgow Room) for help in many ways. To Mrs Marjorie Lingen-Hutton, the owner of copyright for Violet Jacob's work, for permission to publish 'The Yellow Dog'. A tribute must also be paid to Hamish Whyte, whose excellent companion anthology *The Scottish Cat* invited cat-and-dog comparisons where appropriate, particularly in the proverbial and heraldic departments.

We would also like to thank Mrs Wilma Bryce for her typing help. Those who have facilitated the use of copyright material, whether literary or visual, are detailed respectively in an Index at the back of the book or in the text. Our especial thanks, however, go to our friend Morven Cameron, sixteen of whose illustrations were drawn especially to enhance these pages.

INTRODUCTION

I

'Thank God For Dogs,' the widowed Sir Edward Elgar once exclaimed in old age. It is a sentiment that many of us, in less tragic circumstances, must often have echoed, thankful for the friendship and loyalty of a dog that neither criticises nor judges. 'Depend upon it,' Sir Walter Scott remarked, 'if people would speak slowly and with emphasis to their dogs they would understand a great deal more than one gives them credit for.' Perhaps so. Our present companion has no difficulty whatever in making his views and his wishes known.

I have had dogs about me all my life. In my father's house in Glasgow when I was in my teens, a member of the household was Jock, a mongrel that was peculiarly my elder sister's care. During the summer holidays at Innellan, Jock passed under the curious gaze of old MacDiarmid, a former coachman who, then in his eighties, ran a primitive fleet of canvas-topped char-a-bancs that plied between Dunoon and Toward. He still dressed in age-greened coachman's habit and sat inside a protective box—the upper part of which opened—built into the outer walls of his former stables, so that he could check the operational punctuality of his new-fangled fleet of vehicles. Coaching had earned him his living, dog-fancying had fired his life-long enthusiasm. 'Whit kin o a dug's that?' he one day enquired of my sister, fixing Jock with a puzzled, disapproving stare. 'An Irish Cairn,' said my sister promptly, unwilling to compromise the reputation of so dominant a member of our family. 'Ahve nevver heard o thon kin o a dug before,' said old MacDiarmid, tipping his cap forward and scratching the back of his head.

Jock was followed by Nitwit, a mongrel labradorish bitch, that travelled about with me during my army days in England from 1939 until I went to the Staff College at Camberley in 1943, where dogs were not allowed. She finished the War out at Innellan, that one-time paradise of childhood, on the Firth of Clyde, where my father maintained a rented holiday home. During the earlier War years I was frequently billeted in English country houses, but sometimes in farms or, for brief periods, under canvas. Nitwit became a great ratter, her most welcome triumph being the rapid execution by tossing of three of the creatures that had the temerity to run across my camp bed set up in the barn of a Northumberland farmhouse when I was asleep on it.

Not long after we were married, at the end of the War, my wife and I lost no time in introducing dogs to our own newly established household; the dachshunds Blotto and Bunkum, their facetious nicknames devised out of kennel-registered nomenclature representing vintage champagnes. The dachshunds accompanied us in the move from a Glasgow flat to our first home in the country, at Gartocharn, near Loch Lomondside. Blotto was also an enemy of the rat population. To protect ourselves against the unwanted domestic companionship of man's oldest earthly neighbour, we had on one occasion put down rat poison. One large tough rat had eaten the poison, but instead of dying according to the instructions on the label, had somehow managed to crawl under the floor of my study before expiring close to the warmth of the hearth. The origins of the smell that ensued proved difficult to discover, until a prancing Blotto suggested to the man seeking to rid us of the trouble that it might be a good idea to pull up the floorboards.

Dachshunds, unfortunately, suffer in old age from a kind of ossification of the spine. When Blotto and Bunkum left us, both suffering from this painful ailment, we turnd to bassethounds, which somehow manage to combine a similar long-dog appearance of comedy with a remarkably dignified mien. The way to discipline a bassethound, it has been said, is to find out what it wants to do and then ask it to do it. Though originally bred by the French to hunt hares, they like to take their own time about everything else.

Hector, our first basset, became the subject of Edwin Morgan's poem 'An Addition to the Family' and my own 'The Ballad of the Hare and the Bassethound'. The facts in my poem are true. Morgan's facts, gleaned from my old friend George Bruce, are not quite accurate in one respect. While I had declared an affection for the melancholy sound of the basset horn, that lugubriously long-eared member of the clarinet family, I never actually played the instrument, merely collecting its performances on gramophone records.

Hector's companion, Peter, turned out to be a deft tosser-up of hens, arousing the suspicions of local farmers. To avoid discovery and possible summary execution, Peter was despatched to a new home in henless country. There, his new owners discovered that he possessed champion qualities, so he spent his life in exile happily fathering future little prize-winning bassethounds. Toby, our third, and last basset, had a weakness for bitches and at an age when, possibly, he ought to have known better, got himself killed on a busy road in pursuit of one.

His chum for several years had been a friendly black mongrel with hair falling over his eyes and, consequently, permanently obstructed vision. One foggy Christmas Eve in the West End of Glasgow, Woozy attached himself to our youngest daughter while she was taking Toby for his late-night walk. Fed, watered and rested, the black mongrel was next morning returned to the spot from which he had emerged out of the fog, in the hope that he would recover his homing sense of direction. A few hours later, there he was, back on our doormat, obviously determined to adopt himself. In due course, with police approval, his persistence paid off. He gave us a happy seven years. His death from cancer, eagerly game almost to the last, brought deep sadness to us all. He is commemorated in my poem 'Mongrel'.

Siegfreid, our present companion, was reputedly a cross between an alsatian and a collie. He was named not, as some have supposed after the television veterinary surgeon, but after the Wagnerian hero, in the belief that he would mature to the size of one or other of his progenitors. This he has failed to do. Swimming is his passion, as it was, too, of his companion for over two years, Leon, a brindled Bouvier de Flandres. Leon, a trifle thick-headed but an eminently lovable big fellow, was owned by our youngest daughter. A year or so after she acquired him she decided to move to America, so Leon made his home with us while she was settling down. In due course he was summoned to rejoin his mistress in America, travelling with me over the first lap of the long journey in a first class railway carriage to London so that when lying down he would not inconvenience too many passengers, and thereafter flying to the United States in a comfortable cage. My wife and I flew out a fortnight later, by more orthodox means.

In Texas, his new home, dogs, it seems, are liable to a disease called heartworm, which often proves fatal, but against which immunisation can be secured by taking regularly a protective pill. On his arrival in America Leon was at once put onto this heartworm pill. A week after our arrival, while out for a run with his mistress and his substitute owner for two years, doing what he enjoyed best—racing across rough ground and exulting in his natural strength—to our distress he dropped dead of a heart attack. His was another dog-loss I mourned. His place in America has now been taken by Booker (pronounced, not as in the name of the literary prize but in the French manner, with a drawling accent on the last syllable), another handsome Bouvier who does not, however, come into our personal dog story.

II

Whether the horse or the dog is a Scot's oldest companion is perhaps a moot point. As Desmond Morris recently reminded us in a television programme 'The Wolf in the Living Room', the dog is directly descended from the wolf, a creature not always the friend of man. This anthology begins with a charming little mythological tale of the decision of the wolf to come in from the cold and befriend man, by George Mackay Brown. Wolves thereafter flit through the imaginations of two twentieth-century writers, the Gaelic poet Sorley McLean and John Burnside, a representative of the younger generation of poets.

We look, first of all, into the nursery, where children fortunate enough to be brought up with a resident dog learn early to get on good terms with Western man's best friend—the horse long since having been superseded in that role by the motor car, except perhaps among equestrian sportsmen and hill-country farmers. In this section, too, there are artless word-jingles in English and in Scots and even a nineteenth-century translation from Alexander Carmichael's *Carmina Gadelica* (the Songs of the Gael). Those laureates of the nursery, William Soutar and J K Annand, provide a link with the more fully articulated dog-humour which might very well circulate among older youngsters. Here, we range from a Glasgow street ballad, 'The Chip Shop', about a dog who stole a haddie, through George Bruce's prose boyhood recollections of the remarkable determined single-mindedness of Spicey a cross between a Cairn and a Skye terrier; from 'The Ballad of the Hare and the Bassethound' to the wit of Allan Ramsay's 'Tykes' and so back to David Steven and Liz Lochhead in our own day.

Next follows a section devoted to the Allegorical Dog and the dogs of Heraldry. Somewhere amidst the dim myths of Gaelic Scotland ran Finn's own dog, Bran, and a series of grey or black dogs, usually fierce and almost certainly wolf hounds. They form part of the accoutrement of legendary heroes, much as bellying hounds make their fleeting accompanying appearances at the heels of unlucky knights in the world of balladry; appearances too fleeting, however, to justify much inclusion in this anthology. We have therefore contented ourselves with the ghostly sounds of phantom hunters and their dogs as recorded by the anonymous early eighteenth century author of *Albania*, and by a similarly fatal pack that charge through Sir Walter Scott's exciting early ballad, 'The Wild Huntsman'.

Dogs supposedly conversing with each other were used as an allegorical device in late mediaeval times when a writer wanted to lodge a complaint with the king or queen, but knew that to do so directly might prove dangerous. The two poems by William Dunbar and Sir

David Lyndsay of the Mount both illustrate the use of this literary device. Since this is an anthology for the general reader rather than for the specialist in Scottish literature, I have to some degree modernised the spelling in both these early pieces and abbreviated the Lyndsay poem. To a lesser extent I have done this also in 'The Last Dying Words of Bonnie Heck' by William Hamilton of Gilbertfield, near Cambuslang, Glasgow.

Lyndsay, a copy of whose works Sir Walter Scott said once lay alongside the Bible in every peasant's home in pre-Burnsian Scotland, was both a much better poet than he is generally credited with being and a man of considerable literary influence. Leaving aside that veritable corner-stone of Scottish drama, 'Ane Satyre of the Thrie Estates', with which we are not here concerned, it is perhaps worth noting that he was the first writer known to have used (in some of the comic speeches in his great morality play) that troubadours' stanza-form now known in Scotland as 'Standard Habbie' and later strongly associated with Burns. Burns probably knew about Bagsche and his troubles, for his own poem 'The Twa Dugs', in which a town and country animal debate the manners of their respective masters, clearly adopts Lyndsay's idea to suit contemporary eighteenth-century social purpose. It is included here in its entirety.

If one looks for the starting-point of the nineteenth- and early twentieth-century kailyaird movement, as good a place as any, would probably be Burns' 'The Cottar's Saturday Night', particularly the stanza:

> At length his lonely cot appears in view,
> Beneath the shelter of an aged tree;
> The expectant wee-things, toddlin, stacher through
> To meet their Dad, wi' flichterin noise an' glee.
> His wee bit ingle—blinking bonnily.
> His clean hearthstane, his thriftie wifie's smile,
> The lisping infant, prattling on his knee,
> Does a' his weary carking cares beguile,
> An' make him quite forget his labour and his toil.

In such a domestic context, many a field-worn dog stretched himself out gratefully in front of a kailyaird farmhouse fireside. Many a hound, too, exhausted by the chase, slept in front of the log-fire in the ducal hall, or relaxed on warm straw in aristocratic stables. Several kailyaird dogs are featured in these pages, notably those of Hilton Brown and W D Cocker.

The Greyfriars Bobby story, though touching, usually invites re-telling in dreadful kailyaird prose of quite sickening sentimentality. We have therefore settled for two quotations from Forbes MacGregor's piece of investigative journalism into the truth about Greyfriars Bobby, originally published in *The Scots Magazine* in 1988.

Inevitably, our two longest sections deal with *The Working Dog* and *Dog Portraits*. We have defined work in the doggie context as any activity for which the dog has been specially trained, whether about the farm or in the hunting field. In their different styles, Robert Louis Stevenson's boyhood memories of the oldest shepherd in the Pentlands and Alexander Smith's account of the otter hunt he experienced in Skye during a summer in the mid 1850s are particularly vivid pieces of writing.

The *Dog Portraits* focus attention on the characteristics of particular breeds or individual dogs, whether seen collectively, in 'At Crufts' by George Macbeth; as a contrasting duo minutely observed by John Davidson; or lovingly described individually by that nineteenth-century dog-loving medico, Dr John Brown of Edinburgh.

Stevenson appears as a dog lover with reservations in *The Literary Dog* section, along with James Hogg, the Ettrick Shepherd, Thomas and Jane Carlyle, and of course, the most great hearted of them all, Sir Walter Scott.

We invited a number of contemporary Scottish poets, many of them friends, to produce a dog poem or two from their portfolios. To our surprise, several of them turned out to be catophiles, but George Bruce and Alan Bold obliged, while Norman McCaig assured us that only the fact that he lived in an Edinburgh flat had kept him from being a dog owner. Two of his dog poems are included in the *Dogs Remembered* section along with those of my own already referred to, George Bruce's 'Lost', a poem by Alan Bold, a curious poem by the Marquis of Montrose— is it really an honour to be stabbed from behind by a noble who has lost his temper?—a prose elegy by David Stephens and Byron's savagely unforgettable lines on his Newfoundland dog.

Dogs are little affected by the politics of nationalism. We therefore hope that this anthology may give pleasure not only to Scottish dog owners but to those who love dogs everywhere.

MAURICE LINDSAY

PROLOGUE

WOLF—A PROSE POEM

And the wolf roamed here and there through the
great forest that covered the land.

The wolf left tracks in the snow.

The wolf lingered beside a river. The throat of
the wolf was cold with the water that flowed on and on,
singing, from the mountains down to the great water,
the sea. That water in the west was bitter. The wolf
spat it out. But when he wanted to get to another
island, the wolf swam, and he delighted in the cold
surge that all but covered his head, but he could see
through the washed prisms of his eyes the island. The
wolf stood on the shore of the island and shook the sea
from his coat in thrilling showers.

Once the wolf came out of the forest, and he saw
where the river met the sea that a ship had been drawn
up on the beach and a score of men were building huts.
Others cut down the trees with axes. And they dressed
the trunks, and carried them to set into the walls of
a hut.

Already there was a clearing in the forest.

A spasm of fear went through the wolf, for the
first time. These were creatures he would have to keep
an eye on. They were very clever. The thought had
hardly passed through his mind when a slim wooden bird
flashed past him, thrumming and lodged in the next
tree: biting deep into it, and quivering there, just
beside his hesitant paw, an arrow.

The wolf turned and fled for the first time.

Soon men were everywhere. The ships came crowding
out of the east. The little wooden villages were built
at the estuaries, or higher up the river. The great
trees fell, in hundreds and thousands and tens of
thousands. The ground was cleared. Black forests
became green tilth, green pasture. Oxen dragged ploughs,
sheep grazed on the pleasant hillsides.

The axes of the men flashed and bit deeper and deeper into the forest.

Little market villages were built where once the wolf had roamed in perfect freedom and peace and joy.

Now only the wildest places of the land were left to him. He felt like a creature cornered and doomed.

Occasionally he flashed out of the lessening forest and seized a few sheep (new delicious prey, the flesh tender and the blood warm and sweet.)

One evening, when the elders of a tribe were sitting round an open-air fire, the wolf appeared at the edge of the shifting flame-shadows.

The men lifted their spears.

The wolf said, 'I have come to be your servant. I will do what you tell me. I will keep your flocks. I will guard your doors against the night raids of that other tribe across the firth. I will be a good friend to you for ever.'

The chief held out his hand.

And the great smoking tongue of the wolf curled about his fingers: the kiss of peace.

GEORGE MACKAY BROWN

NURSERY DOGS

Children brought up with dogs from a very early age not only do not fear them, but often carry into adult life an empathy with the animal kingdom which, in one sense, we share. Nursery rhymes from two twentieth-century collections are included in this section, along with George Bruce's recollections of Spicey, the dog in his boyhood, two poems by that supreme master of the Scots Bairnsang, William Soutar, two by J K Annand and an amusing plea from a dogless child to his father by a Kirkintilloch schoolmaster, Bill Keys.

MA BONNIE DOGGIE

O he's ma bonnie doggie.
Denty O!
And O, he's ma bonnie doggie,
Denty O!
I widna gie ma bonnie doggie
For a wedder hoggie,
Although I had ma choice o
Twenty O.

(Aberdeen)

I HAD A WEE DOG

I had a wee dog,
It's name was Duff;
I sent him oot
For a box o snuff.

He brak the box,
And skailed the snuff,
And that was a
Ma penny worth.

DOG IN THE MIDDEN

The dog in the midden
He lay, he lay;
The dog in the midden
He lay, he lay.

He lookit abeen him,
And saw the meen sheenin,
And cockit his tail,
And away, away.

                          (Aberdeen)

THE DOG

Dee do
said the white dog
Dee do
said the white dog
Dee do
Often were we
from night time till day
happy and snug
said the white dog.

PAIKS FOR A'

The mouse lowp't oot o' the girnel
And the cat gaed eftir the mouse;
The dug cam in with a breengie bowff
And clear'd the cat frae the house.

The dug was kick't be the maister;
And afore the day was owre
A haik cam crack on the maister's back
And gied him a fearfu' clout.

WILLIAM SOUTAR

BAIRNS' PLAY

I doot, I doot,
Ma fire is out,
An ma little dog's no at hame;
I'll saddle ma cat, an I'll bridle ma dog,
An send ma little dog hame,
Hame, hame again, hame.

WILLIAM SOUTAR

ROON, ROON, ROSIE

Roon, roon, rosie,
Cuppie, cuppie, shell,
The dog's awa tae Hamilton
Tae buy a new bell;
If ye don't take it
I'll tak it masel;
Roon, roon, rosie,
Cuppie, cuppie, shell.

WILLIAM SOUTAR

THE DOGGIES

The doggies gaed tae the mill,
This wey an that wey:
They took a lick oot o this wife's poke,
An they took a lick oot o that wife's poke,
An a loup in the laid, an a dip in the dam,
An gaed wallopin, wallopin, wallopin hame.

LITTLE DOGGIES

Sanny Coutts' little doggies, little doggies,
    little doggies,
Sanny Coutts' little doggies
Lickit Sanny's mou, man.
Sanny ran aboot the stack,
An a's doggies at's back,
An ilka doggie gied a bark,
An Sanny ran awa, man.

THE LIFE AND DEATH OF SPICEY

Like everyone's dog Spicey was a remarkable dog—a cross between a Skye terrier and a Cairn—only more remarkable than any other dog in Fraserburgh in the late and early 1930s. He was well known about the town on account of his independent mind. Once, after accompanying my mother to Macdonald the Grocer's, he stayed on in the shop. He left on his own the next day, but did not return to our house for about three months. Mr Macdonald lived in King Edward Street. In the morning we could see our dog, Spicey, passing our house in the company of Mr Macdonald on his way to his shop. In the evening we could see Spicey returning to Mr Macdonald's home. We never asked any questions of Spicey since he was an adult dog and, if he preferred Mr Macdonald's company and food, that was his business. Then one evening, as Spicey passed our gate, he broke away from Mr Macdonald and came back to us. We pondered the reason. It could not have been the food! Ultimately, we agreed he must have become bored with the company. There were only Mr and Mrs Macdonald in the house and they were not great conversationalists.

Spicey and funerals

Spicey attended all the funerals that went past our house; and they were many, for Victoria Street was on the way to the cemetery one mile or so out the South Road. His habit began at a very important funeral—black horses, plumes and all the best paraphernalia. My father was one of the mourners and in the second row behind the hearse, Spicey tagged on to my father, who indicated his displeasure and shooed him away. Spicey obeyed, but only to the extent of following the heels of the last row of mourners. After that, he felt obliged to attend every funeral that passed our gate. My father approved of this, especially when he did not attend a funeral which for formal reasons perhaps he should have attended— representing the firm for instance. He said he could imagine one of the mourners saying, 'Mr Bruce did not attend the funeral of so-and-so', while another would say, 'No, but his dog did.' So we had a representative.

Spicey and the Picture House

Every Friday the family went to the cinema. Naturally, Spicey went too. We generally sat four or five rows from the back of the stalls. The usher put down a seat for Spicey (which was not paid for), but Spicey liked good value for money and stayed the whole two rounds of the programme, we having gone home at the end of one. He seemed to sleep the entire time, though I was told that when Rin-tin-tin appeared on the screen he barked a response to his canine kind. I heard this some time after the event, for I was not present, nor were the family for we had given up the habit. Not Spicey though. Every Friday at about 6.30 p.m. he made his way to the Picture House. The door was opened for him, the same seat put down, and there he was till *God Save the King*: and all was right and proper until a careless woman sat on him and he squealed. He was so offended he never returned to the cinema.

5   Fishing scene, Fraserburgh *c.* 1905.

Spicey and football

Most Saturdays my father, my brother, Spicey and I went to the Belleslea Park to watch Fraserburgh beat Peterhead or Forres Mechanics or Elgin or Inverness Caley, which they did not always do. Spicey did not always watch beside us. He took a liking to Fraserburgh's centre forward, and would sit by the tunnel leading from the dressing rooms under the grandstand, until he appeared with the team. Then he would run out on to the pitch and sit near the centre of the field. When the players moved into position he generally returned to the side-lines.

On one occasion the visiting team was delayed in arriving and in deference to their opponents Fraserburgh did not take the field until immediately before kick-off, going straight to their positions. Spicey sat down at the centre spot. The game was a cup-tie between Fraserburgh and Peterhead and the most famous referee in Scotland (so we believed) was engaged—Mr Peter Craigmyle, who ran with such speed to the centre that Spicey was still there on the referee's arrival. Mr Craigmyle said 'Shoo', or something like it, to the dog. The dog moved a few yards and sat down. Mr Craigmyle shooed it again with the same result, and so on all the way to the touch-line. Then Mr Craigmyle strode splendidly back—and he was splendid in his importance—to the centre of the field followed at his heels by Spicey, to wild applause and laughter, louder and louder, as Mr Craigmyle never for a moment looked behind him, for *he* could not have been the cause of mirth. But there at the centre-spot sat Spicey. His friend, the centre forward, carried him off the pitch. We, the family, got credit from this encounter. We did not approve of self-importance in Fraserburgh, not even in an international referee.

Unfortunately, all this good in public-relations was undone when Buckie Thistle played Fraserburgh in a cup-tie. Spicey, unusually, had taken up his position at one side of the Buckie Thistle goal and my father at the other side. The ball seemed to be far away from the Thistle goal when suddenly Spicey's friend, the centre forward had the ball at his feet and cunningly directed it just inside the post, well away from the goalkeeper, at Spicey's side who at that moment had taken it into his head to visit my father by crossing on the goal line. The ball hit the rotund, comfortable figure of Spicey, and slipped past the outside of the post. There had been no scoring. All hell broke loose. Oaths, gestures, though (oddly) not kicks were aimed at the traitor dog. All would have been well had he interposed his body at the other end of the pitch. My father laughed outrageously, and dangerously. 'He might have been murdered,' a fisherman said to me later. Spicey never returned to the Belleslea Park.

Spicey and independence in Aberdeen

The family took a flat in Aberdeen near Holburn Junction. We arrived in Aberdeen in the morning. On arrival, Spicey disappeared and did not return till evening. He had been seen in Cults some four miles away. He was, as it were, mapping the place. Shortly after our arrival I looked out on to the Junction, and saw the dog at the centre of the Junction at the policeman's feet, as he was conducting the traffic. Generally he was there until the end of the policeman's roster, though I witnessed the bobby on occasion holding up the traffic to conduct the dog safely to the pavement. It was inevitable that Spicey formed friendships with the shopkeepers of the area, though clandestinely. We were not in on this, as my mother discovered when she went to the tobacconist on behalf of my father. To her surprise there was the dog on a stool, usually used by the owner to reach the higher shelves. She looked at the dog. The dog looked at her, and cut her dead. The tobacconist said: 'A nice wee doggie. He comes to see me every day. I don't know where he's from.' My mother showed no interest. Likewise, she showed no interest when she met Spicey coming out of the butchers with a chop in his mouth.

The death of Spicey

After breakfast it became Spicey's custom to accompany my father to the office. There he would stretch himself out in front of the fire, sleep away part of the morning returning home for his mid-day meal. My father's business took him to other parts of the country, so he was not always regular in his walk to the office.

One morning my mother had a phone call from Andrew, the junior clerk. He had very bad news. There had been an accident. Spicey had been run over by a motor bicycle. Andrew thought he was dead. 'Wrap him in something warm,' my mother had said, 'and bring him home.' Shortly, she saw Andrew carrying a bundle towards our house. 'If Spicey's tail points up,' she said to herself, 'Spicey is alive. If it is down, he is dead.' Not until she ran out to meet Andrew could she determine Spicey's condition. His tail pointed up. Gently, Andrew lowered the dog to the ground. Spicey wandered off down the street back towards the office. It was not yet dinner time.

After some five years in Aberdeen the family went its several ways, my parents returning to Fraserburgh, by which time Spicey had aged. He made only token appearances at funerals, breaking from them at the foot of Victoria Street. One day he did not appear for his mid-day dinner, nor had he put in an appearance by night-fall. By chance my parents were visited by my father's brother-in-law, the Rev Mitchell Hughes, who, being interested in flowers made his way through the drawing room to the conservatory, which could be entered by a sliding glass door. He then made for the garden, but stopped as he looked into a large tub set on the top step that led down to the garden and which collected rainwater from a drain-pipe. In it was the drowned body of Spicey.

The assumption might be made that Spicey was thirsty, had attempted to slake his thirst from the tub, but the ascent into the tub being difficult, had plunged in and been unable to get out. Spicey's only route to the tub, however, was past a dripping tap; the tap being kept at the drip for the dog. (We used to be amused at Spicey's expertise in catching the water on his tongue.) There was only one conclusion, the Reverend gentleman argued. Spicey, having drunk life to the lees, decided he had had enough of it and committed suicide.

I must say I was never convinced by this argument. I suspect that on his return from Aberdeen he decided to inspect all the new arrangements about the house, one of which was the rainwater tub. He had simply heaved himself up to the rim and had fallen in.

GEORGE BRUCE

DOG SHOW

Look at aa thae Poodle dugs
Wi curly hair and floppy lugs
And Yorkies wi their ribboned hair
That snowk at ye wi snooty air.

Pekinese that yap-yap-yap,
Fit only for my leddy's lap,
Big Bulldogs and growling Pugs
Wi slaverin tongues and ugly mugs.

Dugs in orra shapes and sizes
Competin for the cups and prizes;
There's nane amang them that I like
As weel's my ain wee tousie tyke.

J K ANNAND

MY DOGGIE

My wee doggie
Does a lot of tricks,
Fetches the paper,
Brings back sticks,
Chases aa the craws
That steal the hen's feed,
Lowps through a gird,
Kids he's deid,
Sits on his hunkers,
Gies a paw,
Then he gets
A bane to gnaw.

J K ANNAND

A DUG A DUG

Hey, Daddy, wid ye get us a dug?
A big broon alsation? Ur a wee white pug,
ur a skinny wee terrier ur a big fat bull?
Aw, Daddy! Get us a dug. Wull ye?

'n' whose dug'll it be when it messes the flerr?
'n' durties the carpet 'n' pees'n the sterr?
It's me ur yur mammy'll be taen fur a mug.
Away oot an' play. Yur no' needin' a dug,

Bit, Daddy! Thur gien' thum away
doon therr at the RSPCA.
Yu'll get wan fur nothin' so ye wull.
Aw, Daddy, Get us a dug. Wull ye?

Doon therr at the RSPCA!
Dae ye hink Ah've goat nothin' else tae dae
bit get you a dug that Ah'll huftae mind?
Yur no' needin' a dug. Ye urny blind!

Bit, Daddy, it widnae be dear tae keep
'n' Ah'd make it a basket fur it tae sleep
'n' Ah'd take it fur runs away of the hull.
Aw, Daddy. Get us a dug. Wull ye?

Dae ye hear 'im? Oan aboot dugs again?
Ah hink this yin's goat dugs 'n the brain.
Ah know whit ye'll get. A skite'n the lug
if Ah hear any merr aboot this bliddy dug.

Bit, Daddy, thur rerr fur guardin' the hoose
an' thur better'n cats fur catchin a moose
an' wee Danny's dug gies 'is barra a pull.
Aw, hey Daddy. Get us a dug. Wull ye?

Ah doan't hink thur's ever been emdy like you.
Ye could wheedle the twist oot a flamin' coarkscrew.
Noo get doon aff ma neck. Ah don't want a hug.
Awright. That's anuff. Ah'll get ye a dug.

Aw, Daddy! A dug! A dug!

BILL KEYS

7   Scottish terrier. Drawing by Colin Gibson.

GRANDCHILD VISITING
(for Carrie Leigh Barr)

She stands, her chubby knees gently swaying,
before the shapes on the television screen,
unaware of the hate the words are spraying,
or what the murdered falling bodies mean.

Through his own screams a baddie bites the floor.
The colours cease to hold her. *Look, here's me,*
the nosing basset saunters through the door;
and, innocent with love, she cries: 'Toe-*bee*'!

MAURICE LINDSAY

TAILPIECE

I had a wee dog
And he wouched at the mune;
If ma sang be na lang
It's suner dune.
                    (Galloway)

DOG HUMOUR

Dogs do have a sense of humour. Siegfried, the present companion, often delights in making a wide under-cover circle around us when we are calling him back to the car after a country walk, standing quietly at our backs and waiting with obvious relish to see how long it will take us to discover that he is there. Most of the dog humour in this section, however, originates in the minds of their owners, although the Cambuslang poet William Hamilton of Gilbertfield (1670–1751) put words into the mouth of Bonny Heck, a greyhound in Fife about to be hanged for its apparently rather trifling misdemeanours. Dogs readily establish themselves at all social levels, no less readily in the *milieu* of Fred Urquhart's 'The Wedding' than in stately homes and country houses, where they are to be found in other sections of this anthology. Liz Lochhead and Alan Bold add a kind of cabaret quality to dog humour, and the naturalist David Stephen has gentle fun with those who are too genteel to indulge in the naming of parts.

8   Siegfried. Drawing by Morven Cameron.

THE BROAD HINT CUNNINGLY ANSWERED

In ripened years, when blood flows cool,
then mankind cease to play the fool,
grow very cautious, grave, and wise,
and prodigal of good advice,
the courses that themselves run throw,
they hardly to their bairns allow.

Patricius for his merits known
which none who knew him would disown,
was now arriv'd to that same age
which can oppose love's fiercest rage,
tho in his youth, some would debate it,
he took a rug when he could get it.
He had a son, a hearty youth,
who lov'd to smack a pretty mouth,
the lad was lively, brisk, and keen,
not much to ceremony gi'en,
who thought, when nature was inviting,
one should not take too long entreating,
nor cavil much about her laws
when one could show a good because.

Some maiden auld of envious nature,
or chaplain, sour malicious creature,
officiously had told the Laird
that his son John had no regard,
to laws canonical or civil
but amongst lasses played the Devil.
Thought fornication was no sin,
and whored about throw' thick and thin,
unterified at claps and poxes,
repenting-stools or the kirk-boxies.

One evening as the son and father
by a warm ingle sat together
where tired with rambles of the day
upon the hearth lay favourite Tray
to whom thus spoke by way of squint
the squire that son might take the hint:
    'Ye silly cur, whatis't bewitches
you thus to gallop after bitches

the live-lang day oer riggs and bogs
fighting with all the wicked dogs
wasting your strength for little thanks
and getting riven spauls and shanks?'
    John understood his father's drift
when luckily to lend a lift
a little whelp of humour gay
would fain have had some game with Tray
he pauted at his hinging lugs
and sometimes at his tail he druggs
which sport the auld and sullen tike
by snaps and girns seem'd to dislike.
    John to the auld dog spoke, thus slee
get out ye cankered cur cried he,
your eild and sourness gar ye snarl
and with the wanton whelpie quarrel
you have forgot—(your manners tell)
that you was aince a whelp yoursel.

ALLAN RAMSAY

9   Lindy an Irish Setter. Drawing by Morven Cameron.

NEMO CANEM IMPUNE LACESSIT

I kicked an Edinbro dug-luver's dug,
leastweys I tried; my timing wes owre late.
It stopped whit it wes daein til my gate
and skelpit aff to find some ither mug.

Whit a sensation! If a clockwark thug
suid croun ye wi a brolly owre yir pate,
the Embro folk wad leave ye til yir fate;
it's you, maist like, wad get a flee in yir lug.

But kick the Friend of Man! Or hae a try!
The Friend of Wummin, even, that's faur waur
a felony, mair dangerous forbye.

Meddle wi puir dumb craiturs gin ye daur;
that maks ye a richt cruel bruitt, my! my!
And whit d'ye think yir braw front yett is for?

ROBERT GARIOCH

DOG HUMOUR

I have a notion that dogs have humour, and are perceptive of a joke. In the North, a shepherd, having sold his sheep at a market, was asked by the buyer to lend him his dog to take them home. 'By a' manner o' means tak' Birkie, and when ye're dune wi' him just play so' (making a movement with his arm), 'and he'll be hame in a jiffy.' Birkie was so clever and useful and gay that the borrower coveted him; and on getting him to his farm shut him up, intending to keep him. Birkie escaped during the night, and took the entire hirsel (flock) back to his own master! Fancy him trotting across the moor with them, they as willing as he.

DR JOHN BROWN

CHIP SHOP

There's been a murder in the chip shop
Where a wee dug stole a haddie bone
An another dug tried tae tak it aff him
So I hit him wi' a tattie scone.

I went round to see ma Auntie Sarah
But ma Auntie Sarah wisnae in
I looked through a hole in the windae
An shouted Auntie Sarah are ye in?

Her false teeth were lyin' on the table
Her curly wig upon the bed
An I nearly burst ma sides wi' laughin
When I saw her screwin' aff her wooden leg.

Glasgow street song.

THE CHIP SHOP

Lively

There's been a mur-der in the chip shop_____ Where a wee dug stole a hadd-ie bone_____ An' an-oth-er dug tried tae tak it aff him_____ So I hit him wi' a tatt-ie scone

Trad./Arr. A. Trezise ©Kettle Music

There's been a murder in the chip shop
Where a wee dug stole a haddie bone   [dog, haddock
An' another dug tried tae tak it aff him
So I hit him wi' a tattie scone   [potato scone

I went roond tae see ma Auntie Sarah
But ma Auntie Sarah wisnae in   [wasn't
I looked through a hole in the windae   [window
An' shouted Auntie Sarah are ye in?

Her false teeth were lyin' on the table
Her curly wig upon the bed
An' I nearly burst ma sides wi' laughin   [my
When I saw her screwin' aff her wooden leg   [off

Guitar:
Capo 3 up – Key D

This classic street song is still sung today by Glasgow children.

10   The Chip Shop, from *The Singing Kettle*, Cilla Fisher and Artie Trezise, Lynn Breeze, Gary M Coupland, Kettle Music.

THE LAST DYING WORDS OF BONNIE HECK
(a famous Greyhound in the Shire of Fife)

William Hamilton of Gilbertfield (1670–1751) achieved fame at one remove, because his paraphrase into late eighteenth-century Scots of Henry the Minstrel's famous poem The Wallace *'poured a tide of prejudice' into Burns's veins which, said the poet, would 'boil along there till the floodgates of life shut in eternal rest'. It is a feeble enough production compared to the original, the text of which was not available to Burns. However Hamilton's 'The Last Dying words of Bonnie Heck', which appeared in Watson's* Choice Collection of Comic and Serious Scots Poems *(1706), though modelled on Burns, was described by Allan Cunningham as being 'a pretty little pathetic piece of poetry as ever was written'.*

Hamilton served as an army lieutenant in his youth, but spent most of his days on his estate at Gilbertfield, near Cambuslang, Glasgow, though he died at another nearby seat of the family, Latrick.

'Alas, alas,' quo' bonnie Heck,
'On former days when I reflect!
I was a dog in much respect
        For doughty deed;
But now I must hing by the neck
        Without remeed.

O fy, sirs, for black, burning shame,
Ye'll bring a blunder on your name!
Pray tell me wherein I'm to blame?
        Is't in effect
Because I'm cripple, auld, and lame?'
        Quo' bonnie Heck.

'What great feats I have done mysel'
Within clink of Kilrenny bell,
When I was souple, young, and fell,
        But fear or dread,
John Ness and Paterson can tell,
        Whose hearts may bleed.

They'll witness that I was the vier
Of all the dogs within the shire;
I'd run all day and never tire;
    But now my neck,
It must be stretchèd for my hire!'
    Quo' bonnie Heck.

'How nimbly could I turn the hare,
Then serve myself, that was right fair!
For still it was my constant care
    The van to lead.
Now what could sery Heck do mair?
    Syne kill her dead.

At the Kings-muir and Kelly law,
Where good stout hares gang fast awa',
So cleverly I did it claw,
    With pith and speed;
I bure the bell before them a'
    As clear's a bead.

I ran alike on a' kind grounds,
Yea, in the midst of Ardry whins
I gript the maukins by the buns
    Or by the neck;
Where nathing could slay them but guns,
    Save bonnie Heck.

I wily, witty was, and gash,
With my auld felny packy pash;
Nae man might ance buy me for cash
    In some respect;
Are they not then confounded rash,
    That hang poor Heck?

I was a bardy tyke and bauld;
Though my beard's grey I'm not so auld.
Can any man to me unfauld
    What is the feid
To stane me ere I be well cauld?
    A cruel deed!

'Now honesty was aye my drift,
An innocent and harmless shift,
A kail-pot lid gently to lift
    Or aumrie sneck:
Shame fa' the chafts dare call that thift!'
    Quo' bonnie Heck.

'So well's I could play *hocus-pocus*
And of the servants mak' *Jodocus*
And this I did in every *locus*,
    Through their neglect;
And was not this a merry *jocus?*'
    Quo' bonnie Heck.

'But now, good sirs, this day is lost
The best dog in the East-Neuk coast;
For never ane durst brag nor boast
    Me, for their neck.
But now I must yield up the ghost,'
    Quo' bonnie Heck.

'And put a period to my talking,
For I'm unto my exit making:
Sirs, ye may a' gae to the hawking,
    And there reflect
Ye'll ne'er get sic a dog for maukin
    As bonnie Heck.

'But if my puppies ance were ready
Which I gat on a bonnie lady,
They'll be baith clever, keen, and beddy,
    And ne'er neglect
To clink it like their ancient daddy,
    The famous Heck.'

WILLIAM HAMILTON OF GILBERTFIELD

THE WEDDING

Jenny thought it was a lovely wedding. Nearly everybody else thought it was a lovely wedding too, except for the bit of unpleasant excitement when the best man's dog bit Andrew.

At two-thirty in the afternoon, in the Parish Church of Kenlochmore, the Reverend Gerald Teasdale, wearing full clerical regalia over his kilt, long stockings and brogues, married Charlotte Winifred Mathieson, spinster of the parish of St Mary's in Edinburgh, to Henry Havelock Copperwood, bachelor of the parish of St Clement's in Toronto, Canada.

Andrew watched Auntie Lottie take her place beside Uncle Harry, who was wearing a special fancy uniform of red and blue. He was envious of Jenny in her long green dress. She kept lifting up the full skirt to let people admire it and to show off her new black patent leather shoes. Andrew wished he was wearing her wreath of orange blossoms instead of the sailor's hat with *HMS Renown* on its ribbon. And he wished it was Red standing at Uncle Harry's other side. At first, when he came into the church, he'd thought it was Red, and he was going to rush up and embrace him when he saw that, although this was a big man too, it wasn't his friend.

None of them had ever set eyes on the best man until they saw him standing beside Harry in the church. He was someone they'd never even heard mentioned before: Corporal Will Halliwell, a big beefy farmer's son from Saskatchewan. Chrissie didn't pay much attention to him when Harry introduced them after the service; she, like all the others, was so busy throwing confetti at the bride and groom as they got into the Daimler. It was only a few minutes later, preparing with her parents and Granny Colquhoun to get into the Wolseley, that Chrissie became aware of him. He caught her by the elbow and said: 'Jest hold it a minute, honey. I'm goin' with you, and I got to fetch ma dawg.'

He disappeared round the side of the church, and Chrissie, with one foot inside the limousine, was still digesting what he'd said when he came back with a large black labrador on a rope.

Corporal Halliwell boosted Chrissie into the car, handed her the end of the rope and said: 'D'ya mind holdin' him till we get there, honey? In you git, boy!' And he slapped the dog on the rump and it leapt into the back of the Wolseley.

'God Almighty!' cried Mrs Mathieson.

Mrs Colquhoun let out a ladylike squeal. The best man grinned and said: 'He won' hurt you, ladies. He's as tame as a li'l old lamb.' And he banged the door and got into the front beside Mr Jeffrey.

All the way to Stonebiggins Chrissie gibbered with rage. She had to keep pushing away the dog, which not only sat like a load of lead on one of her feet but slobbered all over her new dress. And she glared with dislike from the Corporal's red beefy neck to the big white satin bow and the gift horseshoe fastened to the dog's collar.

Chrissie was in such a temper by the time they reached the house that she just thrust the rope into Corporal Halliwell's hand, left him to assist the old folk from the car, and rushed inside to give her nose a quick dab of powder before welcoming the guests. She did not see the black dog again until she saw Will Halliwell feeding it some of the best slices off a sirloin of beef under the table.

There were so many guests they couldn't all sit down to the wedding breakfast in the same room. So they were split up into three lots. The bride and Chrissie presided over the older and more important ones in the Lovat kitchen; Mrs Grant and Auntie Belle presided over a great number, mostly soldiers, in the Grant kitchen; and Mrs McRae and Nancy Rennie presided over another lot, most of them children, in the McRae kitchen. There was an abundance of food: great sirloins of beef, saddles of mutton, haunches of venison, huge steak-and-kidney pies, as well as all kinds of trifles and cakes. Even though Uncle Archie hadn't managed to come to the wedding, he'd done his duty by Lottie by sending a large suitcase of rationed goods with Auntie Belle.

Andrew had been with the other children in Mrs McRae's, but after a little while he slipped into his own kitchen and sidled into a narrow space at the table between Granny and the best man, to whom he'd taken a fancy. He was watching Will Halliwell slice big hunks off the sirloin of beef and throw them under the table to the dog when he heard Mammy say angrily: 'Listen, mister—er—I don't approve of the way you're feeding all the good beef to your dug. I'd have you remember there's a war on.'

Will Halliwell said: 'Aw, honey, you woulden grudge the pore beast a few bites, would ya?'

'I would,' she said tartly. 'And don't you call me honey.'

'And would you mind taking the dog outside?' Mrs Mathieson chipped in. 'It's not sure whether it's chewing the beef or my feet.'

'Aw, Miz Mathieson—'

'Better get it out, Will,' Lottie said. 'I'm tired of its tail thumping against my legs. It wags its tail so much it's already broken one of Chrissie's vases.'

'I sure am sorry, Lot,' big Will blustered, his face scarlet. 'But I didden reckon the dawg was doin any harm. If you jus' hover a blink I'll put some meat on a plate for it and take it outside.'

He was starting to pile beef on a dinner plate when Chrissie cried: 'Here, not one of my best plates, if you don't mind. Just a minute and I'll get you a tin plate. It's good enough for any dug. Oh and Hecky, would you mind showing Mister—er—whatsisname—where the stable is? He can tie his dug up in there. It'd better be tied up, for fear it eats one o' the horses—though God knows it shouldn't be that hungry. It's had plenty already. Far more than some of the guests.'

Mrs Mathieson pushed back her chair and stood up, to allow Will Halliwell to pull the dog from under the table. Andrew was thrust by her movement against Will. He clutched the big man's thigh and pressed against him as the dog came out from beneath the white linen tablecloth. Whether it was jealousy of the little boy's closeness to its master, or whether it was because it had been deprived of a slice of meat it was harbouring under the table, but the dog suddenly bared its teeth and nipped Andrew's arm.

Andrew screamed.

For a moment there was pandemonium. Mrs Mathieson and Granny Colquhoun vied with each other and Andrew in their ladylike screams. Chrisse shouted: 'Now you've done it, you big clodhopper. Who asked you to bring that bloody dug anyway? If it's hurt this bairn, I'll—'

'Now, Chrissie!' Jim Lovat cried.

'Aw Chris, it ain't nothin' but a li'l old graze,' Harry Copperwood said.

'Sure, it's nothin' but a graze,' Will said. 'The kid ain't hurt.'

'How do you know, you big round O?' Chrissie shouted. 'Get that dug out o' here. Quick!'

Scarlet in the face, Will pulled the dog out of the room. Hecky Grant followed him and, in the confusion, Chrissie trying to comfort Andrew, didn't notice Hecky take away the dinner plate of sliced beef.

Andrew snivelled: 'Re bad dog's tore my sailor soupon, Mammy.'

'Never mind, ducky,' Chrissie said, taking him upstairs. 'Mammy'll soon sew it and your sailor soupon'll be as good as new.'

She bathed the tooth marks on his arm and put disinfectant on them. When they came back to the kitchen Mrs Mathieson and Mrs Colquhoun were having their genteel hysterics remedied by not so genteel glasses of whisky. Jim and Mr Mathieson and Harry were filling everybody's glasses. A somewhat subdued Will Halliwell returned to the table and apologised to Chrissie. She apologised to Will Halliwell. He apologised to everybody else. Mr Teasdale stood up and made a speech, apologising for them all. Then everybody apologised to everybody else, and the toast to the bride and groom was drunk quickly so that their glasses could be refilled for the toast to the bridesmaids. And then, to make amends, big Will Halliwell took Andrew on his knee and made a fuss of him. It was almost like having Red back again. Uncle Will wasn't as nice as Red, his face was too bright and fat, but he was fine and big like Red, so Andrew snuggled against his brawny chest and listened while Uncle Will, who was fond of the sound of his own voice, sang:

> Goodbye-ee, don't sigh-ee,
> wipe the tear
> baby dear,
> from your eye-ee.

'D'you not ken somethin' more cheerful, Will?' Chrissie said. 'Mind this is a wedding you're at, not a funeral.'

So big Will sang 'Itchycoo! Itchycoo! Ain't you got one?'

Then Daddy sang his party piece 'Hey, Bonnie Lassie, Will ye, will ye gang?' And Uncle Harry sang 'If You Were the Only Girl in the World', gazing at Lottie like a rutting stag. Harry's Canadian pals cheered and clapped and stamped, and they wouldn't stop until the bride, glowing from several glasses of port wine, sang:

> Where are the lads of the village tonight?
> Where are the k-nuts we know?

There was even greater applause than there had been for Harry. Mrs Mathieson and Mrs Colquhoun furtively wiped their eyes. Their tears fell again, even more freely, when Grandma sang 'Silver Threads Among the Gold'. But they brightened up when Mr Teasdale made another speech and sang 'I'm Coortin' Bonnie Leezie Lindsay', and by the time he swallowed another glass of whisky and dashed away to get his sermon ready for next day, they were nodding in accompaniment to a Canadian singing 'Alexander's Rag-time Band'.

More Canadians sang: Mr Grant sang a Bothy Ballad, and he and Mr McRae did a sword dance. Even Granny Colquhoun sang a song in Gaelic that nobody could make head or tail of.

At some time, during it all, Lottie and Harry slipped away on their honeymoon, a week at a hotel in Aberdeen. Jenny didn't see them go. By then she was so worn out by all the excitement that she was lying curled up asleep in the corner behind the sofa, her wreath of orange blossoms crushed between her shoulder and the wall. Andrew and Tommy had been put to bed by Mrs McRae in her own house, and Chrissie and Mrs Mathieson, both a little lightheaded with whisky and tiredness, hadn't noticed Jenny slip behind the sofa so that she could hide there for a little while longer before Mrs McRae rounded her up and put her to bed, too.

Two or three days after the wedding Hecky Grant brought Chrissie one of her best dinner plates and said he'd found it in the stable. It was covered with dry horse dung and it stank of urine. 'It's a wonder one o' the horses hasnie tramped on it and broken it, Mistress,' he said with a smirk.

As he went away, grinning, she realised it was not Will Halliwell she had to thank for the plate's condition. In a sudden fury, she threw it on the stone floor and then she jumped on it.

FRED   URQUHART

AN ADDITION TO THE FAMILY

A musical poet, collector of basset-horns,
was buttering his toast down in Dunbartonshire
when suddenly from behind the breakfast newspaper
the shining blade stopped scraping
and he cried to his wife, 'Joyce, listen to this!—
"Two basset-hounds for sale, house-trained, keen hunters"—

Oh we must have them! What d'you think? . . .' 'But dear,
did you say *hounds?*' 'Yes, yes, hounds, hounds—'
'But Maurice, it's *horns* we want, you must be over
in the livestock column, what would we do
with a basset-hound, you can't play a hound!'
'It's Beverley it says, the kennels are at Beverley—'
'But Maurice—''—I'll get some petrol, we'll be there by lunchtime—'
'But a dog, two dogs, where'll we put them?'
'I've often wondered what these dogs are like—'
'You mean you don't even—' 'Is there no more marmalade?'
'—don't know what they look like? And how are we to feed them?
Yes, there's the pot dear.''This stuff's all peel, isn't it?'
'Well, we're at the end of it. But look, these two great—'
'You used to make marmalade once upon a time.'
'They've got cars down to here, and they're far too—'
'Is that half past eight? I'll get the car out.
See if I left my cheque-book on the—' 'Maurice,
are you mad? What about your horns?' 'What horns,
what are you talking about? Look Joyce dear,
if it's not on the dresser it's in my other jacket.
I believe they're wonderful for rabbits—'

So the musical poet took his car to Beverley
with his wife and his cheque-book, and came back home
with his wife and his cheque-book and two new hostages
to the unexpectedness of fortune.
The creatures scampered through the grass, the children
came out with cries of joy, there seemed to be nothing
dead or dying in all that landscape.
Fortune bless the unexpected cries!
Life gathers to the point of wishing it,
a mocking pearl of many ventures. The house
rolled on its back and kicked its legs in the air.
And later, wondering farmers as they passed would hear
beyond the lighted window in the autumn evening
two handome yellow-bosomed basset-hounds
howling to a melodious basset-horn.

                                        EDWIN   MORGAN

BALLAD OF THE HARE AND THE BASSETHOUND

The bassethound's a mournful fellow;
long ears that trail along the ground,
a baying voice that's like a cello,
a tail that circles round and round.

Yet bassethounds were bred for chasing,
through France's royal days of old,
the breathless hare, at first outpacing
the hound who, once he snuffed a hold

of the hare's scent, kept slowly clumbering
ditches, branches, burns and fields
till at the end of all his lumbering,
the limping hare, spring broken, yields.

We're civilised. So basset Billy,
his snuffling anchored to the ground,
was amiable, harmless, silly,
seeking for things he never found.

One sudden day he bumped his snout on
a lump of fur, a sleeping hare.
Poor Billy gazed with wrinkled doubt on
the creature that returned his stare.

At once the hare sent distance arc-ing
as towards the setting sun he sped
while Billy sat upon his barking
then turned and oppositely fled.

But not for long. The old blood-royal
that courses through a basset's veins
is not a thing for time to spoil,
even when it feeds slow-thinking brains.

His massive paws he pushed before him
and slithered to a skidding halt.
In vain did I command, implore him—
ancestral blood cried out, 'Assault!'

So yelping ancient doggy noises,
Billy set off in late pursuit.
Time waits for no such equipoises:
the jinking hare by then had put

two lengthy fields from where he started
and, smalling, breached a hill's horizon,
Billy, essentially kind-hearted,
pulled up with innocent surprise on

his wrinkled features. Body wagging,
he ambled back to where I waited.
With asking eyes he lay there sagging,
face saved and old French honour sated;

as if to say· 'Come on now, praise me
for showing sense; en Français, *sens*;
like you, to kill's a thought dismays me,
so *honi soit qui mal y pense!*'

MAURICE LINDSAY

11   The Basset Hound and the Hare. Drawing by Morven Cameron.

NOT THE WORD FOR IT

A woman, admiring my big German Sheepdog bitch, said to me casually: 'What's its name?'

'It's name,' I said (riding the neuter) 'is Lisa.'

'But that's a girl's name,' she said.

'It is indeed,' I agreed. 'It being a her I could hardly give her a boy's name.'

'Oh!' she said, 'It's so big I thought it was a dog.'

'It is a dog,' I said. 'A German Shepherd bitch.'

'I mean,' she said, 'I thought it was a *dog*, you know—a dog—being so big . . .'

'It is a dog. A bitch dog . . .'

She seemed a little put out at that, and when she was joined by two other women, both of whom patted Lisa, she said to them: 'her name's Lisa. She's a lady dog.'

'But she's huge,' one of the others said.

'She's certainly a big bitch,' I agreed, 'and I'm sure she doesn't mind being called a lady, for she's just that in the best sense of the word.'

I overheard the first one say later: 'You know, I think David Stephen goes out of his way to be coarse.'

God help me; one of the things that never fails to stir my adrenalin is to hear a bitch called a lady dog.

Another is to be asked whether a kitten is a boy or a girl, because boys and girls are people. And cats, like dogs, have their cat and dog names.

I know a lot of people, who readily speak of someone or other bitching about something, or being bitchy, and who use the word bitchiness, but who call a real bitch a lady dog. The only time they use a female dog's name is to insult it.

Not long ago a woman was telling me how she stopped a youth taking young birds from a nest. 'I gave him h-e-l-l,' she said, spelling it out letter by letter.

'I know how to spell it,' I teased her. 'Why don't you just say it?'

Some years ago I gave a talk on ecology to a certain women's organisation. When I was leaving, after tea, the secretary, who was a friend of mine, said to me: 'I think you shocked some of them tonight.'

'Shocked?' I said, shocked. 'I? In God's name how?'

'Well,' she said, 'when you told of the fox that was shot on the dung midden wall, and when you told them about how you analysed badger dung.'

'Oh! for heaven's sake,' I said. 'Did they expect me to call badger dung manure? What a farmer spreads from the midden is dung; what he buys in bags is manure.'

The euphemism is everything. It seems that, even in this age of sewage, the old honest-to-God words whose respectability is beyond reproach are inadmissible in certain quarters.

I'll give you a further example of this. A minister friend of mine, seeking me out for a lecture he wanted me to do, was told by my wife where he could find me. When he found me I was coming off the moor with a polythene bag filled with fox dung. It was a big bag, and I had it slung over a shoulder.

'What have we in the bag?' he asked.

'Fox dung,' I said.

'Tut, tut,' he replied,

When my daughter was a little girl at school she came home one day and asked me if I would dress a kitten belonging to the aunt of a friend. And I told her to tell her school friend I would, and named a time. Whereupon she asked me:

'What are you going to dress the kitten in, Daddy?'

I told her what dressing a cat meant.

DAVID STEPHEN

CAT AND DOG

In a little old house in a forest
Lived a dog and a tabby cat;
The dog was rather a shaggy dog,
The cat was a nine-lived cat.

They kept their cottage tidy
They washed more than once a day,
They hunted when they had to,
They reserved a period for play.

What did they play at? As you ask
They tried to maintain a tone.
The cat played away at cat and mouse,
The dog played dog and bone.

Sometimes the dog lay doggo,
And the cat had catnaps when
The house was still and silent
And the wood was drenched in rain.

In the trees outside the cottage
They heard every sort of sound
But one. Surrounded by beeches
for human beings they pined.

They had their house in the forest,
They kept an open door,
But there were no humans to humour
Though humans had been there before.

On the wall in the hall was a coatstand
With hats and jackets on hooks
And the shelves in the lounge were jam-packed
With rows of leather-bound books.

Where had the humans gone to?
What gives a sparkle to stars?
Why did the chicken cross the road?
Your guess is as good as theirs.

ALAN BOLD

12   Inquiring Jenny. Drawing by Morven Cameron.

IF LIFE HAS ANY MEANING IT'S A PUNNING ONE

At the local Show, the locals show
almost all they can then, consumed, consume.
Shire horses big as shires drag their load,
pulling their weight, not throwing it about.
Sheepdogs dog sheep which are counted in pairs:
'Yan—tan—tethera—but the Judge is asleep.
A machine totes that bale, a red insect tractor bugs the field.

CHRIS BENDON

CAIRNS

Thanks for having me James the Sixth
twisted at the border. Thirteen *chiens
terrieres*, earth dogs, waddled at his
rut—
the Cairn, coursing a pedigree,
emerged with a First.

Tom Leonard has Cairns in his pieces,
eats their ears,
and their wee furry paws.
Edwin Morgan puts Cairns in a space-ship—
tells the clippie
'See they reach Mars.'
Crawford says 'A dog's a dug f'r a' that,'
'We're all happy
Mungo'rels with the word.'

Bitching on the dogs that leave me behind
I doubt Cairns can lead the blind:
guide-wolves drew MacDiarmid.

RICHARD PRICE

A RARA MONGRELLIS

Tourist. " Your dog appears to be deaf, as he pays no attention to me."

Shepherd. " Na, na, sir. She's a varra wise dog, for all tat. But she only speaks Gaelic."

13   A Rare Mongrellis. Reproduced by permission of *Punch*.

IT'S A DOG'S LIFE
(Toby's Song)

Toby Dug: I'm a Mad Bad Dug
I'm Toby the Dug
Alsatian tae the oaxters
wi Labrador's lugs
I've Irish Setter's eyebrows
(ain't they set real neat?)
I've got Bulldog's drumsticks
And Saint Bernard's feet.

I'm a dog.
Top dog.

Girls: Dubby Dooh Wah. Dubby Dooh Wah.

Toby Dug: Ma Da wis half boarder-collie
Half Doberman Pinscher—
Ma Maw goes 'Help Ma Black Boab!'
When ma Da came to winch her
Well, it wis kinuffa a case o'
Lady and the Tramp—
A bit o' a vamp,
A high-class bitch, my Ma—
Nine tenths purebred Alsatian
One part je-ne-sais-quoi—

Girls: Dubby Dooh Wah. Dubby Dooh Wah.

Toby Dug: But I'm a dog.
Top dog.
Stare me straight in the teeth
And I'm sure you'll agree
I've got a high class pedigree
I don't gi'e a monkey's for the world
and its wife
It's a dog's life!

Girls: Top dawg! dubby dooh wah, dop
dubby dooh wah, dop, dop, dop.

LIZ LOCHHEAD

WORKING DOGS

Dogs have been trained to assist man in a variety of ways, from hunting to searching out drugs and explosives aboard aircraft. We do not have any instances of aircraft searching in this selection, but we begin with an early example of deerhunting witnessed by John Taylor (1580–1653), in which we have retained the old spelling, since it adds to the charm of the piece and is easily read. There are several other illustrations of hunting dogs, including an otter-hunt in Skye, and a good selection of what is perhaps the commonest task entrusted to the dog; the control of sheep or cattle. Obviously, a special relationship exists between a shepherd and his dog. Here, perhaps, more than anywhere, the expression of that relationship in kailyaird terms is both understandable and acceptable as a true reflection of country life.

14   Deerhound. Drawing by Colin Gibson.

15 Deerstalking on Jura, by Gourlay Steel. Courtesy of Glasgow Art Gallery and Museum.

HUNTING IN THE HIGHLANDS

In 1618, Ben Jonson, to the considerable amusement of his friends at the Mermaid Tavern, announced that he intended to walk to Scotland, one of his purposes being to converse with the Scottish poet William Drummond of Hawthornden. A few weeks later, a gusty Thames waterman, John Taylor, announced that he intended to follow the famous dramatist's example, 'not carrying any money to or fro, neither Begging, borrowing, or asking Meate, Drinke, or Lodging'. Taylor published a vigorous if eccentric account of his trip, The Pennylesse Pilgrimage, *of which he sold 4,500 copies.*

He penetrated the Highlands, his ready tongue apparently making him acceptable to the aristocracy; for on the Braes of Mar, where he felt so cold that his teeth began to chatter in his head 'like virginal's jacks', he found the Earl of Mar, the Earl of Enzie (a then recently acquired second title of the Marquis of Huntly) and the Earl of Buchan, who welcomed him to their sport.

Once in the yeere, which is the whole month of August and sometimes part of September, many of the nobility of the kingdom (for their pleasure) doe come into these highland countries to hunt, where they doe conform themselves to the habit of the Highlandmen, who for the most part speak nothing but Irish . . . Their habit is shoes with but one sole apiece; stockings (which they call short hose) made of a warm stuff of divers colours, which they call Tartan: as for breeches, many of them, nor their forefathers, never wore any, but a jerkin of the same stuff that their hose is of, their garters being bands or wreaths of hay or straw, with a plaid about their shoulders which is a mantle of divers colours, much finer and lighter stuff than their hose, with blue flat caps on their head, a handkerchief knit with two knots about their neck; and thus they are attired . . .

Their weapons are long bows and forked arrows, swords and targes, arquebusses, muskets, dirks and Lochaber axes . . . As for their attire, any man of what degree soever that comes amongst them must not disdain to wear it: for if they doe, then they will disdain to hunt, or willingly to bring in their dogs: but if men be kind unto them, and be in their habit, then they are conquered with kindness, and the sport will be plentiful . . .

Five or six hundred men doe rise early in the morning, and they doe dispose themselves divers ways, and seven, eight or ten miles compass. They doe bring or chase in the deer in many herds (two, three or four hundred in a herd) to such a place as the noblemen shall appoint them;

then when day is come, the Lords and gentlemen of their companies doe ride or go to the said place, sometimes wading up the middles through burns and rivers, and . . . doe lie on the ground till those foresaid scouts, who are called the Tinchel, doe bring down the deer . . .

After we had stayed there three hours or thereabouts, we might perceive the deer appear on the hills round about us (their heads making a show like a wood), which, being followed by the Tinchel, are chased down into the valley, on each side being way-laid with a hundred couple of strong Irish grey-hounds. they are let loose as occasion serves upon the herd of deer . . . With dog, guns, arrows, dirks and daggers, in the space of two hours four-score fat deer were slain, which after are disposed of some one way, and some another, twenty and thirty miles, and more than enough left for us to make merry withall at our rendezvous.

JOHN TAYLOR

16   Part of a wall mural painting at Traquair House. Courtesy of Peter Maxwell Stuart of Traquair.

THE LAST WOLF

The last wolf in Scotland is supposed to have been killed in 1680 by Cameron of Lochiel but wolves survived into the following century 'on well attested evidence'. Sir Thomas Dick Lauder gives his account of what is supposed to have happened, and the part played in the event by a grey dog.

A poor woman, crossing the mountains with two children, was assailed by the wolf, and her infants devoured, and she escaped with difficulty to Moyhall. The chief of Mackintosh no sooner heard of the tragical fate of the babes, than, moved by pity and rage, he dispatched orders to his clan and vassals to assemble the next day at twelve o'clock, to proceed in a body to destroy the wolf. Pollochock was one of those vassals, and being then in the vigour of youth, and possessed of gigantic strength and determined courage, his appearance was eagerly looked for to take a lead in the enterprise. But the hour came and all were assembled except him to whom they most trusted. Unwilling to go without him, the impatient chief fretted and fumed through the hall, till at length, about an hour after the appointed time, in stalked Pollochock, dressed in his full Highland attire. 'I am little used to wait thus for any man,' exclaimed the chafed chieftain, 'and still less for thee, Pollochock, especially when such game is afoot as we are boune after!' 'What sort o' game are ye after, Mackintosh?' said Pollochock simply, and not quite understanding his allusion. 'The wolf, sir,' replied Mackintosh; 'did not my messenger instruct you?' 'Ou aye, that's true,' answered Pollochock with a good-humoured smile; 'troth I had forgotten. But an' that be a',' continued he, groping with his right hand among the ample folds of his plaid, 'there's the wolf's head!' Exclamations of astonishment and admiration burst from chief and clansmen as he held out the grim and bloody head of the monster at arm's-length, for the gratification of those who crowded round him. 'As I came through the slochk [gully], east the hill there,' said he, as if talking of some everyday occurrence, 'I foregathered with the beast. My long dog there turned him. I buckled wi' him, and dirkit him, and syne whuttled his craig, and brought awa' his countenance, for fear he might come alive again; for they are vera precarious creatures.' 'My noble Pollochock!' cried the chief in ecstasy 'the deed was worthy of thee! In memorial of thy hardihood, I here bestow upon thee Seannachan, to yield meal for thy good grey hound in all time coming.'

SIR THOMAS DICK LAUDER

DEERHOUNDS

Admit the lives more valuable
than our life, than the bodies we bear
more beautiful: tall grey dogs,

what huntsman, what dogboy loosed you
on our slow hearts
and let you slaughter them?

Long dogs, you move with air
belling the vault of your ribcage.
You subdue the miles below your hocks.

Levelled out in speed across wayless country,
over the open grassmoor that is paradise,
the onset of your going undulates the ground.

The bracken hurdles below your height,
the rushes make way for you;
your hard eyes hold in sight the rapid hills.

Brace of deerhounds, a matched two!
Intent, all flame, is what quickens
those long throats thonged with leather.

                                    VALERIE GILLIES

17   John Swanston, gamekeeper, from the Collection at Abbotsford.

MY DOG AND I

This song, which appears in the famous Greig-Duncan Folksong Collection, *was contributed to it by Miss Bell Robertson who, on 2 December 1908, told the collector that 'my brother James used to sing it and mother had bits of it'. The text as printed remarks, somewhat surprisingly, on the absence of gazelle from the Scottish hunting scene. The editor suggested that 'gazelle' was a misprint for gaggle, which I have therefore substituted here.*

My dog and I hae learned a trade,
To go a-hunting when it is late,
When it is late and there's none to spy,
To the hunting goes my dog and I.

In winter when the weather's wet,
My dog and I we warm our feet,
In summer when the weather's dry,
To the hunting goes my dog and I.

My dog and I will catch some hare,
For geese and gaggle will no be there,
They'll no be caught, they fly so high,
To the hunting goes my dog and I.

BELL ROBERTSON

18   Gun Dog. Drawing by Colin Gibson.

AN OTTER HUNT

Alexander Smith, the Kilmarnock-born pattern-designer turned poet and essayist who ended his days as Secretary to Edinburgh University, early in the 1850s made a journey from Glasgow's Broomielaw to Skye aboard a Macbrayne paddle-steamer. In those days, the Macbrayne steamers sailing regularly from the Clyde were almost the only means of supply and communication between places on the Western coast and the islands and the South. Smith recorded his impressions in A Summer in Skye, *first published in 1856 and still one of the most vivid Scottish travel books written. It is from this book that we have taken his description of 'An Otter Hunt'.*

Angus-with the dogs was continually passing over the country like the shadow of a cloud. If he had a home at all, it was situated at Ardvasar, near Armadale; but there Angus was found but seldom. He was always wandering about with his gun over his shoulder, his terriers, Spoineag and Fruich, at his heels, and the kitchen of every tacksman was open to him. The tacksmen paid Angus so much per annum, and Angus spent his time in killing their vermin. He was a deadshot; he knew the hole of the fox, and the cairn in which an otter would be found. If you wanted a brace of young falcons, Angus would procure them for you; if ravens were breeding on one of your cliffs, you had but to wait till the young ones were half-fledged, send for Angus, and before evening, the entire brood, father and mother included, would be nailed up on your barn door. He knew the seldom-visited loch up amongst the hills which was haunted by the swan, the cliff of the Cuchullins on which the eagles dwelt, the place where, by moonlight you could get a shot at the shy heron. He knew all the races of dogs. In the warm blind pup he saw, at a glance, the future terrier or staghound. He could cure the distemper, could crop ears and dock tails. He could cunningly plait all kinds of fishing tackle; could carve *quaichs,* and work you curiously-patterned dagger-hilts out of the black bog-oak. If you wished a tobacco-pouch made of the skin of an otter or a seal, you had simply to apply to Angus. From his variety of accomplishments he was an immense favourite. The old farmers liked him because he was the sworn foe of pole-cats, foxes, and ravens; the sons of farmers valued him because he was an authority in rifles and fowling-pieces, and knew the warm shelving rocks on which bullet-headed seals slept, and the cairns on the sea-shore in which otters lived; and because if any special breed of dog was wanted he was sure to meet the demand. He was a little, thick-set fellow of great physical strength and of the most obliging nature; and he was called Angus-with-the-dogs, because without Spoineag and Fruich at his heels, he was never seen. The pipe was always in his mouth—to him tobacco smoke was as much a matter of course as peat reek is to a turf-hut.

One day after Fellowes had gone to the Landlord's, where I was to join him in a week or ten days, young M'Ian and myself waited for Angus-with-the-dogs on one of the rising grounds at a little distance from the house. Angus in his peregrinations had marked a cairn in which he thought an otter would be found, and it was resolved that this cairn should be visited on a specified day about noon, in the hope that some little sport might be provided for the Sassenach.

A glittering mesh of sunlight stretched across the Loch, blinding, palpitating, ever-dying, ever-renewed. The bee came booming past, the white sea-gull swept above, silent as a thought or a dream. Gazing out on all this, somewhat lost in it, I was suddenly startled by a sharp whistle, and then I noticed that a figure was crossing the bridge below. M'Ian got up; 'That's Angus,' he said; 'let us go down to meet him;' and so, after knocking the ashes out of his pipe and filling it anew, picking up his gun and slinging his shot-belt across his shoulder, he led the way.

At the bridge we found Angus seated, with his gun across his knee, and Spoineag and Fruich coursing about, and beating the bushes, from which a rabbit would occasionally bounce and scurry off. Angus looked more alert and intelligent than I had ever before seen him—probably because he had business on hand. We started at once along the shore at the foot of the cliffs above which we had been lying half an hour before. Our way lay across large boulders which had rolled down from the heights above, and progression, at least to one unaccustomed to such rough work, was by no means easy. Angus and M'Ian stepped on lightly enough, the dogs kept up a continual barking and yelping, and were continually disappearing in rents and crannies in the cliffs, and emerging more ardent than ever. At a likely place Angus would stop for a moment, speak a word or two to the dogs, and they they rushed barking at every orifice, entered with a struggle, and ranged through all the passages of the hollow cairn. As yet the otter had not been found at home. At last when we came in view of a spur of the higher ground which, breaking down on the shore, terminated in a sort of pyramid of loose stones, Angus dashed across the broken boulders at a run, followed by his dogs. When they got up, Spoineag and Fruich, barking as they had never barked before, crept in at all kinds of holes and impossible fissures, and were no sooner out than they were again in. Angus cheered and encouraged them, and pointed out to M'Ian traces of the otter's presence. I sat down on a stone and watched the behaviour

of the terriers. If ever there was an insane dog, it was Fruich that day;
she jumped and barked, and got into the cairn by holes through which
no other dog could go, and came out by holes through which no other
dog could come. Spoineag, on the other hand, was comparatively
composed; he would occasionally sit down, and taking a critical view of
the cairn, run barking to a new point, and to that point Fruich would
rush like a fury and disappear. Spoineag was a commander-in-chief,
Fruich was a gallant general of division. Spoineag was Wellington,
Fruich was the fighting Picton. Fruich had disappeared for a time, and
from the muffled barking we concluded that she was working her way
to the centre of the citadel, when all at once Spoineag, as if moved by a
sudden inspiration, rushed to the top of the cairn, and began tearing up
the turf with teeth and feet. Spoineag's eagerness now was as intense as
ever Fruich's had been. Angus, who had implicit faith in Spoineag's
genius, climbed up to assist, and tore away at the turf with his hands.
In a minute or so Spoineag had effected an entrance from the top, and
began to work his way downwards. Angus stood up against the sky with
his gun in readiness. We could hear the dogs barking inside, and
evidently approaching a common centre, when all at once a fell tumult
arose. The otter was reached at last, and was using teeth and claws.
Angus made a signal to M'Ian, who immediately brought his gun to his
shoulder. The combat still raged within, and seemed to be coming
nearer. Once Fruich came out howling with a bleeding foot, but a cry
from Angus on the height sent her in again. All at once the din of
barking ceased, and I saw a black lurching object flit past the stones
towards the sea. Crack went M'Ian's gun from the boulder, crack went
Angus's gun from the height, and the black object turned half round
suddenly and then lay still. It was the otter; and the next moment
Spoineag and Fruich were out upon it, the fire of battle in their eyes, and
their teeth fixed in its bloody throat. They dragged the carcase backwards
and forwards, and seemed unable to sate their rage upon it. What
ancient animosity existed between the families of otters and terriers?
What wrong had been done never to be redressed? Angus came forward
at last, sent Spoineag and Fruich howling right and left with his foot,
seized the otter by the tail, and then over the rough boulders we began
our homeward march. Our progress past the turf-huts nestling on the
shore at the foot of the cliffs was a triumphal one. Old men, women and
brown half-naked children came out to gaze upon us. When we got
home the otter was laid on the grass in front of the house, where the
elder M'Ian came out to inspect it, and was polite enough to express his
approval, and to declare that it was not much inferior in bulk and
strength to the otters he had seen hunted and killed at the close of last
century. After dinner young M'Ian skinned his trophy, and nailed and

stretched the hide on the garden gate amid the dilapidated kites and ravens. In the evening, Angus, with gun across his shoulder, and Spoineag and Fruich at his heels, started for that mysterious home of his which was supposed to be at Ardvasar, somewhere in the neighbourhood of Armadale Castle.

ALEXANDER SMITH

19   Two gun dogs. Drawing by Edwin Landseer, from *The Works of Sir Edwin Landseer, RA*, published by Cosmo Monkhouse Virtue & Co, London.

AGAINST AND FOR HUNTING

It would be wrong not to represent the point of view of those who object to hunting and to the training which dogs who take part in it undergo. Nowhere is the anti-hunting point of view more eloquently expressed than in 'Autumn', from The Seasons *by James Thomson (1700–48), who was born in Ednam, Roxburghshire, but settled in Richmond, near London, the recipient of a royal pension, holder of the sinecure of Surveyor-General of the Leeward Islands and a member of the literary circle of Pope and Gray.*

> Here the rude clamour of the sportsman's joy,
> The gun fast-thundering and the winded horn,
> Would tempt the Muse to sing the rural game,—
> How, in his mid career, the spaniel struck
> Stiff by the tainted gale, with open nose
> Outstretched and finely sensible draws full,
> Fearful, and cautious on the latent prey;
> As in the sun the circling covey bask
> Their varied plumes, and, watchful every way,
> Through the rough stubble turn the secret eye.
> Caught in the meshy snare, in vain they beat
> Their idle wings, entangled more and more:
> Nor, on the surges of the boundless air
> Though borne triumphant, are they safe; the gun,
> Glanced just, and sudden, from the fowler's eye,
> O'ertakes their sounding pinions, and again
> Immediate brings them from the towering wing
> Dead to the ground; or drives them wide dispersed,
> Wounded and wheeling various down the wind.
> These are not subjects for the peaceful muse,
> Nor will she stain with such her spotless song—
> Then most delighted when she social sees
> The whole mixed animal creation round
> Alive and happy. 'Tis not joy to her,
> This falsely cheerful barbarous game of death,
> This rage of pleasure which the restless youth
> Awakes, impatient, with the gleaming morn;
> When beasts of prey retire that all night long,
> Urged by necessity, had ranged the dark,
> As if their conscious ravage shunned the light

Ashamed. Not so the steady tyrant, man,
Who, with the thoughtless insolence of power
Inflamed beyond the most infuriate wrath
Of the worst monster that e'er roamed the waste,
For sport alone pursues the cruel chase
Amid the beamings of the gentle days.
Upbraid, ye ravening tribes, our wanton rage,
For hunger kindles you, and lawless want;
But lavish fed, in Nature's bounty rolled,
To joy at anguish, and delight in blood,
Is what your horrid bosoms never knew.
    Poor is the triumph o'er the timid hare!
Scared from the corn, and now to some lone seat
Retired—the rushy fen, the ragged furze
Stretched o'er the stony heath, the stubble chapped,
The thistly lawn, the thick entangled broom,
Of the same friendly hue the withered fern,
The fallow ground laid open to the sun
Concoctive, and the nodding sandy bank
Hung o'er the mazes of the mountain brook.
Vain is her best precaution; though she sits
Concealed with folded ears, unsleeping eyes
By Nature raised to take the horizon in,
And head couched close betwixt her hairy feet
In act to spring away. The scented dew
Betrays her early labyrinth; and deep,
In scattered sullen openings, far behind,
With every breeze she hears the coming storm
But, nearer and more frequent as it loads
The sighing gale, she springs amazed, and all
The savage soul of game is up at once—
The pack full-opening various, the shrill horn
Resounded from the hills, the neighing steed
Wild for the chase, and the loud hunter's shout—
O'er a weak, harmless, flying creature, all
Mixed in mad tumult and discordant joy.
    The stag, too, singled from the herd, where long
He ranged the branching monarch of the shades,
Before the tempest drives. At first, in speed
He sprightly puts his faith, and, roused by fear,
Gives all his swift aerial soul to flight.
Against the breeze he darts, that way the more
To leave the lessening murderous cry behind.

20 Old time cattle drover. Drawing by Colin Gibson.

Deception short! though, fleeter than the winds
Blown o'er the keen-aired mountain by the North,
He bursts the thickets, glances through the glades,
And plunges deep into the wildest wood.
If slow, yet sure, adhesive to the track
Hot-steaming, up behind him come again
The inhuman rout, and from the shady depth
Expel him, circling through his every shift.
He sweeps the forest oft; and sobbing sees
The glades, mild opening to the golden day,
Where in kind contest with his butting friends
He wont to struggle, or his loves enjoy.
Oft in the full-descending flood he tries
To lose the scent, and lave his burning sides—
Oft seeks the herd; the watchful herd, alarmed,
With selfish care avoid a brother's woe.
What shall he do? His once so vivid nerves,
So full of buoyant spirit, now no more
Inspire the course; but fainting, breathless toil
Sick seizes on his heart: he stands at bay,
And puts his last weak refuge in despair.
The big round tears run down his dappled face;
He groans in anguish; while the growling pack,
Blood-happy, hang at his fair jutting chest,
And mark his beauteous chequered sides with gore.

*Thomson, however, felt that the predators of the gentler animals were fair
enough game.*

Of this enough. But if the sylvan youth,
Whose fervent blood boils into violence,
Must have the chase, behold, despising flight,
The roused up lion, resolute and slow,
Advancing full on the protended spear
And coward band that circling wheel aloof.
Slunk from the cavern and the troubled wood,
See the grim wolf; on him his shaggy foe
Vindictive fix, and let the ruffian die:
Or, growling horrid, as the brindled boar
Grins fell destruction, to the monster's heart
Let the dart lighten from the nervous arm.
These Britain knows not; give, ye Britons, then
Your sportive fury pitiless to pour
Loose on the nightly robber of the fold.

Him, from his craggy winding haunts unearthed,
Let all the thunder of the chase pursue.
Throw the broad ditch behind you; o'er the hedge
High bound resistless; nor the deep morass
Refuse, but through the shaking wilderness
Pick your nice way; into the perilous flood
Bear fearless, of the raging instinct full;
And, as you ride the torrent, to the banks
Your triumph sound sonorous, running round
From rock to rock, in circling echo tost;
Then scale the mountains to their woody tops;
Rush down the dangerous steep; and o'er the lawn,
In fancy swallowing up the space between,
Pour all your speed into the rapid game.
For happy he who tops the wheeling chase;
Has every maze evolved, and every guile
Disclosed; who knows the merits of the pack;
Who saw the villain seized, and dying hard
Without complaint, though by an hundred mouths
Relentless torn: O glorious he beyond
His daring peers, when the retreating horn
Calls them to ghostly halls of grey renown,
With woodland honours graced—the fox's fur
Depending decent from the roof.

JAMES   THOMSON

THE CLEVEREST—AND LAZIEST—OF DOGS

I was looking at a photograph of him on Christmas Eve, taken just after the war, which showed him at his favourite occupation of doing nothing —unless you can call lying on the garden path, with one of my tame pigeons picking grain from under his nose, doing something.

I suppose if he'd been a man we'd have called him a layabout. Certainly there was nothing he liked better than being unemployed.

Yet he was the most teachable puppy I ever had, and one of the brainiest gundogs anyone ever fired a shot over. He was also a good looker.

The only time he would walk a yard more than he had to was if there was a puddle of water in front of him. He would walk round it. Confronted by a burn six feet wide he would have walked round the parish to avoid crossing it.

He was one puppy you could depend on to sit, and stay seated, until called in. He would have sat for the afternoon at one end of a field while you sat at the other, and when he did come in to the recall he came as though he had fifty-sixers tied to his feet. He was as slow as treacle on a frosty day.

But he had been at the head of the queue when the brains were being handed out; no question about that. People used to say to me he was too brainy to see any future in working like a dog for a man.

Once he had shown he could do a thing, he had made his point, and saw no reason why he should go on doing it. He was the intellectual type—but he was the laziest dog I ever met.

If he had been just another handsome eejit, I would have forgiven him. But he had everything except the will to do.

He could find anything—dummy, dead rabbit, pheasant, or even my bunch of keys. He would range 200 yards downwind, never letting his feet run away with his nose, and find what he was looking for with an almost deadly certainty. Then, having found it, he could never see any sufficient reason why he should have to hump it back to me.

Mind you, he always brought it. You could depend on him to find and bring back, so long as you didn't mind his arriving like a slow goods train.

I tried to put some pace into him by sending him out with a bouncing black dog. A little competition, I thought, would do the trick.

But he went at his own pace, letting the wild black dog run all over the place while he worked down slowly on to whatever was lost and picked it up. Then he looked for somebody to carry it home for him.

He was as certain as tomorrow, as slow as the mills of God, as likeable as could be, and too lazy for words. If I had been one hundred years old, he would have been the perfect dog. And yet . . .

Many a time I put him on a line after two other dogs had given up, and sure as the coming of night he would find what they couldn't find and bring it back as though he hated the very taste of it.

For a dog who hated getting his feet wet, he swam tirelessly when there was an end product. And then would avoid every puddle after he had delivered the goods.

He just didn't like work, or exertion, or discomfort. Usually a clever, eager dog has to be slowed down. This one you couldn't speed up.

He never jumped the gun, or ran in, or chased after exciting scents. All he wanted was not to be asked to go. He knew it all, and he was never so content as when watching other dogs doing the work.

I was very fond of him.

DAVID   STEPHEN

FLASH'S TRAINING BEGINS

'Maybe we could make a start on training your dog. I've got half an hour I can spare afore I look to the sheep,' John Meggetson said after breakfast next day. 'The first thing he has to learn is to answer to his name and to walk behind ye.'

Tom got up from the hearthrug where he had been kneeling beside the black and white puppy, rubbing him gently behind the ears. 'I think he knows his name already, Uncle John. Watch this!' Tom lifted his voice a little. 'Hi, Flash!'

The dog lifted his head alertly.

'Very good!' Uncle John nodded his approval. 'He'll be quick to learn, that one. Now he'll have to go on his lead.' He took the lead down from a hook on the wall and snapped it on to the dog's collar and handed the end of it to Tom. 'We'll take the dog outside to the paddock.'

'Come on, Flash!' Tom said, giving a little jerk to the lead. Flash rose to his feet. The minute Uncle John opened the door, however, Flash made a rush for it, tugging Tom along with him.

'No, no, Flash! That'll not do! It's for your master to lead you, no' for you to lead your master.'

Flash continued his headlong rush outside. John Meggetson followed. 'Hold on to him, Tom. I'll just get my stick.'

Tom looked shocked. 'You—you'll not beat him, Uncle John? He's *my* dog. You wouldn't dare! I'll—I'll——' Tom almost choked.

'Steady on, lad! Ye rush at a thing faster than your wee dog! Of course I shall not beat him! The stick's to guide him, no' to thrash him. I've never found cause to thrash one of my dogs yet.'

Tom felt rather foolish. 'Sorry, Uncle John!'

'Aye, weel, I'm more pleased than vexed at your outburst, laddie.' Uncle John became serious. 'But you're never to let me catch you thrashing your dog, either. No good sheepdog was ever made out o' a cowed animal yet. You've to be *firm* wi' him, but never let anger get the better of you. Now, take the stick in your hand and do as I bid ye.'

Tom took the stick. Flash looked at it out of his eye corner but showed no fear.

'Now pull the dog *behind* you on the lead and at the same time say plainly, "Come behind, Flash!" Hold the lead tight.'

Flash, however, had made up his mind that Tom meant to go for a walk and he bounded ahead

'Come behind, Flash!' Tom called loudly, pulling hard on the lead. Flash was brought up short but he strained at the lead, scrabbling with his feet on the gravel path. Tom tugged at the lead till the little dog, his four feet slipping on the path, was brought behind Tom, though Tom did not achieve it at the first pull. 'My goodness, he's tough!' he panted.

The farmer grinned, 'Aye, he'll need to be if he's to run the hills. Have patience, lad. He'll learn in time.'

At last Tom manoeuvred Flash behind him.

'Now, Tom, every time he tries to pass in front of you, wave the stick from side to side before him.'

'So that's what the stick's for?' Tom remarked.

'Aye, but keep giving him the word of command too.'

'Come behind, Flash!' Tom kept repeating, waving the stick like a sorcerer making an incantation over a cauldron. Flash looked bewildered as he followed the movement of the stick from side to side, but he made no attempt to break away.

'Not so fast, lad! You'll have him mesmerised,' John Meggetson chuckled. 'Now try taking a few steps and see if he'll follow you.'

Still moving the stick, Tom gave a little tug to the lead, saying loudly, 'Come behind, Flash!' Flash bounded forward to the right but the waving stick warned him back. He darted to the left but again the stick was there. After several more ineffectual attempts to get round, he gave it up and meekly followed behind Tom.

'He's learning,' Uncle John approved. 'Now, keep him at that for ten minutes at a time, twice a day, no more.'

'What do I teach him next?' Tom asked eagerly.

'Nothing, lad. One thing at a time till he's mastered it.'

Tom's face fell.

'You see, Tom, a pup's like a child. He can only stand so much teaching at a time. Short lessons of ten minutes repeated twice a day and he'll learn fast enough,' Uncle John explained. 'Don't confuse him with too much to begin with.'

'All right,' Tom agreed, but he still looked a bit disappointed.

'When he's finished his lesson you can give him a pat on his head and say he's a good dog. That'll give him confidence, but no chocolate cake, mind!' There was a twinkle in Uncle John's eye. 'You can take him off the lead now and let him have a good free scamper in the paddock. I must awa' to the sheep.'

John Meggetson summoned Jeff with a whistle and set off at a steady pace towards the nearest hill while Tom continued the lesson with lead and stick. Before the end of the time the little dog seemed to grasp what was required of him. He made fewer darts to elude the stick and began to trot obediently behind Tom. At the end of the lesson Tom stooped and patted the dog on the head. 'Good dog, Flash!'

In delight Flash rolled over on his back, waving all four paws in the air. Tom took the lead off him and in a second Flash was on his feet and capering madly about Tom, leaping in joy at his freedom again. Tom let the little dog run round the paddock for a while, then he turned towards the gate. The dog followed him. 'Come behind, Flash!' he cried, waving the stick. The dog retreated a step or two and fell in behind.

'I do believe you'd follow me of your own accord if I let you out through the gate,' Tom said aloud.

'Not yet, Tom! You've not had him long enough. He's got to learn obedience first.' It was Aunt Jane speaking. She had come out to see how the lesson was going. 'If he got loose he might run away to the hills and goodness knows when you'd see him again.'

Flash went scampering after a bumble bee and Tom took the chance to nip through the gate and close it. The little dog stood forlornly at the end of the paddock.

'Watch this, Aunt Jane!' Tom cried. 'Flash! Flash!'

The dog came bounding towards him.

'Guid sakes! He knows his name already,' Aunt Jane exclaimed, 'He'll be a wonder dog, that one!' But she was not looking at the the dog but at Tom, a different transfigured Tom from the unhappy silent boy who had come to them at first.

Uncle John insisted that only Tom should feed Flash and when, each evening, Tom put down the dish of meat for the dog and called his name, the dog appeared instantly.

'Aye, he's learned his name and to come to you now,' Uncle John remarked when Flash ran up without hesitation. 'The next lesson we'll take him off the lead, but you must still keep the stick to direct him and give him the usual command, "Come behind!" Always use the same words, so the dog gets used to them.'

After making a round or two of the paddock Tom slipped off the lead and cried, 'Come behind, Flash!' For a moment Flash seemed surprised at the lack of the restraining lead, then by newly acquired habit he fell in at Tom's heels and trotted solemnly round the paddock, keeping a wary eye on the stick which warned him not to venture too far in front.

'Grand! Grand!' Meggetson commented. 'he's learned his first lesson weel.'

'Can I take him out for a walk now without the lead, Uncle John?'

The farmer shook his head. 'Not yet.'

'But *you* said he'd learned his lesson,' Tom protested, slightly rebellious.

'Aye, but he's got other lessons to learn first. There are far ower many sheep on those hills to let him loose yet. If he gets running wild among them, scattering them he'll always want to *chase* sheep, not herd them.'

'What lesson next, then?' Tom asked.

'He's got to learn to lie down on his stomach at the word "Down!"' Then if he's working wi' sheep, you've got control over him.'

Tom looked perplexed. 'How do I teach him that?'

'Put the lead on him again.'

Tom snapped the lead on Flash's collar.

'Now press downward on his collar, saying "Down!" quite clearly as you do so.'

Tom gently forced the little dog into a crouching position saying 'Down!' in a loud voice. Surprised, Flash obeyed, but immediately tried to rise again. Tom repeated the pressure again and again.

'Now pat him on the head when he does stay down of his own accord,' Uncle John instructed.

At about the twentieth try Flash seemed to get the notion of what was wanted and stayed crouching at Tom's feet. Tom patted him affectionately and praised him and Flash shot out his tongue and licked Tom's hand.

'Practise "Come behind" and "Down" several times a day, Tom, off the lead in the paddock, but until he has learned absolute obedience you mustn't let him off the lead outside the paddock.'

'Can I take him for a walk *on* the lead? Tom asked.

'Aye, he might do that, but take the stick and see he keeps behind ye. Go down the farm road by the river and keep him well away from the sheep. We'll introduce him to them later on.'

'Can't I *run* him on the lead?'

Uncle John smiled. 'A bit of exercise'll be good for both of you. The minute you slow down to a walk, though, see he jogs *behind* you. That's his place and he's got to know it.'

Tom and Flash scampered down to the river. Mrs Meggetson came to the gate. She shaded her eyes against the setting sun and watched the pair of them.

'He's a different laddie since that dog came to the farm,' she pronounced. 'Flash seems to have given him a kind of purpose.'

When Flash had thoroughly mastered his two lessons and was quick to obey the words. 'Come behind!' and "Down!", Uncle John said, 'Now it's time he got used to the sheep. We'll try him loose in the farmyard first, though, with the gates shut.' There was a twinkle in his eyes.

Tom made sure the gates on the steading were closed before he slipped the lead from Flash's neck. He wondered how his uncle would try out Flash without any sheep present. Just then a number of ducks began to waddle in procession across the farmyard to a small pond. Flash flew at them barking. The ducks scattered, quacking angrily.

Horrified, Tom yelled at the top of his voice, 'Down, Flash! Down!' fearful of his uncle's wrath.

Flash hesitated, looked desperately at the ducks, then stopped in the middle of his run and crouched low, growling a little. The ducks huddled together in a corner of the farmyard and stood there, lifting one flat webbed foot and then another, letting out indignant quacks. Flash, his head raised between his forepaws, never took his eyes off them. They seemed to be mesmerised by him.

'I'm sorry, Uncle John! I'd forgotten about the ducks when I let him off the lead,' Tom apologised.

'I hadn't!' Mr Meggetson said. Tom was surprised to find his uncle chuckling. 'I wanted to see how Flash would go on with the ducks. Look at him with his eyes fixed on them! That dog's got the eye all right!'

'The eye?' Tom looked puzzled. 'What do you mean?'

'It's a power some sheepdogs have, Tom, the power to hold the sheep in one place just by staring at them. They don't all have it, but the dogs that do, they make the champions.'

'And Flash has it?'

'Look at him, lad! The ducks darena' stir from the corner for his eye being fixed on them.'

Tom could hardly hide his delight at this information.

'Call him off now and see if he'll come at your bidding,' his uncle suggested.

'Flash! Flash! Come behind!' Tom cried in his most commanding voice.

Somewhat reluctantly Flash rose to his feet and took his eyes off the ducks. He trotted obediently to Tom who pointed to the ground at his feet and said 'Down!' Flash obeyed and Tom stooped and patted him.

As if released from a magic spell the ducks began waddling quickly towards the pond, fluttering their wings now and again to quicken their pace. Only when they were safely floating on the surface of the pond did they quack defiance at Flash.

'Aye, the dog's learned obedience to your command,' Uncle John commented. 'For such a young dog he's shaping very well indeed. You can let him herd the ducks to the water now and again. It'll be fun for both o' you, but be sure that he doesna take hold o' the ducks wi' his mouth, or your aunt'll no' be sparing wi' her tongue on either of us.'

Tom and his uncle grinned at each other. It was as though they had entered into a secret alliance.

'Wait a wee while and we'll try Flash wi' a few sheep,' Uncle John promised.

Then one day he asked Tom if he'd like to walk up the hill and look at the sheep with him after supper and take Flash too. On the way he talked to the boy about Flash, as if anxious to take his mind off the letter.

'It seems a good chance to introduce Flash to the sheep,' he said, 'but ye'll need to keep him on the lead yet till he's got used to them. It wouldna' do for him to go after them like he went after the ducks.'

When they reached the first small flock on the hill Tom said 'Come behind!' very sternly and Flash obeyed, eyeing the sheep between Tom's leg and the poised stick.

'Walk Flash on the lead round the sheep and let him have a good look at them,' John Meggetson instructed Tom.

The puppy quivered and strained a little at the lead but Tom held fast and walked him several times round the sheep bunched together on the hillside. As they moved round, the sheep kept moving round too, keeping their heads to the dog, watching him warily but not trying to break away. Flash never took his eyes off them.

'What did I tell you? Yon dog has got the power of the eye,' Uncle John said with satisfaction. 'You can take him a bit closer to them, but dinna' let him run *at* the sheep.'

Tom went closer in several times and Flash behaved well, walking behind him sedately on the lead.

'That's grand,' Uncle John approved. 'Tomorrow we'll start him learning to drive a few sheep in the paddock.'

Next day Uncle John had a few sheep placed in the small field known as the paddock which was next to the house.

'Keep the lead on Flash yet, but let him drive the sheep bit by bit into the corner of the paddock. Make him go down on his stomach every few steps so that he does not frighten the sheep but moves them along quietly.'

Tom led Flash towards the sheep. The dog, still on the lead, ran forward two or three yards. The sheep began to move away towards the corner, then Tom cried, 'Down!' In an instant the puppy was crouching on his stomach, his eyes glaring at the sheep. The sheep stood still, watching him. Another move towards them and they bunched towards the corner. At each move of a few yards Tom ordered Flash to go down and the little dog obeyed, though once or twice it was rather reluctantly, as though he would like to hurry up the job. At last the sheep were penned in the corner.

'Weel done!' Uncle John said. 'Now take the lead off him, Tom, but tell him to stay down and we'll see what happens.'

Tom bent down and released the dog, pushing Flash's head down as he did so and saying 'Down!' Like a miracle Flash obeyed!

For a couple of minutes neither sheep nor dog stirred. Flash holding them by his steadfast stare, then Tom put the lead on him again and the spell was broken. Flash gave a burst of barking and strained at the lead.

'Quiet lad!' the farmer said. 'Quiet, Flash!' The best sheepdogs dinna' bark unless they want to call the master's attention.'

With a final bark and growl Flash settled down.

'That's shown Flash the power he has over the sheep. No' bad! No' bad!' From John Meggetson 'No bad!' was the highest praise. 'Ye've to keep at that drill now, Tom, for two or three weeks till Flash is quite sure what is required of him. I'll leave a few sheep in the paddock every day but ye must never let him run at them and scatter them.'

Through the warm summer days the training went on and Tom and the dog became more and more absorbed in each other. Out on the hills the green grass took a tawny tinge and the heather buds appeared.

'Ye'd think that dog knew what the lad was *thinking*. Tom scarcely needs to say a word to him,' Aunt Jane remarked one evening when Tom was out for a walk with Flash.

'Aye, the lad's done far better than ever I thought he would,' Uncle John agreed. 'Mind, though, he's got the best o' material to work on in Flash. That dog comes of the best strain of Border collies.'

KATHLEEN FIDLER

COLLIES

Sir Thomas Dick Lauder (1784–1848) was a follower of Scott in the field of the historical novel. Unfortunately, his most famous tale, The Wolf of Badenoch, *suffers from his inability to reach a convincing solution in coping with mediaeval speech, a difficulty he did not have to face in his exciting factual account of* The Great Moray Flood *(1830). His amusing account of collies in action comes from his book* Scottish Rivers *(1847).*

We quite well remember sitting on a dike by the roadside for nearly an hour with a shepherd of those parts, whilst, at our request, he despatched his dog over to the opposite hill, the face of which rose steeply backwards for nearly two miles, and stretched for double that space to right and left. The intelligence displayed by the creature was infinitely beyond anything we could have previously conceived. The moment he had compelled the brigade of bleaters to perform the evolution which his master's first signal had dictated, he sat down in his distant position with his eyes fixed on him; and, though certainly not nearer to us than half-a-mile to a mile, as the crow would fly, he at once caught up every successive signal, however slight, of his commanding officer, and put the troops into active motion, to carry the wished-for manoeuvre into effect. In this manner, they were made to visit every part of the hill-face in succession— at one time keeping in compact phalanx, as if prepared to receive cavalry, and at another scouring away and scattering themselves over

21   Sheepdog trials. (Courtesy of *The Scottish Farmer*).

the mountains, as if skirmishing, like *tirailleurs* against some unseen enemy advancing from over the hill-top beyond; and it appeared to us that, great as we had already considered the talents of Lieutenant Lightbody, the able adjutant of the distinguished corps we had recently left, we must feel ourselves compelled to declare that he was a mere tyro compared to this wonderful canine tactician.

And then, as to council, as well as war, we have seen some half-dozen of these highly gifted animals meet together from different parts of the mountains and glens, as if by appointment, at a sunny nook of some *fauld dike*, and then, seated on their haunches, hold a conference in which we, who were watching them, could have no doubt matters of vital importance to the collie population of the parish were discussed. No body of Presbyterian elders of kirks could have behaved with greater decorum, or could have shaken their heads more wisely; and when the conference broke up, we had not a single lingering doubt in our mind that the important business which had been under discussion, had been temperately settled in the wisest and most satisfactory manner.

SIR THOMAS DICK LAUDER

22   Auld Tam. Drawing by Colin Gibson.

THE OLDEST HERD IN THE PENTLANDS

When the boy Robert Louis Stevenson knew John Todd, he had been all his days faithful to that curlew-scattering sheep-collecting life that is the shepherd's.

He spoke in the richest dialect of Scots I ever heard; the words in themselves were a pleasure and often a surprise to me, so that I often came back from one of our patrols with new acquisitions; and this vocabulary he would handle like a master, stalking a little before me, 'beard on shoulder', the plaid hanging loosely about him, the yellow staff clapped under his arm, and guiding me uphill by that devious, tactical ascent which seems peculiar to men of his trade. I might count him with the best talkers; only that talking Scots and talking English seem incomparable acts. He touched on nothing at least, but he adorned it; when he narrated, the scene was before you; when he spoke (as he did mostly) of his own antique business, the thing took on a colour of romance and curiosity that was surprising. The clans of sheep with their particular territories on the hill, and how, in the yearly killings and purchases, each must be proportionally thinned and strengthened; the midnight busyness of animals, the signs of the weather, the cares of the snowy season, the exquisite stupidity of sheep, the exquisite cunning of dogs: all these he could present so humanly, and with so much old experience and living gusto, that weariness was excluded. And in the midst he would suddenly straighten his bowed back, the stick would fly abroad in demonstration, and the sharp thunder of his voice roll out a long itinerary for the dogs, so that you saw at last the use of that great wealth of names for every knowe and howe upon the hillside; and the dogs, having hearkened with lowered tails and raised faces, would run up their flags again to the masthead and spread themselves upon the indicated circuit. It used to fill me with wonder how they could follow and retain so long a story. But John denied these creatures all intelligence; they were the constant butt of his passion and contempt; it was just possible to work with the like of them, he said—not more than possible. And then he would expand upon the subject of the really good dogs that he had known, and the one really good dog that he himself had possessed. He had been offered forty pounds for it; but a good collie was worth more than that, more than anything to a 'herd'; he did the herd's work for him. 'As for the like of them!' he would cry, and scornfully indicate the scouring tails of his assistants.

Once—I translate John's Lallan, for I cannot do it justice, being born *Britannis in montibus*, indeed, but alas! *inerudito saeculeo*—once, in the days of his good dog, he had bought some sheep in Edinburgh, and on the way out, the road being crowded, two were lost. This was a reproach to John, and a slur upon the dog; and both were alive to their misfortune. Word came, after some days, that a farmer about Braid had found a pair of sheep; and thither went John and the dog to ask for restitution. But the farmer was a hard man and stood upon his rights. 'How were they marked?' he asked; and since John had bought right and left from many sellers and had no notion of the marks—'Very well,' said the farmer, 'then it's only right that I should keep them.'—'Well,' said John, 'it's a fact that I cannae tell the sheep; but if my dog can, will ye let me have them?' The farmer was honest as well as hard, and besides I daresay he had little fear of the ordeal; so he had all the sheep upon his farm into one large park, and turned John's dog into their midst. That hairy man of business knew his errand well; he knew that John and he had bought two sheep and (to their shame) lost them about Boroughmuirhead; he knew besides (the Lord knows how, unless by listening) that they were come to Braid for their recovery; and without pause or blunder singled out, first one and then another, the two waifs. It was that afternoon the forty pounds were offered and refused. And the shepherd and his dog— what do I say? the true shepherd and his man—set off together by Fairmilehead in jocund humour, and 'smiled to ither' all the way home with the two recovered ones before them. So far, so good; but intelligence may be abused. The dog, as he is by little man's inferior in mind, is only by little his superior in virtue; and John had another collie tale of quite a different complexion. At the foot of the moss behind Kirk Yetton (Caer Ketton, wise men say) there is a scrog of low wood and a pool with a dam for washing sheep. John was one day lying under a bush in the scrog, when he was aware of a collie on the far hillside skulking down through the deepest of the heather with obtrusive stealth. He knew the dog; knew him for a clever, rising practitioner from quite a distant farm; one whom perhaps he had coveted as he saw him masterfully steering flocks to market. But what did the practitioner so far from home? and why this guilty and secret manoeuvring towards the pool?—for it was towards the pool that he was heading. John lay the closer under his bush, and presently saw the dog come forth upon the margin, look all about to see if he were anywhere observed, plunge in and repeatedly wash himself over head and ears, and then (but now openly and with tail in air) strike homeward over the hills. That same night word was sent his master, and the rising practitioner, shaken up from where he lay, all innocence before the fire, was had out to a dykeside and promptly shot; for alas! he was that foulest of criminals under trust, a sheep-eater; and it was from the maculation of sheep's blood that he had come so far to cleanse himself in the pool behind Kirk Yetton.

R L STEVENSON

DANDIE

Come in ahint, ye wan'erin' tyke!
Did ever body see yer like?
Wha learnt ye a' thae poacher habits?
Come in ahint, ne'er heed the rabbits!
Noo bide there, or I'll warm yer lug!
My certie! ca' yersel' a doug?
Noo ower the dyke an' through the park:
Let's see if ye can dae some wark.
'Way wide there, fetch them tae the fank!
'Way wide there, 'yont the burn's bank!
Get roon' aboot them! Watch the gap!
Hey, Dandie, haud them frae the slap!
Ye've got them noo, that's no' sae bad:
Noo bring them in, guid lad! guid lad!
Noo tak' them canny ower the knowe—
Hey, Dandie, kep that mawkit yowe!
The tither ane, hey, lowse yer grip!
The yowe, ye foumart, no' the tip!
Ay, that's the ane, guid doug! guid doug!
Noo haud her canny, dinna teug!
She's mawkit bad; ay, shair's I'm born
We'll hae tae dip a wheen the morn.
Noo, haud yer wheesht, ye yelpin' randie,
And dinna fricht them, daft doug Dandie!
He's ower the dyke—the de'il be in't!
Ye wan'erin' tyke, come in ahint!

                                    W D COCKER

'GLEN', A SHEEPDOG

I ken there isnae a p'int in yer heid,
   I ken that ye're auld an 'ill,
An' the dogs ye focht in yer day are deid,
   An I doot that ye've focht yer fill;
Ye're the dourest deevil in Lothian land,
But, man, the he'rt o' ye's simply grand;
Ye're done an' doited, but gie's yer hand
   An' we'll thole ye a whilie still.

A daft-like character aye ye've been
   Sin the day I brocht ye hame,
When I bocht ye doon on the Caddens green
   An' gied ye a guid Scots name;

Ye've spiled the sheep and ye've chased the stirk,
An' rabbits was mair tae yer mind nor work,
An' ye've left i' the morn an' stopped till mirk,
   But I've keepit ye a ' the same.

Mebbe ye're failin' an' mebbe I'm weak,
   An' there's younger dogs tae fee,
But I doot that a new freen's ill tae seek,
   An I'm thinkin I'll let them be;
Ye've whiles been richt whaur I've thocht wrang,
Ye've liked me weel an' ye've liked me lang,
An' when there's ane o' us got tae gang—
   May the guid Lord mak' it me.

HILTON BROWN

DOMESTIC DOGS

A series of dog portraits in prose and verse, and a plea by Dr John Brown for the establishment of an Edinburgh dog home to accommodate strays; a plea that remained unanswered.

23   The Letter of Introduction, by Sir David Wilkie, RA. Courtesy of The National Galleries of Scotland.

FAITHFUL TO THE END

Several accounts of the execution of Mary, Queen of Scots have come down to us. They were collected by the Honourable Mrs Maxwell Scott in her book, The Tragedy of Fotheringay, *published in 1912. Here is part of one of them.*

Then she lying very still on the block, one of the executioners holding of her slightly with one of his hands, she endured two strokes of the other executioner with an axe, she making very small noise or none at all, and not stirring any part of her from the place where she lay; and so the executioners cut off her head, saving one little gristle, which being cut asunder he lifted up her head to the view of all the assembly and bade God save the Queen. Then her dressing of lawn falling off from her head it appeared as grey as one of threescore and ten years old, and polled very short, her face in a moment being so much altered from the form she had when she was alive as few could remember her by her dead face. Her lips stirred up and down almost a quarter of an hour after her head was cut off. Then Mr Dean said with a loud voice, 'So perish all the Queen's enemies,' and afterwards the Earl of Kent came to the dead body, and standing over it with a loud voice said, 'Such be the end of all the Queen's and the Gospel's enemies.'

Then one of the executioners pulling off her garters espied her little dog, which was crept under her clothes, which could not be gotten forth but by force. It afterwards would not depart from the dead corpse, but came and laid between her head and her shoulders, which being imbrued with her blood was carried away and washed, as all things else were, that had any blood, was either burned or clean washed, and the executioners sent away with money for their fees; not having any one thing that belonged unto her. And so every man being commanded out of the hall except the Sheriff and his men she was carried by them up into a great chamber lying ready for the surgeons to embalm her.

From *the Tanner Manuscript*

24   Portrait of Shandy, a Cairn Terrier. Courtesy of Jim Macdonald.

TOWSER

The Paisley poet Robert Tannahill (1742–1810) was much attached to his dog, Cyrus who accompanied him on his rambles on Gleniffer Braes. When Cyrus suddenly died, Tannahill celebrated his memory in the following poem, which first appeared in The Paisley Repository *in July 1806. John Kaspar Lavater, referred to by the poet, was a physionomist born in Zurich in 1741 but who died a Protestant minister in 1801.*

'Dogs are honest creatures,
Ne'er fawn on any that they love not;—
And I'm a friend to dogs—
They ne'er betray their masters.'

In mony an instance, without dout,
The man may copy frae the brute,
An by th' example grow much wiser;—
Then read the short memoirs o Towser.

Without ae spark o wit or glee
To licht them through futurity.
E'en be it sae;—poor Towser's story,
Though lamely tauld, will speak his glory.

   'Twas in the month o cauld December,
When Nature's fire seem'd just an ember,
An growlin Winter bellow'd forth
In storms an tempests frae the north—
When honest Towser's loving master,
Regardless o the surly bluster,
Set out to the neist borough town
To buy some needments o his own;
An, case some purse pest soud waylay him,
He took his trusty servant wi him.

   His bus'ness done, 'twas near the gloamin,
An ay the king o storms was foamin,
The doors did ring—lum pigs down tuml'd—
The strawns gush'd big—the sinks loud rum'ld;

Auld grannies spread their looves, an sich't
Wi 'O sirs! what an awfu nicht!'
Poor Towser shook his sides a draigl'd,
An's master grudg'd that he had taigl'd;
But, wi his merchandising load,
Come weel, come wae, he took the road.
Now cluds drave o'er the fiel's like drift,
Nicht flung her black cleuk o'er the lift;
An thro the naked trees an hedges
The horrid storm redoubl'd rages:
An, to complete his piteous case,
It blew directly in his face.
Whiles 'gainst the footpath stabs he thumped,
Whiles o'er the coots in holes he plumped;
But on he gaed, an on he waded,
Till he at length turn'd faint an jaded.

    With def'rence tae our great Lavaters,
Wha judge a mankind by their features,
There's mony a smiling, pleasant-fac'd cock
That wears a heart no worth a custock,
While mony a visage, antic, droll,
O'erveils a noble, gen'rous soul.
With Towser this was just the case:
He had an ill-faur't tawtie face,
His mak was something like a messin,
But big, an quite unprepossessin;
His master caft him frae some fallows
Wha had him doom'd untae the gallows
Because (sae hap'd poor Towser's lot)
He wadna tear a comrade's throat;
Yet, in affairs o love or honour,
He'd stan his part amang a hunner,
An whare'er fighting was a merit,
He never failed to shaw his spirit.

    He never girn'd in neighbour's face
Wi wild, ill-natur'd scant-o-grace,
Nor e'er accosted ane wi smiles,
Then, soon as turn'd, wad bite his heels,
Nor ever kent the courtier airt,
To fawn wi rancour at his heart;
Nor aught kent he o cankert quarlin,

Nor snarlin just for sake o snarlin;
Ye'd pinch him sair afore he'd growl,
Whilk ever shaws a magnanimity o soul.

But what adds maistly to his fame,
An will immortalise his name—
Immortalise!—presumptive wicht!
Thy lines are dull as darkest nicht,
To gang he could nae langer bide,
But lay doun by the bare dykeside.
Now, bairns an wife rush'd on his soul—
He groan'd—poor Towser loud did howl,
An, mournin, couret doun aside him;
But, oh! his master couldna heed him,
For now his senses 'gan to dozen.
His vera life-streams maist war frozen;
An't seemed as if the cruel skies
Exulted o'er their sacrifice,
For fierce the win's did o'er him hiss,
An dasht the sleet on his cauld face.

As on a rock far, far frae lan,
Twa shipwreck'd sailors shiv'ring stan,
If chance a vessel they descry,
Their hearts exult wi instant joy,
Sae was poor Towser joy'd to hear
The tread o trav'llers drawing near;
He ran, an yowl'd, an fawn' upon 'em,
But couldna mak them understan him,
Till, tugging at the foremost's coat,
He led them tae the mournfu spot
Where, cauld an stiff, his master lay,
Tae the rude storm a helpless prey.

Wi Caledonian sympathy
They bore him kindly on the way,
Until they reach'd a cottage bien.
They tauld the case—war welcomed in—
The rousin fire, the cordial drop,
Restor'd him soon tae life an hope;
Fond raptures beam'd in Towser's eye,
An antic gambols spake his joy.
                                    ROBERT TANNAHILL

HOUND LEAPING

The hound Joyous
waits on our threshold.
Late at night
her master opens the door.
She floats towards him,
buoyant, for him to catch her.

She lies out on the air,
the breath of her brisket lifts her
like a hawk hunting with hanging feet.
She glides in, mouth open,
her slip of pink tongue showing:
the one red tile
in the whole hound mosaic.

VALERIE GILLIES

WEE FREENLY DOUG

Wee freenly doug that rins aroon,
What cantrip's this? Get doon! Get doon!
I'm no yer maister. Hoots! gang hame!
I dinna ken ye, what's yer name?
I like the way ye cock yer lug,
Wee freenly doug.

I've clapped yer heid, noo rin awa',
What's that? Ye want to gie a paw!
Ay, dougs an' men, ma canine brither,
Are kind o' sib to ane anither,
Noo dinna bark, ye'll fricht that speug,
Ye randy doug.

Keep aff ma knees, ye daft wee loon,
Ye'll fyle ma claes! Keep doon! keep doon!
Buscuits? I've nane. I un'erstaun',
Ye only want to lick ma haun'.
There, lick awa', I'm no' a fyke,
Wee freenly tyke.

Ye'll wag yer tail aff wi' guid-natur',
Puir thing, ye're no' a bad wee cratur',
Did ye jalouse ma he'rt was wae,
An' did ye mean to mak' me gay?
Ay! glower at me, an' cock yer lug,
Wee freenly doug!

W D COCKER

25   Dog with Slipper. Drawing by Morven Cameron.

CELIA, THE WIFE O THE LAIRD

MRS MACKINTOSH, wi heather-mixture suit,
hauds oot frae Brechin in a blacke coupé:
we condescendan mien she gies a toot
an scatters sheep an fairmers frae her way.

Wi gracefu ease she purrs alang the road,
jinkan roun corners, shearan aff the hedge,
content wi smeddum that gat her sic a load
o whisky, meat an cigarettes for Reg.

Beside her, Pooh, her Pomeranian dug,
snuffles the air an stoiters roun the seat,
syne stretches oot upon the tartan rug
with twitchan nose fowr inches frae the meat.

Mountains and woods flow past her like a flick—
Charming, she thinks, the Scottish Rural Scene—
Wi artfu glances Pooh begins to lick
the paper whaur a pund o mince had been.

A line o cedars sweepan up a lawn,
an, hame again the weekly journey's done.
The heather-mixture's crinkl't sit-upon
gets oot an stretches like a yeastfu bun.

In green plus-fowrs and cheery Oxford cry,
Reggie comes amblan oot tae greet his wife.
Anither week the warld can whiffle by;
the laird's weil-bieldit frae the blasts of life

MAURICE LINDSAY

26 Servants at Dalkeith House, by J Ainsley. Courtesy of the Duke of Buccleuch and Queensberry, KT.

DONALD FRASER'S DOG
(after the Gaelic of Rob Donn)

D'ye wonder I'm wild
at ye, bawsant-faced collie,
that runs at my heels
like a pestering child?

Ye make me affronted,
the speak of the parish.
Folk say it's my trade
when a dog-catcher's wanted!

Ye're nae guid to me,
sae gang back to your maister,
thon daft Donald Fraser
that lets you run free!

Take thon look frae your een
—or I'll learn ye a lesson!
Ye ken fine what I mean,
ye'd better awa!
I canna keep ye,
                    my honest wee messan!
Bawsant-faced collie . . .
                    sae leal and sae braw!

DONALD CAMPBELL

THE DUG
(*after the Italian of Belli*)

My dug? If he wes killed, ye'll unnerstaun,
I'd murn as sair as gin they'd killed my brither.
Thon dug, ken this, there isnae sic anither,
Ye'll niver find his marra in the laun.

Ye suid jist see him eating breid, and gaun,
the dear wee thing, to seek things fir me, whither
to fesh my hat, or sneeshin-mull, whitiver,
and he duis things like we wad dae by haun.

When I win hame he wringles like an eel,
syne in the morn, ye suid see him stalk
to greet me, and he taks ma bairns to schuil.

He'll gae the messages, save me a walk
doun til the baker's and the pub . . . I feel
that the wan thing he cannae dae is talk.
Sonnet No 985 El cane
18 ottobre 1833

ROBERT GARIOCH

WHAT WILL I DO GIN MY DOGGIE DEE?
(Air: '*O'er the hills an' far away*')

Oh! what will I do gin my doggie dee?
He was sae kind an' true to me,
Sae handsome, an' sae fu' o' glee—
What will I do gin my doggie dee?
My guide upon the wintry hill,
My faithfu' friend through guid an' ill,
An' aye sae pleased an' proud o' me—
What will I do gin my doggie dee?

27 Grandfather's Return, by John Burr. Courtesy of The National Galleries of Scotland.

He lay sae canty i' my plaid,
His chafts upon my shouther-blade,
His hinder paw upon my knee,
Sae crouse an' cosh, my doggie an' me.
He wagged his tail wi' sic a swirl,
He cocked his leg wi' sic a curl,
An' aye snook't out his nose to me—
Oh! what will I do gin my doggie dee?

He watched ilk movement o' my ee,
When I was glad he barkit tae;
When I was waefu', sae was he—
Oh! I ne'er lo'ed him as he lo'ed me.
He guarded me baith light an' dark,
An' helpit me at a' my wark;
Whare'er I wandered there was he—
What will I do gin my doggie dee?

Nae ither tyke the country roun',
Was ever fit to dicht his shoon;
But now they'll hae a jubilee,
He's like to be removed frae me.
'Twas late yestreen my wife an' he—
Deil hae the loons that mauled them sae!
They're baith as ill as ill can be—
What will I do gin my doggie dee?

                                   GEORGE OUTRAM

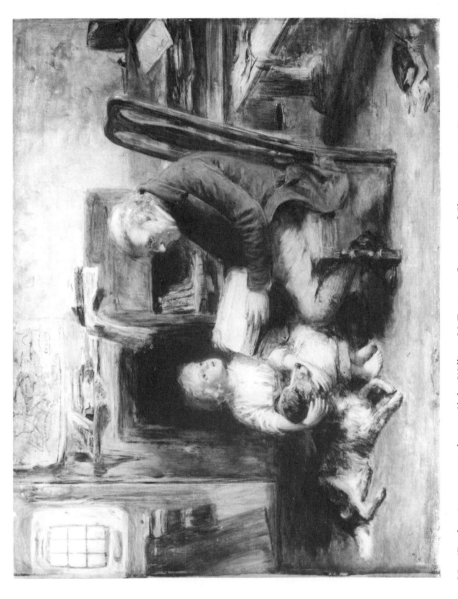

28   'Do doggies gang tae heaven?', by William McTaggart. Courtesy of Glasgow Art Gallery and Museum.

TRIO

Coming up Buchanan Street, quickly, on a sharp winter evening
a young man and two girls, under the Christmas lights—
The young man carries a new guitar in his arms,
the girl on the inside carries a very young baby,
and the girl on the outside carries a chihuahua.
And the three of them are laughing, their breath rises
in a cloud of happiness, and as they pass
the boy says, 'Wait till he sees this but!'
The chihuahua has a tiny Royal Stewart tartan coat like a teapot-
        holder
the baby in its white shawl is all bright eyes and mouth like favours
        in a fresh sweet cake,
the guitar swells out under its milky plastic cover, tied at the neck
        with silver tinsel tape and a brisk sprig of misletoe.
Orphean sprig! Melting baby! Warm chihuahua!
The vale of tears is powerless before you.
Whether Christ is born, or is not born, you
put paid to fate, it abdicates
                        under the Christmas lights.
Monsters of the year
go blank, are scattered back,
can't bear this march of three.

—And the three have passed, vanished in the crowd
(yet not vanished, for in their arms they wind
the life of men and beasts, and music,
laughter ringing them round like a guard)
at the end of this winter's day.

EDWIN MORGAN

MIDSUMMER NIGHT'S DOG
(Toby's song)

I'm a mad bad dog
I'm a Midsummer Dog
And I'll tummle your world right over
And my wildest night's dream
Cowps this hale bleak housing scheme
And rolls it in the Clover

Bow Wow   Bow Wow

The Christians hate the Muslims
I seen it on the News—
The Cathlicks hate the Proddys
And the Arabs hate the Jews

Bow Wow   Bow Wow

The poor hate the rich
And the ugly hate the pretty
Whites hate black
And the country hates the city

Bow Wow   Bow Wow

Men have hated Women
Since the world began—
The haves hate the havenots—
And Woman hates Man

Bow wow   Bow Wow

I canny thole intolerance
That's wan thing I detest—
The old hate the young
And East hates West

Bow Wow   Bow Wow

So I'm a glad bad dog
To be a Midsummer dog
And to roll you in the clover
While this magic moon shall sail
In two shakes of my tail
I'll tummle your sane World over

So no more underdog
I'm a blood and thunder dog
I'm not a sleeping dog and I won't lie!
I'll not say please
And I'll not beg
Sniff your kickers and the vicars
Hump your leg—
I'm not a sleeping dog and I won't lie!
I'll nosh your sausages
And snap at the nippers

I'll shit on your doorstep
And I'll chew your slippers—
I'm not a sleeping dog and I won't lie!

Men have hated Women
Since the world began—
The haves hate the havenots
And Woman hates Man

Bow Wow   Bow Wow

LIZ   LOCHHEAD

29   'Wha daur meddle wi me?'. Drawing by Morven Cameron.

CHILDLESS

Little doggie, eat your beefies
and I'll take you for a walkies;
then a bone to clean your teefhies—
pity that we can't have talkies.

MAURICE LINDSAY

THE SHEEP-DOG

The dog leapt over the hurdle—
I did but stare at sheep
Sharing the God-like languor
Those solemn heads did keep

I stared and the sheep stared,
Each twitching a soft nose,
Moist to strange airs that flowed
From my face, hands and clothes.

Wagged tails of thick-legged lambs
Wild in their milky pleasure
Impatient sheep moved on
Scouting their full measure.

Then that dog leaping hurdle
Rolled on me like a log
O that my guardian angel
Were a shaggy sheep-dog

ANDREW YOUNG

30   Sheepdog. Drawing by Morven Cameron.

THE LOST COLLIE

No' a face that I ken,
   Thrangity, reek an' noise,
Naething but strange-like men,
   An' weans wi' their ain bit ploys.
Seekin' him far an' near,
   My he'rt dunts faster an' faster:
Shairly somebody here
   Kens whaur he's gane, my master!

Cockin' my anxious lugs,
   Hidin' my fears doon deep,
Speirin' at daft-like dugs
   That hae na the smell o' sheep;
Tryin' to fin' some trace
   In a' the streets I've crossed,
Keekin' in ilka face,
   Does naebody ken, I'm lost?

W D COCKER

PLEA FOR AN EDINBURGH DOG HOME

An inveterate lover of dogs, Dr John Brown added his voice to a plea by a Mr William Chambers of Glenmoriston that a dog home should be set up for Edinburgh strays. Originally printed in The Scotsman, *the letter was subsequently published in the final selection of Brown's Essays,* Horae Subsecivae.

It need not be an expensive institution—if the value of the overplus of good eating that, from our silly over-indulgence, makes our town dogs short-lived, lazy, mangy, and on a rare and enlivening occasion *mad,* were represented by money, all the homeless, starving dogs of the city would be warmed and fed, and their dumb miseries turned into food and gladness. When we see our Peppers, and Dicks, and Muffs, and Nellys, and Dandies, and who knows how many other cordial little ruffians with the shortest and spiciest of names, on the rug, warm and cosey—pursuing in their dreams that imaginary cat—let us think of their wretched brethren or sisters without food, without shelter, without a master or a bone. It only needs a beginning, this new ragged school and home, where the religious element happily is absent, and Dr Guthrie may go halves with me in paying for the keep of a rescued cur. There is no town where there are so many thorough-bred house-dogs. I could produce from my own dog acquaintance no end of first-class Dandy Dinmonts and Skyes; and there is no town where there is more family enjoyment from dogs—from Paterfamilias down to the baby whose fingers are poked with impunity into eyes as fierce and fell as Dick Hatteraick's or Meg Merrilies's.

Many years ago, I got a proof of the unseen and therefore unhelped miseries of the homeless dog. I was walking down Duke Street, when I felt myself gently nipped in the leg—I turned, and there was a ragged little terrier crouching and abasing himself utterly, as if asking pardon for what he had done. He then stood up on end and begged as only these coaxing little ruffians can. Being in a hurry, I curtly praised his performance with 'Good dog!' clapped his dirty sides, and, turning round, made down the hill; when presently the same nip, perhaps a little nippier—the same scene, only more intense—the same begging and urgent motioning of his short, shaggy paws. 'There's meaning in this,' said I to myself, and looked at him keenly and differently. He seemed to twig at once, and, with a shrill cry, was off much faster than I could. He stopped every now and then to see that I followed, and by way of putting off the time and urging me, got up on the aforesaid portion of his body, and, when I came up, was off again. This continued till, after going through sundry streets and by-lanes, we came to a gate, under which my short-legged friend disappeared. Of course I couldn't follow him. This astonished him greatly. He came out to me, and as much as said, 'Why the—— don't you come in?' I tried to open it, but in vain. My friend vanished and was silent. I was leaving in despair and disgust, when I heard his muffled, ecstatic yelp far off round the end of the wall, and there he was, wild with excitement. I followed him to a place where, with a somewhat burglarious ingenuity, I got myself squeezed into a deserted coachyard, lying all rude and waste. My peremptory small friend went under a shed, and disappeared in a twinkling through the window of an old coach body, which had long ago parted from its wheels and become sedentary. I remember the arms of the Fife family were on its panel; and I daresay, this chariot, with its C springs, had figured in 1822 at the King's visit, when all Scotland was somewhat Fifeish. I looked in, and there was a pointer bitch with a litter of five pups; the mother like a ghost, and wild with maternity and hunger; her raging,

29   Queen Elizabeth with her corgis. Photograph courtesy of the *Scotsman Publication Ltd*.

yelling brood tearing away at her dry dugs. I never saw a more affecting or more miserable scene than that family inside the coach . . . What the relief was when we got her well fed and cared for—and her children filled and silent, all cuddling about her asleep, and she asleep too—awakening up to assure herself that this was all true, and that there they were, all the five, each as plump as a plum,

> All too happy in the treasure,
> Of her own exceeding pleasure,

what this is in kind, and all the greater in amount as many outnumber one, may be the relief, the happiness, the charity experienced and exercised in a homely, well-regulated *Dog Home*. *Nipper*—for he was a waif—I took home that night, and gave him his name. He lived a merry life with me—showed much pluck and zeal in the killing of rats, and incontinently slew a cat which had—unnatural brute, unlike his friend—deserted her kittens, and was howling offensively inside his kennel. He died, aged sixteen, healthy, lean, and happy to the last. As for *Perdita* and her pups, they brought large prices, the late Andrew Buchanan, of Coltbridge, an excellent authority and man—the honestest 'dogman' I ever knew—having discovered that their blood and her culture were of the best.

I have subscribed to the London 'Home' ever since I knew of it, and will be glad to do as much more for for one of our own, as Edinburgh is nearer and dearer than the city of millions of dogs and men. And let us remember that our own dogs are in danger of being infected by all the dog-diseases, from the tragic *rabies* down to the mange and bad manners, by these pariah dogs; for you know among dogs there is in practical operation that absolute equality and fraternity which has only been as yet talked of and shot at by and for us.—I am, &c.

BAD DOGS

There are, of course, bad dogs, and these are two of them, although usually it has seemed to us that often execution should be performed on the careless or neglectful owner rather than on the animal.

ARRAN BANNER 17 MAY

Here is a photograph
of Farmer Jim Bone
with his twelve dead
lambs and sheep
the caption says
attacked by dogs:
not a sharp picture
there seem to be only
two sheep and eight lambs
count them, count them.

HAMISH WHYTE

THE DOG RUNS AWAY

The dog runs away
with the hen in his mouth.
Catch him!

He must not be allowed such traffic.
What bundle of feathers will be safe from him?
He will scratch the cockerel from the dawn . . .

IAIN CRICHTON SMITH

DOG PORTRAITS

It has been claimed that the oldest Scottish dog is the wolfhound, of which the most famous is undoubtedly Sir Walter Scott's Maida, to be found in the section on literary dogs. The variety of breeds that has evolved from the wolfhound down the centuries is astonishing, an astonishment, indeed, neatly commemorated in George Macbeth's 'At Crufts'. In this section you will also meet a selection of Dr John Brown's Edinburgh dogs, Greyfriar's Bobby, likewise from Edinburgh, competing dogs, fighting dogs, a dog on the lookout for a good home—all too common a problem in a nation that is supposedly a nation of animal-lovers—and, lastly, a dog that went to sea.

32   Dog Portrait. Drawing by Morven Cameron.

GREYFRIARS BOBBY

In Edinburgh, outside Greyfriars Burial Ground, above the Grassmarket, the statue of a small dog stands on a plinth. He is Greyfriars Bobby, the telling of whose touching little tale has provoked so much sentimentality that it is not easy to find a concise readable account of it. In 1979, Forbes Macgregor set out to investigate the truth about Greyfriars Bobby, and uncovered the fact that the story first appeared in the Inverness Advertiser *on 10 May 1864, told by T. Wilson Reid, an Ayrshire journalist. Here is his account.*

My attention has for some time back been attracted to a case of canine fidelity which has not yet found its way into the newspapers, but which is, I think, much more remarkable than most cases of the kind that are on record. One day, some five years ago, several burials took place in that ancient and famous place of interment Old Greyfriars Churchyard. The whole of the following night a little terrier dog whined mournfully among the graves, and, under the shelter of an old pillared tombstone, that little dog has remained in the grave-yard almost ever since. I say *almost* ever since, because, after the had watched every night for somewhere about twelve months, Bob—for such is the name he goes by—was one day unfortunate enough, while out on a message for provender from one of the numerous friends he has made in the vicinity of Old Greyfriars, to get himself run over by a passing cab. He was nearly killed, but being taken up and nursed tenderly, Bob recovered in a few weeks, and returned to his old quarters in the kirkyard. Since then he has taken an occasional night's lodgings with some of his acquaintances, but he prefers to be among the mools. Indeed, on more than one occasion he became very violent when attempts were made to keep him in at night. Nobody knows whose death he mourns, or where he comes from, although the general belief is that he came from the country along with a funeral cortege. I saw the modest little animal today coming out of Gryfriars gateway, but he is now looking old and grey, although he yet keeps his tail high, and trots cleverly across the street to get a little 'creature comfort' in the shape of a biscuit or a sandwich from the publican or the baker. Bob never leaves the vicinity of Greyfriars. With a somewhat intimate friend, Sergeant Scott of the Royal Engineers, he sometimes takes a walk to the end of George IV Bridge, but there his head nods and his tail wags farewell and he trots back to the graveyard. Unlike many of his species and his betters, Bob was never known to do

33 Greyfriars Bobby. Photograph courtesy of the *Scotsman Publications Ltd.*

a dishonest action, and it is believed he would rather starve than steal. I make no excuse for giving you this interesting little history of certainly the most remarkable and faithful animal I ever knew.

This story was subsequently copied by several other Scottish newspapers, emerging as one of what W Gordon Smith described as Scotland's 'bydand myths'. In 1989, McGregor published the 'polished' version in The Scots Review, *the version treated in fictional form by Eleanor Atkinson in 1912.*

In 1858, in central Edinburgh, close to the Castle, the Grassmarket and Greyfriars Burial Ground, on each weekly market day, Wednesday, when the One O'clock Gun fired, a shepherd, Auld Jock, from Cauldbraes Farm on the Pentland Hills, accompanied by a faithful Skye terrier, was in the habit of taking his midday meal at John Traill's restaurant in Greyfriars Place. The terrier, named Bobby, was always rewarded with a bap, or other titbit.

One stormy November day, John Traill was surprised to see Bobby enter alone, showing signs of fatigue and distress. Not finding his master in the coffee-house, the dog went in search of him in the nearby closes and derelict buildings. Later that day Bobby returned to the restaurant with Auld Jock who was obviously very ill. Traill offered to fetch a doctor, but Jock refused and with Bobby went back into the storm. The next day the police found Jock's dead body and arranged for the funeral in Greyfriars Burial Ground.

That evening Bobby began a long vigil near his master's grave. Several days after he was discovered doing this he came to the restaurant for a midday snack.

Thereafter for many years Traill encouraged him to come for his dinner at the sound of the One O'clock Gun.

The story then continues through 14 years, relating such incidents as the near-escape of Bobby when he was in danger from the 1867 Dog Duty Act which required dog-owners to have a licence. In Bobby's case, it was paid by the Lord Provost.

In a skilful piece of investigative journalism, Macgregor discovered that there was neither a shepherd nor a farmer called Auld Jock, and that Bobby's milieu was urban rather than rural. Bobby was a police watch-dog owned by a constable, John Gray. On coming off night duty, guarding the cattle awaiting the next day's sale, Gray would walk to Hall's Court, change into civilian clothing and, still accompanied by Bobby, go to have a meal. After the death of his master Bobby was fed, and frequently slept, either at number 38 Candlemaker Row, overlooking Greyfriars Yard, the home of a Mr Ritchie and his daughter, or at number 28 where one James Anderson lived, and where in bad weather the little dog slept. Macgregor thus sums up:

The main facts then, are these: Greyfriars Bobby was a police watch-dog owned by John Gray, a market policeman, who resided in the area of his beat in Hall's Court, a slum cul-de-sac off the Cowgate in Central Edinburgh. He died there of pulmonary tuberculosis (aged 45) at 8.45 p.m. on Monday 8 February 1858 having been attended for three months by the police surgeon Dr Henry D Littlejohn. This proves that he had at least two years police service. Bobby was probably a puppy he had acquired about 1856.

Gray and Bobby, with three other officers, guarded the animal pens in the Grassmarket from 10 p.m. to 6 a.m. weekly for three nights before the Wednesday market. After duty Gray changed into civilian clothes and with Bobby took lunch at the Greyfriars Place coffee-house. Owing to the peculiar nature of his disease he probably continued to visit the coffee-house until shortly before his death.

Bobby, along with Gray's son (Young Jock) and others, attended his master's funeral on Market Day 10 February. Being unwilling to leave the grave he was carried back to Hall's Court from which, on several occasions, he returned to the graveyard. For the next 14 years he regarded Greyfriars Churchyard as his home.

FORBES MACGREGOR

That, however, is not quite the end of the tale. Macgregor later discovered that in an unnamed 'autobiographical book', Reid claimed that he and another journalist made up the story when short of copy.

But was this claim true? A note written by Ritchie, who had been a clockmaker, was given to Macgregor by a Glasgow descendant of Ritchie, Alice M Clark, attesting to Bobby's regular presence at the grave of John Gray from the time of the funeral on 10 February 1858.

So—did he exist or didn't he? No wonder the statue of the little dog wears a slightly quizzical look.

THE GREYHOUND

Often I use the quick-turning quarry's art
To reach the reclusion of my heart.

Yet He comes on like a longbacked hound
Able to stand over a lot of ground,

Free running like the scytheswing of a mower
His action shows great driving power.

His is the sound formation I would liken
To whatever God has made breathtaking.

A muscular and balanced grace
Can cleanly run, back doubling to the pace,

That back like a beam, head of a snake
—So the good greyhound shows his make.

A heart has room in that chest, nerved
In deep underline to form a curve.

Shoulderblades laid back over the lungs' panting
Set sharp bones in angulation long and slanting,

Articulate to bring the length of leg in line.
Concussion of the earth speeds him up an incline.

The thoroughbred throws forward low and straight
Those forelegs with unstilted gait.

That supple neck can reach to level-bite
The swerving flanks of prey in flight.

Out from among a world of beauties, God sent
The longdog to grip my mind with what He meant.

VALERIE GILLIES

TOBY, PETER AND BOB

The Scottish physician John Brown (1810–82) was born in Biggar, son of the Reverend John Brown, a secessionist who believed in complete atonement, and who was tried for heresy, and acquitted, in 1845 by those who believed in limited atonement. Dr John Brown, a much admired essayist in his day, wrote charmingly of Sir Walter Scott's short-lived little friend, Marjory Fleming, 'Pet Marjory', and of his own wide-ranging interests, both professional and general. These were collected in the two volumes of his Horae Subsecivae *(Leisure Hours, 1851–61). Some of his best essays describe his dogs, 'Rab and his Friends'. We have chosen three of the friends, Toby, Peter and Bob.*

TOBY

Was the most utterly shabby, vulgar, mean-looking cur I ever beheld: in one word, a *tyke*. He had not one good feature except his teeth and eyes, and his bark, if that can be called a feature. He was not ugly enough to be interesting; his colour black and white, his shape leggy and clumsy; altogether what Sydney Smith would have called an extraordinarily ordinary dog: and, as I have said, not even greatly ugly, or, as the Aberdonians have it, *bonnie wi' ill-fauredness*. My brother William found him the centre of attraction to a multitude of small blackguards who were drowning him slowly in Lochend Loch, doing their best to lengthen out the process, and secure the greatest amount of fun with the nearest approach to death. Even then Toby showed his great intellect by pretending to be dead, and thus gaining time and an inspiration. William bought him for twopence, and as he had it not, the boys accompanied him to Pilrig Street, when I happened to meet him, and giving the twopence to the biggest boy, had the satisfaction of seeing a general engagement of some severity, during which the twopence disappeared; one penny going off with a very small and swift boy, and the other vanishing hopelessly into the grating of a drain.

Toby was for weeks in the house unbeknown to any one but ourselves two and the cook, and from my grandmother's love of tidiness and hatred of dogs and of dirt, I believe she would have expelled 'him whom we saved from drowning', had not he, in his straighforward way, walked into my father's bedroom one night when he was bathing his feet, and introduced himself with a wag of his tail, intimating a general willingness to be happy. My father laughed most heartily, and at last

Toby, having got his way to his bare feet, and having begun to lick his soles and between his toes with his small rough tongue my father gave such an unwonted shout of laughter that we—grandmother, sisters, and all of us—went in. Grandmother might argue with all her energy and skill, but as surely as the pressure of Tom Jones' infantile fist upon Mr Allworthy's forefinger undid all the arguments of his sister, so did Toby's tongue and fun prove too much for my grandmother's eloquence. I somehow think that Toby must have been up to all this, for I think he had a peculiar love for my father ever after, and regarded grandmother from that hour with a careful and cool eye.

Toby, when full grown, was a strong coarse dog: coarse in shape, in countenance, in hair, and in manner. I used to think that, according to the Pythagorean doctrine, he must have been, or been going to be, a Gilmerton carter. He was of the bull-terrier variety, coarsened through much mongrelism and a dubious and varied ancestry. His teeth were good, and he had a large skull, and a rich bark as of a dog three times his size, and a tail which I never saw equalled—and indeed it was a tail *per se*; it was of immense girth and not short, equal throughout like a policeman's baton; the machinery for working it was of great power, and acted in a way, as far as I have been able to discover, quite original. We called it his ruler.

When he wished to get into the house, he first whined gently, then growled, then gave a sharp bark, and then came a resounding, mighty stroke which shook the house; this, after much study and watching, we found was done by his bringing the entire length of his solid tail flat upon the door, with a sudden and vigorous stroke; it was quite a *tour de force* or a *coup de queue*, and he was perfect in it at once, his first *bang* authoritative, having been as masterfully and telling as his last.

With all this inbred vulgar air, he was a dog of great moral excellence—affectionate, faithful, honest up to his light, with an odd humour as peculiar and as strong as his tail. My father, in his reserved way, was very fond of him, and there must have been very funny scenes with them, for we heard bursts of laughter issuing from his study when the two were by themselves: there was something in him that took to that grave, beautiful, melancholy face. One can fancy him in the midst of his books, and sacred work and thoughts, pausing and looking at the secular Toby, who was looking out for a smile to begin his rough fun, and about to end by coursing and *gurrin'* round the room, upsetting my father's books, laid out on the floor for consultation, and himself nearly at times, as he stood watching him—and off his guard and shaking with laughter. Toby had always a great desire to accompany my father up to town; this my father's good taste and sense of dignity, besides his fear of losing his friend (a vain fear!), forbade, and as the decision of character of each was great and nearly equal, it was often a drawn game. Toby, ultimately, by making it his entire object, triumphed. He usually was nowhere to be seen on my father leaving; he however saw him, and lay in wait at the head of the street, and up Leith Walk he kept him in view from the opposite side like a detective, and then, when he knew it was hopeless to hound him home, he crossed unblushingly over, and joined company, excessively rejoiced of course.

One Sunday he had gone with him to church, and he left him at the vestry door. The second psalm was given out, and my father was sitting back in the pulpit, when the door at its back, up which he came from the vestry, was seen to move, and gently open, then, after a long pause, a black shining snout pushed its way steadily into the congregation, and was followed by Toby's entire body. He looked somewhat abashed, but snuffing his friend, he advanced as if on thin ice, and not seeing him, put his fore-legs on the pulpit, and behold there he was, his own familiar chum. I watched all this, and anything more beautiful than his look of happiness, of comfort, of entire ease when he beheld his friend—the smoothing down of anxious ears, the swing of gladness of that mighty tail—I don't expect soon to see. My father quietly opened the door, and Toby was at his feet and invisible to all but himself; had he sent old George Peaston, the 'minister's man', to put him out, Toby would probably have shown his teeth, and astonished George. He slunk home as soon as he could, and never repeated that exploit.

I never saw in any other dog the sudden transition from discretion, not to say abject cowardice, to blazing and permanent valour. From his earliest years he showed a general meanness of blood, inherited from many generations of starved, bekicked, and down-trodden forefathers and mothers resulting in a condition of intense abjectness in all matters of personal fear; anybody, even a beggar, by a *growl* and a threat of eye, could send him off howling by anticipation, with that mighty tail between his legs. But it was not always so to be, and I had the privilege of seeing courage, reasonable, absolute, and for life, spring up in Toby at once, as did Athené from the skull of Jove. It happened thus:—

Toby was in the way of hiding his culinary bones in the small gardens before his own and the neighbouring doors. Mr Scrymgeour, two doors off, a bulky, choleric, red-haired, red faced man—*torvo vultu*—was, by law of contrast, a great cultivator of flowers, and he had often scowled Toby into all but non-existence by a stamp of his foot and a glare of his eye. One day his gate being open, in walks Toby with a huge bone, and making a hole where Scrymgeour had two minutes before been planting some precious slip, the name of which on paper and on a stick Toby made very light of, substituted his bone, and was engaged covering it, or thinking he was covering it up with his shovelling nose (a very odd relic of paradise in the dog), when S spied him through the inner glass-door, and was out upon him like the Assyrian, with a terrific *gowl*. I watched them. Instantly Toby made straight at him with a roar too, and an eye more torve than Scrymgeour's, who, retreating without reserve, fell prostrate, there is reason to believe, in his own lobby. Toby contented himself with proclaiming his victory at the door, and returning finished his bone-planting at his leisure; the enemy, who had scuttled behind the glass-door, glaring at him.

From this moment Toby was an altered dog. Pluck at first sight was lord of all; from that time dated his first tremendous deliverance of tail against the door, which we called 'come listen to my tail'. That very evening he paid a visit to Leo, next door's dog, a big, tyrannical bully and coward, which its master thought a Newfoundland, but whose pedigree we knew better; this brute continued the same system of chronic extermination which was interrupted at Lochend—having Toby down among his feet, and threatening him with instant death two or three times a day. To him Toby paid a visit that very evening, down into his den, and walked about, as much as to say 'Come on, Macduff!' but Macduff did not come on, and henceforward there was an armed neutrality, and they merely stiffened up and made their backs rigid, pretended each not to see the other, walking solemnly round, as is the manner of dogs. Toby worked his new-found facility thoroughly, but with discretion. He killed cats, astonished beggars, kept his own in his own garden against all comers and came off victorious in several well-fought battles; but he was not quarrelsome or foolhardy. It was very odd how his carriage changed, holding his head up, and how much pleasanter he was at home. To my father, next to William who was his Humane Society man, he remained staunch. He had a great dislike to all things abnormal, as the phrase now is. A young lady of his acquaintance was calling one day, and, relating some distressing events, she became hysterical. Of this Toby did not approve, and sallying from under my father's chair, attacked his friend, barking fiercely, and cut short the hysterics better than any *sal volatile* or valerian. He then made abject apologies to the patient, and slunk back to his chair.

And what of his end? for the misery of dogs is that they do die so soon, or, as Sir Walter says, it is as well they do; for if they lived as long as a Christian, and we liked them in proportion, and they then died, he said that was a thing he could not stand.

His exit was lamentable, and had a strange poetic or tragic relation to his entrance. My father was out of town; I was away in England. Whether it was that the absence of my father had relaxed his power of moral restraint, or whether through neglect of the servant he had been desperately hungry, or most likely both being true, Toby was discovered with the remains of a cold leg of mutton, on which he had made an ample meal; this he was in vain endeavouring to plant as of old, in the hope of its remaining undiscovered till tomorrow's hunger returned, the whole shank-bone sticking up unmistakably. This was seen by our excellent and Rhadamanthine grandmother, who pronounced sentence on the instant; and next day, as William was leaving for the High School, did he in the sour morning, through an easterly *haur*, behold him 'whom he saved from drowning', and whom, with better results than in the case of Launce and Crab, he had taught, as if one should say 'thus would I teach a dog,'—dangling by his own chain from his own lamp-post, one of his hind feet just touching the pavement, and his body preternaturally elongated.

William found him dead and warm, and falling in with the milk-boy at the head of the street, questioned him, and discovered that he was the executioner, and had got twopence, he—Toby's every morning crony, who met him and accompanied him up the street, and licked the outside of his can—had, with an eye to speed and convenience, and a want of taste, not to say principle and affection, horrible still to think of, suspended Toby's animation beyond all hope. William instantly fell upon him, upsetting his milk and cream, and gave him a thorough licking, to his own intense relief; and, being late, he got from Pyper, who was a martinet, the customary palmies, which he bore with something approaching to pleasure. So died Toby; my father said little, but he missed and mourned his friend.

There is reason to believe that by one of those curious intertwistings of existence, the milk-boy was that one of the drowning party who got the penny of the twopence.

PETER

One day lately a friend sent in a young Skye puppy for our judgement. We kept him for a day to study him, and the upshot is that we keep him still. He was so funny, so confidential, so plucky, his nose and the roof of his mouth were so black and comely, his genius for oddity, for unexpectedness so decided, his tail so glorious, that we could not let him go; and then, best of all, Dick tolerated him, adopted him, allowed him to take liberties with *his* tail that no mortal dog had ever before dared to do unbitten. Not that Dick played with him, or showed any approach to hilarity or acute interest, but he permitted himself and his dignity and his tail to be interfered with by this inveterate imp in a way that made the question of succession clear. You'll observe that I give him no name; this was our distress—no name would fit him. You know doubtless what one comes through in selecting a name for a dog; it is infinitely

worse than doing the same by a child; if it is your seventeenth, you can
fall back upon Scripture, or the Anglo-Saxons, or the cardinal virtues;
but with a dog there must be what Goethe calls an elective affinity
between the dog and the name. Well, we tried him for a week in vain
with all sorts of compact and cordial words, till one evening after dinner,
when we were sleepy and the room darkening, this young and genial
ruffian was seen perched in the arm-chair. 'Peter!' we all exclaimed, and
Peter he is—not any particular Peter, but Peter absolute. I don't know
him well enought yet to speak definitely, but I incline to think well of
him, he is an original, and stands on his own bottom. Dogs, like men,
have generally some dominant quality; thus Toby was eminently wide-
awake, though he was much else; Wylie, in the same way, was more
eident than any one other thing; Wasp more impassioned; Jock more
daft; Crab more deep—a very deep dog was Crab; John Pym more full o'
fechtin; Puck more of a simpleton; Rab more huge (in head, in heart, and
in affection); and Dick like another Richard, more judicious; but Peter
is, in his essence and in every action—especially of his tail—which he
waves aloft like a feather or banner—*ludicrous*, he can't help it, he does
not mean it, he is it; he is like the great actor Liston, his mere look makes
you laugh, not that you laugh at him, or in any way think lightly of his
understanding; he is the cause, not the object of laughter, as many a
good man and great has been before him; he is not the least of a foolish
or hare-brained dog,—he is a dog of affection and *nous*. He is a dark
brindle, and as plucky and procacious as Mr Roebuck, whom I am told
he resembles, but then he is young. If I survive him, which I almost hope
may not be, I shall perhaps write his life, which I promise will not be as
long as his tail and shorter than his temper, which, with all his boyish
wilfulness, I can see is as sweet and faithful as was Jonathan's (the
grandson of Kish) or Colonel Newcome's. If he survives me, I am sure of
one true mourner. *Macte esto puer!*

'Man is the god of the dog,' says Burns after Lord Bacon; it were well
for us if we served our Master as our dog serves his.

BOB

If Peter was the incarnation of vivacity, Bob was that of energy. He
should have been called Thalaba the Destroyer. He rejoiced in
demolition—not from ill temper, but from the sheer delight of energising.

When I first knew him he was at Blinkbonny toll. The tollman and his
wife were old and the house lonely, and Bob was too terrific for any
burglar. He was as tall and heavy as a foxhound but in every other
respect a pure old-fashioned, wiry, short-haired Scotch terrier,—red as
Rob Roy's beard,—having indeed other qualities of Rob's than his

hair—choleric, unscrupulous, affectionate, staunch,—not in the least magnanimous, as ready to worry a little dog as a big one. Fighting was his 'chief end', and he omitted no opportunity for accomplishing his end. Rab liked fighting for its own sake too, but scorned to fight anything under his own weight; indeed, was long-suffering to public meanness with quarrelsome lesser dogs. Bob had no such weakness.

After much difficulty and change of master, I bought him, I am ashamed to say, for five pounds, and brought him home. He had been chained for months, was in high health and spirits, and the surplus power and activity of this great creature, as he dragged me and my son along the road, giving battle to every dog he met, was something appalling.

I very soon found I could not keep him. He worried the pet dogs all around, and got me into much trouble. So I gave him as Night-watchman to a goldsmith in Princes Street. This work he did famously. I once, in passing at midnight, stopped at the shop and peered in at the little slip of glass, and by the gas-light I saw where he lay. I made a noise, and out came he with a roar and a bang as of a sledge-hammer. I then called his name, and in an instant all was still except a quick tapping within that intimated the wagging of his tail. He is still there,—has settled down into a reputable, pacific citizen—a good deal owing, perhaps, to the disappearance in battle of sundry of his best teeth. As he lies in the sun before the shop door he looks somehow like the old Fighting Téméraire.

I never saw a dog of the same breed; he is a sort of rough *cob* of a dog—a huge quantity of terrier in one skin; for he has all the fun and briskness and failings and ways of a small dog, begging and hopping as only it does. Once his master took him to North Berwick. His first day he spent in careering about the sands and rocks in the sea, for he is a noble swimmer. His next he devoted to worrying all the dogs of the town, beginning, for convenience, with the biggest.

This aroused the citizens, and their fury was brought to a focus on the third day by its being reported alternatively that he had torn a child's ear off, or torn and actually eaten it. Up rose the town as one man, and the women each as two, and, headed by Matthew Cathie, the one-eyed and excellent shoemaker, with a tall, raw divinity student, knock-kneed and six feet two, who was his lodger, and was of course called young Dominie Sampson. They bore down upon Bob and his master, who were walking calmly on the shore.

Bob was for making a stand, after the manner of Coriolanus, and banishing by instant assault the 'common cry of curs', but his master saw sundry guns and pistols, not to speak of an old harpoon, and took to his heels, as the only way of getting Bob to take to his. *Aurifex*, with much *nous* made for the police station, and with the assistance of the constables and half a crown, got Thalaba locked up for the night, safe and sulky.

Next morning, Sunday, when Cathie and his huge student lay uneasily asleep, dreaming of vengeance, and the early dawn was beautiful upon the Bass, with its snow cloud of sea-birds 'brooding on the charmed wave', Bob was hurried up to the station, locked into a horse-box—him never shall that ancient Burgh forget or see.

DR JOHN BROWN

The Duchess.

35   Dr John Brown's Scottie, 'The Duchess'.

AT CRUFT'S

Old English Sheepdog
Eyes
drowned in fur:
an affectionate,

rough cumulus
cloud, licking
wrists and

panting: far
too hot
in your

'profuse' coat
of old wool. You
bundle yourself

about on
four shaggy
pillars

of Northumberland
lime-stone,
gathering sheep.

Weimaraner
On long
monkey's-paws
like

olive-branches, you
loll, awkwardly
leaning

your dun muzzle against
the veined
oak: your

eyes are what
matter most, those
bottomless, dreaming

yellows, orbed
in
the fine bone

of a German
hunter's-rifle
head

Chow
With ears
of a Teddy bear: your
tail

over-curled
as if attempting
to open

yourself
like a tin
of pilchards: your tongue

seal-blue: you
roll
in a cuddly

world
of
muscular

bunches, bouncy as
Chinese
India-rubber

Shih Tzu
Top-knot
in a safety-
pin, this

grand-master,
flexible
as a rug, flops

inclines
his grave head,
is a blur

to the Japanese
photographer,
some foreign

bitch, is he
thinking,
as he wraps

his fleece
in imaginary
sleeves.

Chinese Crested
Raw
as a skinned
chicken, the

goat's plume
on your brow
ruffled, you

swing a
furred
switch

in the ring
behind you
fastidiously

tripping
more like a gazelle
than a dog

as you move:
Manchurian,
shivering.

Schnautzer
In that
severe
square hook

of a head, he
holds outlines
of his own

dour
elegance to be
scissored

in air: braced
legs
erect

his arched
eyebrows: in grey
mournful

exactitude, his
jaw swivels and:
schnapps!

Bulldog
With a face
as crumpled
as crushed

paper, he
shoulders
grumpily

36 Waiting, by Sir Edwin Landseer, from *The Works of Sir Edwin Landseer, R.A.* published by Cosmo Monkhouse Virtue & Co, London.

over the sawdust:
someone pats
his

rear, he is
sure,
nevertheless, there

is still
a war on. Everything
everywhere,

pace Leibnitz,
is for
the worst.

Dobermann
Always
on the attack, the lips
drawn

hard back, the
minute
immaculate

teeth, bared
in a snarl, no
love

lost, is
there, then,
between us, or

wasted; in
smooth black
and orange

killing skin
you sit,
spring-coiled.

Shetland Sheep-dog
Am I being
so thoroughly
powdered

to win
a prize, or
just

to please
this ingenious
powderer

in her
pink anorak, you
seem to ask,

with your bright
ice-chips
ripping

the prejudice from
your over-
fluffy ruff.

Pyrenean Mountain Hound
As if
absorbing the whole
heat of snow

into his noble
coat, he
lifts,

heavy-lidded, the
sombre
gaze

of a glacier-
liver,
knowing

not only how
to revive
the frozen

with brandy, but
what
being wanted means.

Newfoundland
Is
a black
solid bodied

one this, with
a look
of lying

beside a
banked fire,
stretched

in his log
-cabin, his nose
twitching

to the sound
of owls or
coyotes, or even

coal
dropping
in the grate.

Clumber Spaniel
If ears
are for hearing
with,

she seems to
waste
acres of expensive

37 A Poodle, by Edwin Landseer, from *The Works of Sir Edwin Landseer, R.A.* published by Cosmo Monkhouse Virtue & Co. London.

velvet, her
brindled
flaps relaxing

in
friendly
fingers, although,

quite definitely,
closed: at any rate she
goes

on
dozing
without saying a word.

Great Dane
To be as
big
you could

easily
over-leap my
six feet with your

coat of
many
colours, fawn,

black, harlequin,
is,
after all,

remarkable
enough, so
why whip

my legs
to a jelly
with your tail?

Boston Terrier
Neat
enough for
a tea-party

in that flat
alpaca coat, you
maintain, though, something of

a lawyer's look,
my mid-Victorian,
Yankee

dandy, round-
supercilious-
eyed, fresh

from the courts
after quartering
someone, perched

on your four
ebony
sticks.

Samoyed
As if
presenting the
spun glitter of

a new
steel wool: or an
ice tasting

of glacier-
mint: this
polar bundle of

huggable
whiteness, clear
hair

emerging
like tufts
of grown

glass from her
deep skin,
glows.

Alsatian
and yet
without exactly the
appearance of

being violent
that heavy
tail, tucked

under the firm
hind-quarters,
occasions

doubts about the
advisability
of treating

this law-dog
as if
he was really only

a sheep
in wolf's-
clothing.

Irish Setter
Touch the flowing
thorough-bred
insouciance

of the Old
Ascendancy: the
superior-tweed

mahogany
fur, glossy
as if wet

from the best kind
of trout-stream
recently,

ruffles, furrows
a little
over

the interrogating,
courteous arrogance
of the eyes.

Boxer
On a strong
rope,
aggressive,

restrained, you
tug
at your corner,

eager
for the bell, and
to be in,

dancing
round the ring,
belligerent in

your
gloved skin,
muscled

as if to
let fists
emerge, clenched.

GEORGE MACBETH

A DOGFIGHT

Four and thirty years ago, Bob Ainslie and I were coming up Infirmary Street from the High School, our heads together, and our arms intertwisted, as only lovers and boys know how, or why.

When we got to the top of the street, and turned north, we espied a crowd at the Tron Church. 'A dogfight!' shouted Bob, and was off; and so was I, both of us all but praying that it might not be over before we got up! And is this not boy-nature? and human nature too? and don't we all wish a house on fire not to be out before we see it? Dogs like fighting; old Isaac says they 'delight' in it, and for the best of all reasons; and boys are not cruel because they like to see the fight. They see three of the great cardinal virtues of dog or man—courage, endurance, and skill—in intense action. This is very different from a love of making dogs fight, and enjoying, and aggravating, and making gain by their pluck. A boy—be he ever so fond himself of fighting, if he be a good boy, hates and despises all this, but he would have run off with Bob and me fast enough: it is a natural, and a not wicked interest, that all boys and men have in witnessing intense energy in action.

Does any curious and finely-ignorant woman wish to know how Bob's eye at a glance announced a dogfight to his brain? He did not, he could not see the dogs fighting; it was a flash of an inference, a rapid induction. The crowd round a couple of dogs fighting, is a crowd masculine mainly, with an occasional active, compassionate woman, fluttering wildly round the outside, and using her tongue and her hands freely upon the men, as so many 'brutes'; it is a crowd annular, compact, and mobile; a crowd centripetal, having its eyes and its heads all bent downwards and inwards, to one common focus.

Well, Bob and I are up, and find it is not over: a small thoroughbred, white bull-terrier, is busy throttling a large shepherd's dog, unaccustomed to war, but not to be trifled with. They are hard at it; the scientific little fellow doing his work in great style, his pastoral fighting enemy fighting wildly, but with the sharpest of teeth and a great courage. Science and breeding, however, soon had their own; the Game Chicken, as the premature Bob called him, working his way up, took his final grip of poor Yarrow's throat—and he lay gasping and done for. His master, a brown, handsome, big young shepherd from Tweedsmuir, would have liked to have knocked down any man, would 'drink up Esil, or eat a crocodile', for that part if he had a chance:

it was no use kicking the little dog; that would only make him hold the closer. Many were the means shouted out in mouthfuls of the best possible ways of ending it. 'Water!' but there was none near, and many cried for it who might have got it from the well at Blackfriars Wynd. 'Bite the tail!' and a large, vague, benevolent, middle-aged man, more desirous than wise, with some struggle got the bushy end of Yarrow's tail into his ample mouth, and bit with all his might. This was more than enough for the much-enduring, much-perspiring shepherd, who, with a gleam of joy over his broad visage, delivered a terrific facer upon our large, vague, benevolent, middle-aged friend,—who went down like a shot.

Still the Chicken holds; death not far off. 'Snuff! a pinch of snuff!' observed a calm, highly-dressed young buck, with an eye-glass in his eye. 'Snuff, indeed!' growled the angry crowd, affronted and glaring. 'Snuff! a pinch of snuff!' again observes the buck but with more urgency; whereon were produced several open boxes, and from a mull which may have been at Culloden, he took a pinch, knelt down, and presented it to the nose of the Chicken. The laws of physiology and of snuff take their course; the Chicken sneezes, and Yarrow is free!

The young pastoral giant stalks off with Yarrow in his arms,—comforting him.

But the Bull Terrier's blood is up, and his soul unsatisfied; he grips the first dog he meets, and discovering she is not a dog, in Homeric phrase, he makes a brief sort of *amende*, and is off. The boys, with Bob and me at their head, are after him: down Niddry Street he goes, bent on mischief; up the Cowgate like an arrow—Bob and I, and our small men, panting behind.

There, under the single arch of the South Bridge, is a huge mastiff, sauntering down the middle of the causeway, as if with his hands in his pockets: he is old, grey, brindled, as big as a little Highland bull, and has the Shaksperian dewlaps shaking as he goes.

The Chicken makes straight at him, and fastens on his throat. To our astonishment, the great creature does nothing but stand still, holding himself up, and roar—yes, roar; a long, serious remonstrative roar. How is this? Bob and I are up to them. *He is muzzled!* The bailies had proclaimed a general muzzling, and his master, studying strength and economy mainly, had encompassed his huge jaws in a home-made apparatus, constructed out of the leather of some ancient *breechin*. His mouth was open as far as it could; his lips curled up in rage—a sort of terrible grin; his teeth gleaming, ready, from out the darkness; the strap across his mouth tense as a bowstring; his whole frame stiff with indignation and surprise; his roar asking us all round, 'Did you ever see the like of this?' He looked a statue of anger and astonishment, done in Aberdeen granite.

We soon had a crowd: the Chicken held on. 'A knife!' cried Bob; and a cobbler gave him his knife: you know the kind of knife, worn away obliquely to a point, and always keen. I put its edge to the tense leather; it ran before it; and then!—one sudden jerk of that enormous head, a sort of dirty mist about his mouth, no noise,—and the bright and fierce little fellow is dropped, limp, and dead. A solemn pause: this was more than any of us had bargained for. I turned the little fellow over, and saw he was quite dead: the mastiff had taken him by the small of the back like a rat, and broken it.

He looked down at his victim appeased, ashamed, and amazed; snuffed him all over, stared at him, and taking a sudden thought, turned round and trotted off. Bob took the dead dog up, and said, 'John, we'll bury him after tea.' 'Yes,' said I, and was off after the mastiff. He made up the Cowgate at a rapid swing; he had forgotten some engagement. He turned up the Candlemaker Row, and stopped at the Harrow Inn.

There was a carrier's cart ready to start, and a keen, thin, impatient, black-a-vised little man, his hand at his grey horse's head, looking about angrily for something. 'Rab, ye thief!' said he, aiming a kick at my great friend, who drew cringing up, and avoiding the heavy shoe with more agility than dignity, and watching his master's eye, slunk dismayed under the cart,—his ears down, and as much as he had of tail down too.

What a man this must be—thought I—to whom my tremendous hero turns tail! The carrier saw the muzzle hanging, cut and useless, from his neck, and I eagerly told him the story, which Bob and I always thought, and still think, Homer, or King David, or Sir Walter, alone were worthy to rehearse. The severe little man was mitigated, and condescended to say, 'Rab, ma man, puir Rabbie,'—whereupon the stump of a tail rose up, the ears were cocked, the eyes filled, and were comforted; the two friends were reconciled. 'Hupp!' and a stroke of the whip were given to Jess; and off went the three.

Bob and I buried the Game Chicken that night (we had not much of a tea) in the back-green of his house, in Melville Street, No 17, with considerable gravity and silence; and being at the time in the Iliad, and, like all boys, Trojans, we of course called him Hector.

DR JOHN BROWN

THE SPUDDY

When the pubs closed the crew returned to the *Silver Crest*. 'What's he doin' aboard?' they asked, seeing the Spuddy.

'Ship's dog,' replied Jake laconically.

'Where's his kid, then?' asked the youngest crewman. recognising the dog and when Jake gave a brief explanation they murmured small pretended grumbles about having a dog aboard and hoped he would not be responsible for another run of bad luck.

'Not him.' Jake spoke with conviction as he gave the Spuddy a rough stroking. 'He's goin' to be our mascot, you'll see.'

And as their mascot they came to regard him since on his first night at sea with them they ran into an enormous shoal of herring and came back gunwale deep with their load. The crew were jubilant with the knowledge that their run of ill-luck had ended.

'I told you he'd be our mascot,' Jake reminded them and the crew accepted his remark with such seriousness that the Spuddy, had he allowed it, would have become more of a ship's pet than a ship's dog.

'He's worth his weight in steak every week,' asserted the cook as if daring any of them to question the sudden increase in the butcher's bill.

The Spuddy took readily to life at sea and as he saw the catches of herring coming aboard the obvious excitement of the men infected him and he raced from stem to stern, from stern to stem, careful to keep out of everybody's way yet still making sure he was sharing in the activity. By the third night he was so anxious to join in that he grabbed at the net ropes as the men were hauling and bracing himself pulled with every ounce of muscle in his body.

'By God! We've got a dog an' a half,' the crew congratulated one another.

After the third successive night of good catches the *Silver Crest* seemed to lose the shoal and on the fourth night again they searched in vain while the Spuddy spent his time running rootlessly around the deck or sitting wistfully in the bow staring in the night-black water. He was repeating this performance the following night when Jake, in the wheelhouse, was surprised to hear him start to bark. Jake was puzzled, it was the first time since he had been aboard that the Spuddy had been heard to bark. Jake was even more puzzled when a few moments later the dog came aft and began scratching at the wheelhouse door. Jake liked to have the Spuddy's company when he was alone on deck and kicking open the door he waited for the dog to come in. Instead of joining him the Spuddy only pawed at him and whined.

'What is it, boy?' Jake asked. But the dog ran back to stand with his two feet on the bow while he peered down into the water and his tail wagged ecstatically. Jake eased the throttle and immediately a head appeared at the fo'c'sle hatch. 'See what's botherin' him!' Jake shouted.

The youngest member of the crew came aft, pulling on an oilskin. 'What's wrong, skipper?'

'See what's botherin' the Spuddy,' Jake repeated. 'He's behavin' kind of queer, as if he can see or hear somethin',' The man went forward and as he reached the bow the Spuddy's tail began to thrash even more ecstatically and again he started to bark. The young man knelt down beside him, concentrating his attention on the sea. The cook came aft to join Jake.

'What's excitin' the dog?' the cook asked.

'Damned if I know,' admitted Jake, and added uncertainly, 'You'd think he must be hearin' or seein' somethin' the way he's actin'.'

The man in the bow stood up and turning gave a wide negative sweep of his arms.

'He can't see anythin' seemingly,' said the cook.

Shouting to the Spuddy to be quiet Jake throttled the engine down to a murmur and handing over the wheel to the cook with the instruction to steer in a wide circle he went out on deck and listened and looked intently. A minute later he was back in the wheelhouse.

'Go an' tell them to stand by to shoot the nets,' he snapped. 'It's my belief that dog's tryin' to tell us there's herrin'.'

Flashing him an incredulous glance the cook rushed forward to pass the command. An hour later they were gloatingly hauling in their loaded nets while the Spuddy looked on with smug triumph. Afterwards down in the fo'c'sle the crew looked at one another in amazement and asked, 'How did he do it, d'you reckon? By smell or by sight or by hearin'?'

'It's enough that he did it,' the oldest crew member declared. 'What we must wait an' see now is, can he do it again?'

The Spuddy not only did it again and again but he became such a reliable herring spotter that if he showed no interest in the area they were searching for fish they knew there was little likelihood of finding any there. In Gaymal when the stories got around the Spuddy, instead of being regarded as a stray, became a star and though there were some fishermen who at first refused to believe in the dog's ability to detect the presence of herring the *Silver Crest's* consistently good catches were irrefutable evidence of his powers and it was not long before skipper Jake was pointing out to his crew how even the most sceptical of the

38 The Spuddy, from *The Spuddy* by Lillian Beckwith, Arrow Publications.

fishermen tended when at sea to keep the *Silver Crest* close company in the hope of sharing the Spuddy's largesse.

When Andy heard of the Spuddy's faculty for herring spotting he was both thrilled and proud to know he was his friend for though Andy was attending school now, on Saturday mornings he was always waiting at the pier for the *Silver Crest* to come in so that he could greet the Spuddy and take him for the long hill walks Jake said the dog needed after the week at sea. In the evenings when the time came for him to return to his aunt's house Andy liked, before giving the Spuddy a special farewell fussing, to accompany him aboard the boat and watch him eat one of the meals the cook had left for him. When the Spuddy had become a sea dog he had to get used to taking his meals in the evening the same as the crew and when at weekends he was left in charge of the boat the cook always put two bowls of food out for him—one at each end of the galley—explaining to the dog that one was to be eaten on the Saturday night and the other on the Sunday night. To test his theory that the Spuddy was intelligent enough to understand and obey, the cook came down to the boat on the first Sunday morning and found to his satisfaction that only one of the meals had been eaten; the other was untouched. When he came down later that evening again to test his theory he found the second meal had been eaten. For three successive weekends the cook visited the boat, not always at the same times, and invariably he found that the Spuddy did not touch the second bowl of food until the Sunday evening.

A year passed and the Spuddy became a cherished and indispensable member of the crew of the *Silver Crest*. In addition to herring spotting he had resumed his war with the gulls, protecting the herring at unloading time as fiercely as he had at one time protected the fish for which Joe had been responsible. At weekends he guarded the boat like a sentry so that crews from other boats moored outside the *Silver Crest* were heard to complain that though the Spuddy allowed them to cross his boat in daylight when returning drunk at night they had to 'give the password like bloody soldiers before he'd let you cross'.

On board he could be trusted to keep out of the way of the crew's feet when they were busy on deck, except for falling overboard one pitch black night into a heaving sea while the skipper and crew were all too busy hauling to notice his disappearance he did nothing that would cause them concern. That night the Spuddy had been really frightened but sensibly he had fought the sea to swim round the boat to the side where the nets were being hauled and gripping the footrope of the net with teeth and legs he clung on. It was not until the incredulous crew saw him being hauled in with the net that they realised he must have fallen overboard and how near they must have been to losing him.

Jake's fear had erupted in a flash of anger and he swore at the Spuddy vehemently, ordering him down to the fo'c'sle but afterwards when things had quietened down Jake laughed to himself, thinking he had never seen the dignified Spuddy look so utterly ridiculous and dejected as he had when he was being hauled aboard along with a load of herring. Jake called the dog back to the wheelhouse to give him a teasing and patting but following that night he aways made sure the Spuddy was safely in the fo'c'sle when they were actually fishing and he never dared tell Andy of the incident.

There was no doubt the *Silver Crest* became a happier boat after the Spuddy had become its mascot. The crew liked him to be there because it made the boat seem more homely. Jake was glad of the companionship in the wheelhouse during the long hours alone on deck; glad too of the dog's apparent need of him for though Jake knew there wasn't a skipper in the port who wouldn't be glad to offer the Spuddy 'bunk and bait' he felt that the dog, having accepted him as his skipper, would feel betrayed if Jake were to desert him now. As for the Spuddy, he now had what he had always wanted: a home and a man on whom he could at last bestow the loyalty and love which he had not previously cared to give. He was in no danger of forgetting Andy but his feeling for him was that of a staunch friend; a loved companion and a playmate. But his skipper was his skipper and friend in the Spuddy's eyes supreme. After the weekends Jake would come down to the boat on Monday mornings and step straight into the Spuddy's welcome and as Jake gave him the accustomed rough caress the dog's top lip would lift in an attempt at a smile and he would snort and paw at Jake until the skipper bent down to receive the approving lick behind the ear which the dignified Spuddy never bestowed on any of the crew.

LILIAN   BECKWITH

TWO DOGS

The Greenock-born poet John Davidson (1857–1909) spent most of his working life in London and, latterly, Penzance. He was associated with the Yellow Book group, but he never outgrew his Scots dourness nor characteristically individual way of looking at things. He committed suicide in the English Channel in the mistaken belief that he was suffering from cancer.

Two dogs on Bournemouth beach: a mongrel one,
With spaniel plainest on the palimpsest,
The blur of muddled stock; the other, bred,
With tapering muzzle, rising brow, strong jaw—
A terrier to the tail's expressive tip,
Magnetic, nimble, endlessly alert.

The mongrel, wet and shivering, at my feet
Deposited a wedge of half-inch board,
A foot in length and splintered at the butt;
Withdrew a yard and crouched in act to spring,
While to and fro between his wedge and me
The glancing shuttle of his eager look
A purpose wove. The terrier, ears a-cock,
And neck one curve of sheer intelligence,
Stood sentinel: no sound, no movement, save
The mongrel's telegraphic eyes, bespoke
The object of the canine pantomime.

I stooped to grasp the wedge, knowing the game;
But like a thing uncoiled the mongrel snapped
It off, and promptly set it out again,
The terrier at his quarters, every nerve
Waltzing inside his lithe rigidity.

'More complex than I thought!' Again I made
To seize the wedge; again the mongrel won,
Whipped off the jack, relaid it, crouched and watched,
The terrier at attention all the time.
I won the third bout: ere the mongrel snapped

His toy, I stayed my hand; he halted, half
Across the neutral ground, and in his pause
Of doubt I seized the prize, a vanquished yelp
From both; and then intensest vigilance.

Together, when I tossed the wedge, they plunged
Before it reached the sea. The mongrel, out
Among the waves, and standing to them, meant
Heroic business; but the terrier dodged
Behind, adroitly scouting in the surf,
And seized the wedge, rebutted by the tide,
In shallow water, while the mongrel searched
The English Channel on his hind-legs poised.
The terrier laid the trophy at my feet;
And neither dog protested when I took
The wedge: the overture of their marine
Diversion had been played out once for all.

A second match the reckless mongrel won,
Vanishing twice under the heavy surf,
Before he found and brought the prize to land.
Then for an hour the aquatic sport went on,
And still the mongrel took the heroic rôle,
The terrier hanging deftly in the rear.
Sometimes the terrier when the mongrel found
Betrayed a jealous scorn, as who should say,
'Your hero's always a vulgarian! Pah!'
But when the mongrel missed, after a fight
With such a sea of troubles, and saw the prize
Grabbed by the terrier in an inch of surf,
He seemed entirely satisfied, and watched
With more pathetic vigilance the cast
That followed.

      'Once a passion, mongrel, this
Retrieving of a stick, ' I told the brute,
'Has now become a vice with you. Go home!
Wet to the marrow and palsied with the cold,
You won't give in; and, good or bad, you've earned
My admiration. Go home now and get warm,
And the best bone in the pantry.' As I talked
I stripped the water from his hybrid coat,
Laughed and made much of him—which mortified
The funking terrier.

'I'm despised, it seems!'
The terrier thought. 'My cleverness (my feet
Are barely wet!) beside the mongrel's zeal
Appears timidity. this biped's mad
To pet the stupid brute. Yap! Yah!' He seized
The wedge and went; and at his heels at once,
Without a thought of me, the mongrel trudged.

Along the beach, smokers of cigarettes,
All sixpenny-novel-readers to a man,
Attracted Master Terrier. Again the wedge,
Passed to the loyal mongrel, was teed with care;
Again the fateful overture began.
Upon the fourth attempt, and not before,
And by a feint at that, the challenged youth
(Most equable, be sure, of all the group:
Allow the veriest dog to measure men!)
Secured the soaked and splintered scrap of deal.
Thereafter, as with me, the game progressed,
The breathless, shivering mongrel, rushing out
Into the heavy surf, there to be tossed
And tumbled like a floating bunch of kelp,
While gingerly the terrier picked his steps
Strategic in the rear, and snapped the prize
Oftener than his more adventurous, more
Romantic, more devoted rival did.

The uncomfortable moral glares at one!
And, further, in the mongrel's wistful mind
A primitive idea darkly wrought:
Having once lost the prize in the overture
With his bipedal rival, he felt himself
In honour and in conscience bound to plunge
For ever after it at the winner's will.
But the smart terrier was an Overdog,
And knew a trick worth two of that. He thought—
If canine celebration works like ours,
And I interpret canine mind aright—
'Let men and mongrels worry and wet their coats!
I use my brains and choose the better part.
Quick-witted ease and self-approval lift
Me miles above this anxious cur, absorbed,
Body and soul, in playing a game I win.

Without an effort. And yet the mongrel seems
The happier dog. How's that? Belike, the old
Compensatory principle again:
I have pre-eminence and conscious worth;
And he his power to fling himself away
For anything or nothing. Men and dogs,
What an unfathomable world it is!'

JOHN DAVIDSON

LOST OR FOUND DOG

'Go home, dog,' Uncle Andrew Keith ordered, in his strictest voice. 'Off with you now! We don't want you. Home!'

The dog sat down on its haunches on the sea-grass a few yards away, put its head on one side, pink tongue hanging out, and smiled— positively smiled at them.

'No, no,' the man said. He pointed, away across the blue waters of the great bay towards the village, over a mile away. 'You're a stupid animal! don't you understand what home means? Go *home*!'

The dog thumped its brown tail on the grass, but made no other move.

'Don't send him away, Uncle,' Angus pleaded. 'He's nice. Isn't he, Anna?'

Angus's sister Anna nodded her dark head. 'Yes, he is. But he's not a he, you know—he's a she!'

'Oh! Well. Um. Maybe you're right. But she's still a jolly nice dog, for all that.'

Their Uncle Andrew stooped and picked up a piece of driftwood. All the wide saltings, the grey-green grasslands that surrounded the wide shallow bay and were covered by the high tides, were littered with such whitened sticks and other things washed up in stormy weather.

'Off with you, I say!' he cried. And raising his hand, he threw the stick hard.

'Oh, I say! That's not fair,' Angus said.

'Uncle Andrew!' Anna reproached him. 'How could you? What a shame! Throwing things at the poor beast! When she's being so friendly . . .'

'Sillies!' their uncle said. 'I didn't throw it *at* her. Just near her. To let her see she's not wanted. Don't you think I'm a better thrower than that! I'm . . .' He stopped staring. 'Goodness me! Well, I'm . . .'

The dog had not even blinked her brown treacle-ball eyes as the stick flew past. Turning her head to note where it fell, however, she got up quite unhurriedly and trotted away. But only as far as the stick. Picking it up in her mouth, she came trotting back again with it, tail swinging slowly from side to side. Coming up to Mr Keith, she dropped the stick at his feet, and went back to sit where she had been before.

The youngsters laughed heartily. Soon after they had crossed the long wooden footbridge which led from the road out across the wide shallows where the Peffer Burn entered the salt water of Aberlady Bay, the dog had appeared from nowhere in particular. One moment they were walking by themselves, the next it was there. It had taken up a position a yard or two behind the man and two children, and proceeded to follow them out into the empty salt-marsh.

She was a medium-sized dog, mainly golden-brown Labrador retriever, but not entirely so, clearly, for she had a keen, rather pointed face, intelligent round eyes, and a white tip to her thin tail—which no retriever should have. But, most obviously she had retriever-ish ideas, especially where sticks were concerned.

'It's all right for you two to laugh,' their uncle complained. 'Very funny, I must say! But you asked me to bring you here, into the Bay, to watch birds. This is a Nature Reserve. You can't go bird-watching with a dog. It will frighten all the birds away.'

'She's not frightening that lark, anyway,' Angus pointed out. A lark, which had been soaring up and down, up and down, whistling joyfully, just ahead of them, dropped down as though on a string, to land on the sea-grass just a few yards away, and began to run back and forwards, coming quite close—close enough for them to see the little cocky crest on its head. It had stopped singing the moment that it touched the ground.

'Probably got a nest nearby, and wants to distract our attention from it,' Mr Keith said. 'Anyway, we didn't come out here just to see the larks. You can see them almost anywhere. It's waders and sea-birds we want to see—and wildfowl. And this dog will scare *them* off, you may be sure.'

'Let's give her a chance, at least,' Angus pleaded 'If she turns out to be a nuisance, we can send her away then.'

'I don't see that we've got any choice—do you?' Anna said. 'If you ask me, this beast's coming with us whatever we say!'

Mr Keith made a last attempt. Lifting up a long string of dried seaweed, he strode towards the dog, to make a swipe at it with seaweed, using it like a whip, and telling the beast to be off in no uncertain voice.

The creature jinked out of the way with the utmost ease—but merely circled round, to sit down again, watching them all with the most friendly interest.

'Oh, well—I give up!' their uncle declared disgustedly. 'Come on, then.' 'There's something written on her collar,' the keen-eyed Anna said. She ran forward, and the dog made not the least attempt to dodge or move away. When she patted the animal's head, she got a brief lick on the wrist from a warm pink tongue in return. Stooping, she turned the loose collar round.

It was not a proper dog's collar, just an old piece of leather strap, pretty thin and worn. And on it, in big badly-made capital letters was the name TESS, scrawled in copying-ink. That was all.

'Tess!' Anna cried. 'Your name's Tess?'

The dog wagged her tail hard, and licked the girl's wrist again.

'Tess! Good dog, Tess!' Angus called.

Mr Keith groaned. 'Goodness—we'll never get rid of it now,' he said. 'Come along—let's get moving at least.'

They went striding around over the saltings, seawards, clumping hollowly as they went—for they were all wearing wellington boots;

their feet would not have remained dry for half-a-minute otherwise, for the entire area around the tidal mud-flats was waterlogged and though they did not sink in, the grey-green sea-grass oozed water at every step. All about them the saltings were dotted with hundreds of little pools and runnels and shallow ditches. Tess trotted at their heels happily, a fine spray of water splashing up from her feet.

'Where are the wildfowl, Uncle?' Angus asked, after a little while. The whole great spread of the salt-marsh seemed to be utterly empty of all life or movement, save for themselves. 'I don't see a thing.'

Mr Keith halted them. 'Just stand still, and listen,' he said.

When they did that, at first they heard only the sigh of the wind and the distant roar of the waves breaking on the sand-bar that stretched across the mouth of the bay, two miles away. Then they began to hear two other distinct kinds of sounds, above that. One was from below them, it seemed—the quiet whisper and trickle and bubbling of water; the other was from above them, carried on the wind, a thin piping, trilling, whistling, cheeping sort of noise that went on all the time, so high-pitched and faint as hardly to be noticed.

'Is that . . . them?' the boy asked.

'Yes, those are the small waders. Hundreds, thousands of them, Knots, dunlin, sanderling, redshanks, oyster-catchers—things like that. They're all around us. Along the tide's edge. In the pools, and all the hollows and runnels and ditches. If you were to look hard, with the field-glasses, you'd see that the whole place was alive with them. They're very well camouflaged, you see—their colours blend in perfectly with the background. But we'll see some of them much better when we get out nearer to the tide-line—see whole flocks of them at once . . .'

Just then there was a sudden interruption. Their Uncle Andrew almost bit his tongue. Only a yard or two from their feet what had looked like a patch of darker sea-grass became a large hare, which came to life and set off at a great pace towards the distant sand-hills, long ears battened along its brown back. And like an arrow from a bow Tess was after it, almost knocking the youngsters aside as she shot between them in whimpering pursuit.

'Goodness!' Mr Keith exclaimed. 'Look at that! What did I tell you? Just the sort of thing I expected. Chasing a hare. And in a Nature Reserve.'

'She's fairly going at a lick!' Angus declared, admiringly. 'Look at the water she's spraying out! Like a hovercraft or something. D'you think we'd better call her back, though?' Not waiting for an answer, he raised his voice to shout, 'Tess! Tess! Come here! Here, Tess—here!'

If the dog heard him, she paid no attention.

'She'll never catch that hare, anyway,' Anna said, 'no need to get into a flap. The hare's not really trying, I think! Look how easily she's taking it.'

'Well, a hare must be one of the fastest things alive,' Angus said. 'I think Tess is putting up a pretty good show, actually.' He started to shout again.

'Don't do that,' their uncle told him. 'Let the dog go. If she chases the hare far enough, perhaps she won't come back, and we'll be rid of her. And it's *not* a good show for a dog to chase animals, Angus, however fast. It shows that the beast's not properly trained. Let's hope nobody sees all this, and connects the brute with us.'

'There's not a soul in sight, as far as the eye can see, Uncle.'

'In a Nature Reserve like this there may be more people than you can spot, at first glance. Because they're hidden. Watching the birds. With glasses. Hiding behind a pile of driftwood or a clump of reeds. You never know.'

'M'mmm. I don't think I like that awfully much,' Anna said. 'The feeling that there may be people hidden and watching, in all this emptiness.'

'A funny place for a hare to be, anyway,' Angus put in. 'Wasn't it? Down here in this wet salt-marsh?'

'They come here quite often. They seem to like it. There are dozens of them live in this Bay area. Perhaps they like the salt taste in the grasses. One man I know suggested that they nibbled seaweed, to get the iodine from it. Very good for them. Come on, you two.'

They plodded on, with Tess and the hare disappearing into the distance.

Two large birds flew over, close together and fairly low, in a heavy,

powerful flight. They were mainly white but with black and red and rich brown splashes on them, and they grunted as they flew. They planed down amongst the reeds about 400 yards away. They were shelduck, Uncle Andrew said—not really ducks at all, but a kind of goose. If the three of them were to stalk up very quietly, towards those reeds, they might just get near enough to have a good look at the birds through the glasses. They were not common, although there were usually a few pairs nesting in Aberlady Bay.

This was the sort of thing that they had come out to do, and the youngsters were very keen. Taking note of a landmark, in the shape of an old fish-box, so that they did not lose the clump of reeds amongst the many in that great flat expanse of saltings, they moved cautiously on, even tip-toeing at first, until they realised that this was foolish. Presently they stopped crouching too, for they were only getting cricks in their necks and backs, and it was only taking an inch or two from their heights anyway. They were thankful that they did not have to crawl on their stomachs, for they would have been soaked in a yard or two.

They managed to reach the fish-box itself without the shelducks flying up. Here they were within fifty or sixty yards of the birds, and got an excellent view of them. Angus almost went into fits, trying not to laugh at the way one of them, the male their uncle said, kept arching its neck and throwing its head about this way and that, showing off in front of the lady—who actually seemed to be asleep anyway—croaking in a throaty gabble all the time.

It was while they were watching this, very pleased with themselves, that Anna heard the faint panting sound behind her, and turned to find Tess crouching there, head flat on paws, eyes upturned modestly, and trying not to puff too hard. She must have crept up exceedingly quietly.

Mr Keith did not know quite what to do. To have given the dog a good row for chasing the hare would have meant making a noise and probably disturbing the shelducks. Any shooing-away movement would have given away their position, too; and it was no good just frowning at Tess—who kept her glance carefully on Anna and Angus, anyway. So, sighing, he did nothing, and concentrated on watching the birds, and in a whisper pointing out to the young people various special things about them, such as the touches of green on the wings and the pink legs and scarlet bills. Unlike so many birds, the female was just as colourful as the male.

They had two pairs of field-glasses with them, Mr Keith's own, and an old pair between the two youngsters. Angus was rather hogging the second pair, so that it was Anna again, whose eyes were not glued to eye-pieces, who noticed the new development.

'Goodness!' she exclaimed, loudly enough for her uncle to shush at her. 'Look at Tess! What on earth is she doing?'

Tess was still flat on her stomach, but not behind them any more, and not lying still. She was away off to their right front, fully fifty yards away, crawling over the sodden sea-grass, slowly but determinedly, head down, not sinking but actually creeping.

'The wretched brute!' Mr Keith declared, rather forgetting to whisper. 'She's going to ruin this afternoon for us, that's obvious. She'll frighten away those shelduck . . .'

'Maybe not,' Angus said. 'She's being very careful. Look how she keeps down. I've never seen a dog do that before. I wonder what she thinks she's doing?'

'I think she's doing the same thing that we are,' Anna said. 'She's stalking those ducks. She must have seen that we were watching them. Probably smelt them. And now she's showing that she can do it better than we can!'

Their uncle snorted, but again there was nothing he could do about Tess without rousing the shelduck.

It quickly became clear that the dog wasn't just creeping up on the birds directly; she was working round behind them. Doing it very skilfully, too . They had not seen her yet, nor sensed her presence.

When Tess was perhaps twenty yards the other side of the ducks, she turned to face them. Slowly, not jerkily, she rose to her feet. She did not move, except slowly to wag her tail. She just stood there.

After a while the shelducks seemed to become aware of her. They both stood up, craning their necks in her direction. Still she did not move more than her tail. The great birds cocked their dark heads this way and that, comically, not knowing whether to be frightened or not. But when Tess did not come towards them, they seemed to decide she was not dangerous at the moment, and sank down again. But clearly they were keeping an eye on her.

After a while the dog sank down too, and began to crawl forward again, very slowly. She moved only a few yards, and then quietly stood up again, tail wagging gently. Again the ducks raised their heads to stare.

Even Mr Keith was most impressed by this time, wondering what Tess was up to. He was not worried about her catching and harming the ducks, being quite sure that they would never let the dog come close enough for that; anyway they were fairly powerful birds.

When Tess repeated the same performance again, even more slowly and cautiously, and then rose up only about ten yards from the ducks, she obviously had *them* much interested too; not actually alarmed, but curious, wondering what this strange thing could be, and only frightened enough to move just a little bit away from Tess.

The dog sank down once more, and after a minute or so began to creep forward again. The ducks moved still a little further away. Then the process was repeated. And each time, the birds moved closer towards the waiting humans.

It was Angus who put into words what was in all their minds. 'You know,' he whispered, 'I do believe that she's doing this deliberately. To drive the ducks towards us, without frightening them off. She's moving them to us. She probably thinks we want to catch them, and can't get near enough.'

'Of course she is,' Anna agreed. 'She's doing this to make up for her being naughty and chasing that hare! I'm sure of it.'

Uncle Andrew rubbed his chin thoughfully. 'Well . . .' he said. He was really more interested in the shelducks, however, than in why they were acting as they did. He had never been so close to them. They were now not a dozen yards away. There was no need to use the glasses any more. The birds were walking slowly directly towards them now, their heads turned all the time, and looking back at Tess.

It was just fortunate for all concerned that it was Mr Keith himself who knocked over the fish-box, which had been standing on its side, as he tried to get lower down behind it, with the ducks coming closer still. It did not make much of a bump—but it was more than enough to change the entire situation. In a single second, heavy as the birds seemed, they were into the air, croaking hoarsely, their powerful wings beating and whistling. Twice they circled round above, as though reluctant to leave without discovering what this strange brown thing had been, before they flew away seawards and were soon out of sight.

Mr Keith cleared his throat loudly. 'A pity,' he said. 'Just one of those things. Most interesting, though. The best view I've ever had of shelduck. Fine birds.'

'Yes. And for that you've got to thank Tess!' Angus pointed out strongly. 'That was a jolly good show, you must admit, Uncle. I'd no idea that a dog could do that sort of thing.'

'Well, I suppose that sheepdogs do much the same, really. And pointers do something of the sort, too. But they're trained, of course.'

'I think this one has been trained, too—despite the hare,' Anna said. 'In fact I think Tess is a very clever dog, indeed.'

'M'mmm. Well,' Mr Keith was not going to admit this—but on the other hand he could hardly claim now that having the dog with them was going to ruin the bird-watching.

They set out for the tide-line once more, with Tess now trotting happily beside them.

41   Dog Portrait. Drawing by Morven Cameron.

They spent a pleasant hour out on the hard wet sand of the open bay itself, watching the great flocks of waders flying and swooping and banking in the air. They were wonderful to see, particularly when a huge flock of perhaps two hundred birds in swift flight, all changed direction in a split second. How it was done even Mr Keith could not explain, though he muttered something about natural radar. Obviously, if even one bird made a botch of it, and turned in the wrong direction, or not quickly enough, or did not turn at all, the others would be all crashing into it and into each other. How did they know to turn just then, the youngsters demanded? Who decided that they would turn? Was there a signal given? And so on. Their uncle could not answer their questions, only being able to say that these were mainly dunlin, knots and sanderling, and that Nature was very wonderful.

On that note they turned, for the two-mile walk back to the village for tea. Tess turned with them, as though part of the family.

NIGEL TRANTER

ALLEGORICAL AND LEGENDARY GHOST DOGS

There are several kinds of allegorical dog. From mediaeval times poets wrote about the imaginary foibles of dogs representing humans when it might have been dangerous to pen an open attack. Sir David Lyndsay's Bagsche is such a dog, as are Burns's 'Twa Dogs', though Burns was using an established literary convention for its own sake rather than to avoid any risk of personal retribution. William Dunbar, however, called Mr Dog, the Queen's wardrober, a dog, and got away with it. Then there are the dogs who people Gaelic legends and Lowland fables, represented here by 'Finn and the Grey Dog' and 'The Yellow Dog', amongst others. There is the dog of the poet's imagination; and, as a tailpiece, James Bridie's witty piece of youthful moralising, echoing a mediaeval Scots literary tone.

42   Fionn, from 'Fionn's Journey to Lochlan' in *Scottish Folk Tales and Legends*, retold by Barbara Ker Wilson, Oxford University Press.

149

FINN AND THE GREY DOG
(Argyllshire)

One day Finn and his men were hunting on the hill. They had killed many deer. When they were preparing to go home, they saw a tall lad coming. He greeted Finn, and Finn returned his greeting.

Finn asked him where he came from and what he wanted.

'I have come from the East and from the West, seeking a master,' he said.

'I need a lad,' said Finn, 'and if we can agree, I'll employ you. What reward do you want at the end of a year and a day?'

'Not much,' said the lad; 'only that you go with me, at the end of the year and the day, to a feast at the palace of the King of Lochlan.'

Finn engaged the lad, and he served him faithfully to the end of the year and a day.

On the morning of the last day the tall lad asked Finn if he was satisfied with him. Finn said he was perfectly satisfied.

'Well,' said the lad, 'I hope I shall have my reward, and that you'll go with me as you promised.'

'You'll have your reward,' said Finn, 'and I'll go with you.'

'It is the day I have to keep my promise to the lad,' Finn told his men, 'and I don't know when I shall return. But if I am not back within a year and a day, let the man who is not whetting his sword be bending his bow to revenge me on the shore of Lochlan!'

When he had said this, he bade them farewell and went into his house. His fool was sitting by the fire.

'Are you sorry I am going away?' Finn asked.

'I am sorry you are going that way,' said the fool, weeping, 'but I'll give you advice if you'll take it.'

'Yes,' said Finn, 'for often the King's advice has come from the fool's head. What is your advice?'

'It is,' said the fool, 'to take Bran's chain in your pocket with you.'

Finn did so, bade him farewell and went away. He found the tall lad waiting for him at the door.

'Are you ready to go?' said the lad.

'I am ready to go,' said Finn. 'Lead the way, you know the road better.'

The tall lad set off, and Finn followed. Yet, though Finn was swift, he could not touch the tall lad with a stick all the way. When the tall lad was disappearing through a gap in the mountains, Finn would be appearing on the ridge behind him. They kept that distance between them till their journey's end.

They entered the palace of the King of Lochlan, and Finn sat down wearily. But, instead of a feast, the lords of the King of Lochlan were considering how to bring about his death.

'Hang him!' said one. 'Burn him!' said another. 'Drown him!' said a third.

'Send him to Glenmore!' said another. 'He'll not go far there before he's killed by the Grey Dog. There would be no death more disgraceful, in the opinion of the Feinne, than their King's death from a cur.'

They all clapped their hands, and agreed with him.

At once they took Finn to the Glen where the Dog was. They had not gone very far up the Glen before they heard the Dog howling. When they saw him, they said it was time to run. So they left Finn at the Dog's mercy.

If Finn ran away, the men would kill him, and if he stayed, the Dog would kill him. He would as soon be killed by the Dog as by his enemies. So he stayed.

The Grey Dog came with his mouth open and his tongue hanging to one side. Every breath from his nostrils burned everything three miles in front of him and on both sides of him. Finn was tortured by the heat, and knew he could not stand it long. If Bran's chain was going to be of any use, now was the time to take it out. He put his hand in his pocket, and when the Dog was near him he took the chain out and shook it. The Dog at once stopped and wagged his tail. He came to Finn, and licked all his sores from head to foot, healing with his tongue what he had burned with his breath. At length Finn put Bran's chain round the Grey Dog's neck and went down the Glen with the Dog on a leash.

An old man and woman, who had fed the Grey Dog, lived at the foot of the Glen. The old woman was at the door, and when she saw Finn coming with the Dog she ran into the house crying.

'What do you see?' said the old man.

'I saw as tall and handsome a man as ever I saw, coming down the Glen with the Grey Dog on a leash.'

'If all the people of Lochlan and Ireland were together,' said the old man, 'not one of them could do that, but Finn, King of the Feinne, and Bran's golden chain with him.'

'Whether it's he or not, he's coming,' replied the old woman.

'We'll soon know,' said the old man, going out.

He met Finn, and they greeted each other. Finn told him why he was there, and the old man invited him into the house for a rest and a meal.

The old woman told Finn he was very welcome to stay for a year and a day, and Finn accepted the invitation.

At the end of the year and a day the old woman was standing on a knowe near the house. She looked toward the shore and saw a great army on the beach of Lochlan. She ran into the house, her eyes big with fear.

'What did you see?' said the old man.

'I saw something I never saw before. There's a great army on the beach, and among them a red-haired man with a squint. I don't think there's his equal, as a fighter, this night under the stars.'

'They are my companions,' said Finn. 'Let me go to meet them.'

Finn and the Grey Dog went down to the shore. When his men saw him coming they shouted, so that it was heard in the four corners of Lochlan. They and their King greeted each other, and no less friendly was the greeting between Bran and the Grey Dog, for they were brothers taken together from the castle.

They took vengeance on the men of Lochlan for their treatment of Finn. They began at one end of Lochlan and did not stop till they went out at the other end.

After they had conquered Lochlan they went home, and in the Hall of Finn they made a great feast that lasted a year and a day.

NORAH AND WILLIAM MONTGOMERIE

from the **LAY OF THE BLACK DOG**
(*Leather na Feinne*, p 91)

The Lord of the Fionn rose early
before the sun rose on the plain;
they saw coming from the hill
a red-hooded man with a black dog.

He was pleasant to look at:
his cheeks were red as raspberries,
his teeth whiter than chalk,
his hair, however was black.

(The stranger is looking for a dog-fight)

They all unleashed their dogs,
and it was not their wont to retreat;
the black dog's attack was rough:
he killed nine times fifty dogs.

It was then that Fionn spoke:
'This is quite a shindy,'
turning away from the crowd
he looked darkly at Bran.

Bran shook the golden chain,
the crowd saw that his anger was great,
Bran became fierce and surly
wanting to get at the Black Dog.

They set the dogs snout to snout,
and they shed blood in sight of the host,
fighting closely and hard
until the Black Dog was dead.

(TR) DERRICK THOMSON

TUNDRA'S EDGE

Here is the wolf,. the wind, the sound of rain,
the kitchen light that falls across the lawn—
these things are his. The house is his domain.

Here is the wolf. He slips in with the dawn
to raid your mirrors. Shadows will persist
for days, to mark the distance he has gone

in search of you. Yet still you will insist
the wolf died out in these parts long ago:
everyone knows the wolf does not exist.

You catch no scent. And where the mirrors glow
those are not eyes, but random sparks of light.
You never dream of running with the snow.

Yet here is wolf. He rustles in the night.
Only the wind, but you switch on the light.

JOHN BURNSIDE

43   Near the Finish, by Sir Edwin Landseer, from *The Works of Sir Edwin Landseer, RA,*
published by Cosmo Monkhouse Virtue & Co, London.

THE COMPLAINT AND PUBLIC CONFESSION
OF THE KING'S AULD HOUND CALLIT BAGSCHE
DIRECTIT TO BAWTIE, THE KING'S BEST-BELOVIT DOG,
AND HIS COMPANIONS

Alas! whom to should I complain
    In my extreme necessity:
Or whame to shall I mak my maine
    In Court, na dog will do for me,
    Beseekand some for charity,
To bear my supplicatioun,
    To Scudlar, Luffra, and Bawtie,
Now, or the King pass off the toun.

I have followit the Court so lang,
    whill, in guid faith, I may no mair;
The country knaws I may nocht gang,
    I am so cruikit, auld and sair,
    That I wait nocht whare to repair;
For, when I had authority,
    I thocht me so familiar,
I never dred necessity.

I rue the race that Geordie Steil
    Brocht Bawtie to the King's presence,
I pray God lat him never do weil,
    Sen syne I gat na audience;
    For Bawtie now gets sic credence.
That he lies on the King's nicht goun,
    Where I, perforce, for my offence,
Maun in the close lie like ane loun.

For I have been, ay to this hour,
    Ane worrier of lamb and hog;
Ane tyrant and ane tulzeour,
    Ane murdressar of mony ane dog;
    Five fowls I chased out throch the scrog
Wharefore their mothers did me warie;
    For they were drownit all in ane bog;
Speir at John Gordon of Pitarie,

Whilk in his house did bring me up,
    And usit me to slay the deer,
Sweet milk and meal he gart me sup,
    That craft I leirnit soon, perquier;
    All other virtue ran arrear
When I began to bark and flyte
    For there was neither monk nor friar,
Nor wife, nor bairn, but I would bite.

When to the King the case was knawin
    Of my unhappy hardiness,
And all the sooth unto him schawin,
    How everilk dog I did oppress;
    Then gave his Grace command express
I should be brocht to his presence;
    Notwithstanding my wickedness;
In Court I gat great audience . . .

I was that na man durst come near me,
    Nor put me furth of my ludging;
Na dog durst fra my dinner scare me,
    When I was tender with the King:
    Now everilk tyke does me doun thring,
The whilk before by me war wrangit,
    And sweirs I serve na other thing,
But in ane Halter to be hangit.

Thocht you be hamely with the King,
    Ye Luffra, Scudlar, and Bawtie,
Beware that ye do nocht doun thring,
    Your neighbours throw authority:
    And your example mak by me,
And believe weil ye are but doggis
    Though ye stand in the hiest gree,
See ye bite neither lambs nor hoggis.

Though ye have now great audience
    See that ye be yow nane opprest;
Ye will be punished for your offence,
    From time the King be weil confessed;
    There is na dog that has transgressed
Through cruelty, and he may fang him,
    His Majesty will tak na rest
Till on ane gallous he gar hang him.

                      SIR DAVID LYNDSAY OF THE MOUNT

OF JAMES DOG, KEEPER OF THE QUEEN'S WARDROBE

James, or Jame, Dog is first mentioned as looking after James IV's clothing in 1488. He subsequently became the Queen's wardrober, having charge not only of her apparel but also of furniture not in use. Despite Dunbar's dislike of him, Dog held the office until at least 1527, by which time the courtier-poet had been dead for several years.

The wardrober of Venus bour
To gif a doublet he is as dour
As if it were ane syd fut frog:
    Madame, ye heff a dangerous dog.

When that I schaw to him your wrytin,
He girns that I am red for bytin;
I wald he had ane heavy clog:
    Madame, ye heff a dangerous dog.

When that I speal til him friendlyk,
He barkis lyk ane midding tyke,
War chassand cattle throu a bog:
    Madame, ye heff a dangerous dog.

He is ane mastif, meikle of mycht,
To keep your wardrobe ouer nycht,
From the great Sowdan Gog-ma-Gog;
    Madame, ye heff a dangerous dog.

He is owre meikle to be your messan,
Madame, I red ye get a less ane,
His gang gars all your chalmers shog;
    Madame, ye heff a dangerous dog.

WILLIAM DUNBAR

THE YELLOW DOG

'Aye, a doag's grand company.'

The platitude floated out in the murky air of the smiddy in which three men were smoking; it hung for a minute, unanswered, and the shepherd took his pipe out of his mouth and emitted a solemn 'aye'.

Outside, the late October afternoon dwindled to evening; work being over, the smith sat on his anvil facing the shepherd and old Robert Spence.

'Grand, grand company,' said Spence again.

The blacksmith pushed his cap back. He was very much younger than his companions and perhaps had not outgrown the taste for disagreeing with his elders.

'Weel,' he said slowly, 'I kent a man—I didna exactly ken him weel, though I kent plenty about him—that wasna just benefited by the company o' a doag.'

'It isna ilka body that understands doags,' said Spence.

'The man I'm tellin' ye o' was a lang time or he understood ane o' them.'

The shepherd made no comment, but the quality of contempt in his silence was a challenge to the smith.

'It was ma wife's uncle,' he began, 'that had a fairm oot yonder at the fit o' the Sidlaws—a cantankered-like carle that hadna very muckle tae say til onybody. He'd naethin' tae say tae me, at ony rate, for I was coortin' at the time, and the lassie had an awfae wark tae get ootbye tae meet me. I daur'd na come near the hoose. Ye see, he was that set against me, but whiles we'd hae a word thegither, her an' me, ahint a dyke, when it was possible. Weel, there was ae nicht we was there and we could hear the treid o' a man runnin' an' pechin' up the brae and we were fair fleggit, Bell an' me, but the auld deevil gae'd by an' never saw naethin'. He was that pit aboot. Ye could see the heid o'm against the sma' licht there was i' the sky and his hair was tousled an' his bonnet lost.'

'Was't a doag chasin' him?' asked Spence.

'Na, na—but listen you till I tell ye—it had been him chasin' a doag—'

'The fule,' broke in the shepherd.

'Ye micht think that, perhaps. But I mind when Bell got the chance tae tell me the richts o' it, I was whiles fear'd tae gang oot i' the dairk ma lane—aye was I.'

'Feech!' exclaimed the shepherd, 'ye were owre young tae be oot late—coortin' tae! Ye're no muckle mair nor a laddie the noo.'

'I'm a married man this twa year,' rejoined the smith, 'and there's a wean at hame and anither comin'. But that's nae matter. Mind you what I'm tae tell ye. It'll gar ye think. Yon man, Bell's uncle, had got sheep awa' upo' the hill and he'd been oot seekin' a yowe that was missin' frae the flock.'

At the mention of a flock the shepherd's humour began to change and the two old men fixed their eyes on the smith's face.

'Aye, he was up amang the hills an' he couldna get word o' the yowe and he was fair done, what wi' traivlin' the bogs he didna ken, an' trampin' a' kind o' places an' duntin' himsel' amang the stanes. It was i' the autumn, a day like this; the afternoon was gettin' on an' he couldna see whaur he was, for he was newly come tae the farm and he wasna accustomed tae the hills. He was a Fife body. I'se warrant ye he said some queer things, for he was an ill-tongued man, and at last he thocht he wadna fash himsel' ony mair wi' the yowe an' just leave the bizzer tae dee in her sins. Forbye there was a pucklie mist, and it was takin' him a' his time tae win doon tae ceevilisation or sunset.

'At last he got his feet on flat ground and he cam' upon a warld o' whins; there wasna a hoose nor a beast tae be seen, an' when he was through the whins it was the same; naethin' but a muckle green place wi' clumps o' rashes and ne'er a peewee nor a whaup tae cry owre his heid. He was standin' like a fule when a dairk-like thing cam oot frae ahint a tree-stump aboot as far aheid as he micht see, an' it had the appearance o' a doag. It cam' towards him wi' its heid doon an' he could tell through the gloamin' that it was a kind o' a yella colour; its tail was hangin' atween its legs. It lookit queer, he thocht. (Man, I dinna like thae things!)'

He paused for breath; the old men said nothing, for the smith was transporting them into places whose like they had seen many a time.

'It cam' and stoppit a wee bittie in front o' him; syne it startit rinnin' roond him. Whiles it ran in a muckle circle, whiles in sma' anes. But aye it ran; roond an' roond wi' its heid hangin', and whiles it lookit up at him wi' its yella een, whiles no. He couldna say what tae mak' o' it, but it seemed as if the cratur kent somethin' that gar'd it behave yon way. His he'rt was like tae dee, he said, yon thing had that ill look aboot it; he tried strikin' oot wi' his stick, but he couldna reach it, and at last he just steppit forrit though he didna ken the road he was taklin'; a' he thocht was tae get rid o' the brute. But it was nae use, for it gae'd on afore him, turnin' its heid an' lookin' back tae see if he was comin'. He stude still when he saw that and the doag commenced tae rin roond him the same as before. Whatever he tried, he couldna get quit o'm.'

'I dinna believe ye,' said Spence.

'I'm no carin',' replied the smith, 'but I can haud ma tongue gin ye like. Am I tae gang on?'

44   The Yellow Dog, from *The Lum Hat and Other Stories, Last Tales of Violet Jacob*, edited by Ronald Garden, Aberdeen University Press.

Spence and the shepherd put their pride in their pockets, and the smith continued.

'Weel, it cam' intill the man's mind that the beast micht be makin' for its hame, and gin he was to folla it he'd maybe land at some hoose whaur he'd get put on his road, so he began to think shame o' himsel' for no seein' that it was just a nat'ral thing, and awa' they went, him an' the doag. There was bogs an' ditches, broom an' tracks runnin' in and oot o' the lang grass, amangst the black shaws o' the weepies that was deein' i' the autumn. He didna ken foo lang they'd traivelt, and gin he stude tae tak's breith the thing afore him wad stap an' turn back, and though he tell't himsel' that a doag was a doag and nae mair, he couldna thole the notion o' it comin' near an' maybe runnin' roond him again. There wasna a body tae be seen nor a man's voice tae hear as they gaed ane ahint the ither, but at last the doag loupit through a broken place whaur the stanes had whummled oot o' the dyke on till a road. It was a narra road and there was a bittie green grass at the side o' it, and he was fine an' pleased when he saw it, for he kent it, and yonder no' far aheid was the muckle grey stane that stickit up like the figure o' a man, by the arn trees i' the weet ditch. He wasna mair nor a mile frae hame and the kent, nat'ral look o't made him bauld, the same as a suppie whusky micht hae done, and anger't him aye the mair at the doag though it had brocht him sae far on his journey. As I tell't ye, he was a thrawn cratur and he up an' hurled his stick and struck the beast i' the side. It didna cry nor rin; it just cam back till him and ran a great circle roond him. He didna like that and saw he'd get nae peace till he was at his ain door and could clap it i' the dog's face; sae he gaed on again, an' it rinnin' afore him, and as they passed the stane amang the arn trees the beast stoppit that quick he was near steppin' on it. He lookit doon tae his feet, and it was gone. There was nae doag there.'

'Nae doag there?' cried the shepherd.

'Aye, naethin'. There was naethin'. The road was toom but for himsel', and he was that terrified that he started awa wi' the cauld sweit drippin' on his cheeks and ran till his breith was done. That was the nicht Bell an' me saw him come hame.'

The smith stopped and looked at his companions.

'Noo, what div ye mak' o' that?' he asked, as neither of them spoke.

'I wad say that yon man had been a leear,' replied the shepherd judicially; 'and, ony way, it's time I was awa'. Come on min.'

The collie rose at the summons and followed his master to the door.

The smith turned to Spence.

'Ah weel, ye see,' said the old man. 'I wasna there mysel', and I couldna exactly say . . .'

He began to bestir himself too.

'But will ye no bide and hear the end o' it?' called the smith to the shepherd's back, which square and heavy, filled the doorway.

'An' is that no' the end?'

'Na, there's mair.'

The young man had not moved from the anvil; but the shepherd, though he turned round, stayed in the doorway; to have approached would have been a concession to folly, to youth, to all sorts of officially negligible things.

'It was a while after when I got this job here an' was married,' began the smith again. 'I was acquaint wi' yon business o' the doag and we'd speak aboot it at times, her an' me. But the man himsel' couldna thole tae hear aboot it, for there was some that made a joke o't an' wad cry oot when he passed, *"Whaur's yer doag, Fifie? hae ye gi'en him a holiday?"* But there wasna very muckle use for him tae be pretendin' wi' us that had seen him thon nicht comin' hame dementit-like, and Bell had been i' the hoose and got the tale frae his ain lips. But we said naethin' tae upset him, and noo that the lassie an' me was man an' wife, and the smiddy daein' weel, he didna tak sae ill at me, and we'd gang tae the fairm, noo and again, o' Sawbaths, for her auntie likit Bell.

It was ane o' thae days that we was there. There was just the auntie at hame, for her man had gane awa' aifter the kirk was oot and tell't her he wad be hame for tea time. A braw November day it was, saft and freish, and I mind we went oot i' the yaird when dinner was done, for Bell had wrocht wi' the turkey when she was at fairm and was seekin' tae see what like birds her auntie had gotten this year. The turkey-hens were steppin' aboot an' the bubblyjock scrapin' his wings alang the ground because I was whustlin' at him tae gar him rage; we was lauchin' at him when a little lassie lookit ower the palin' an' cried on us.

"Mistress Donal'! Mistress Donal'! Yer man tell't me tae come for ye, for he's no verra weel—he's got a sair pain in his he'rt an' he canna stand. He bad me mak' haste. He's doon this way!"

We a' set aff, and the lassie brocht us tae the same road that he'd traiv'led wi' the doag mair nor a year syne. Puir Mistress Donald was no' that quick on her feet for she was stoot and no just young, and I left Bell wi' her an' ran. When I got roond a turn I could see the arn trees that were bare but for a wheen broun leaves, wi' the muckle stane stickin' up below them frae the rank grass, an' there was a dark heap lyin' terrible still at the stane's fit.

It was him, deid. It took me a while tae mak' sure, and when I raised mysel' tae see whether Bell and the puir body was comin', I heard a kind o' movin' an lookit roond.

Aboot a stane's thraw frae's, there was a yella doag standin' lookin' at me.'

VIOLET JACOB

THE TYKES TOOLY

Of all the rangers of the moor
fair Juno was the greatest whore,
none froister scowered the knows and bogs,
She was a toast among the dogs,
but, ah! what dire mischiefs are spred!
from ills, by love and beauty bred,
Empires distroy'd, and private jars,
assassinations, bloody wars,
thus fierce were toolys 'mongst the tykes
for Juno, when she took the sykes,
even blood-relation pled no grace
'mongst the love-bitten barking race,
The father in the madest ire
'gainst the son's thraple did conspire,
and uncle curst thought it no sin
to rive his yowling nevoy's skin,
for Juno's love, the panting croud
shew'd all their fangs, & gowld aloud,
Ringwood, Ranger, Tray & Towser,
ventured their heart's blood to espouse her,
The rageing pack, all in a fury
gowl, snarl, & bite, & tear, & worry,
'till many a dog with gamping wound,
and horrid yelling, bit the ground,
and meikle blood, and dirt, was shed,
before the amorous plea was redd.
Like them the human race appears
who go togither by the ears,
and think it an heroick play
to murder thousands in a day,
and when the bloody race is run
by either side there's nothing won,
Our tale, this Mortall fairy teaches
Mankind act oft like dogs & bitches.

ALLAN RAMSAY

THE TWA DOGS

Robert Burns's poem 'The Twa Dogs' first appeared in his Poems Chiefly in the Scottish Dialect, *published in 1786. The tradition of using animals to voice human sentiments is a mediaeval one.*

> *A Tale*
> 'Twas in that place o' Scotland's isle,
> That bears the name o' Auld King Coil,
> Upon a bonie day in June,
> When wearing thro' the afternoon,
> Twa dogs, that were na thrang at hame,
> Forgather'd ance upon a time.

The first I'll name, they ca'd him Caesar,
Was keepit for his Honor's pleasure;
His hair, his size, his mouth, his lugs,
Shew'd he was nane o' Scotland's dogs,
But whalpit some place far abroad,
Whare sailors gang to fish for Cod.

His locked, letter'd, braw brass collar
Shew'd him the gentleman and scholar;
But tho' he was o' high degree,
The fient a pride, na pride had he,
But wad hae spent an hour caressin,
Ev'n wi' a tinkler-gypsey's messin:
At kirk or market, mill or smiddie,
Nae tawted tyke, tho' e'er sae duddie,
But he wad stan't, as glad to see him,
And stroan't on stanes an' hillocks wi' him.

The tither was a ploughman's collie,
A rhyming, ranting, raving billie,
Wha for his friend and comrade had him,
And in his freaks had Luath ca'd him,
After some dog in Highland sang,
Was made lang syne, Lord knows how lang.

He was a gash an' faithful tyke,
As ever lap a sheugh or dyke.
His honest, sonsie, baws'nt face
Ay gat him friends in ilka place;
His breast was white, his touzie back
Weel clad wi' coat o' glossy black;
His gawcie tail, wi' upward curl,
Hung owre his hurdies wi' a swirl.

Nae doubt but they were fain o' ither,
An' unco pack an' thick thegither;
Wi' social nose whyles snuff'd and' snowkit,
Whyles mice an' moudieworts they howkit;
Whyles scour'd awa in lang excursion,
An' worry'd ither in diversion;
Till tir'd at last wi' mony a farce,
They sat them down upon their arse,
And there began a lang digression
About the *lords o' the creation*.

CAESAR

I've aften wonder'd, honest Luath,
What sort o' life poor dogs like you have;
An' when the gentry's life I saw,
What way poor bodies liv'd ava.

    Our Laird gets in his racked rents,
His coals, his kain, and a' his stents:
He rises when he likes himsel;
His flunkies answer at the bell;
He ca's his coach; he ca's his horse;
He draws a bonie, silken purse
As lang's my tail, whare thro the steeks,
The yellow letter'd Geordie keeks.

    Frae morn to e'en it's nought but toiling,
At baking, roasting, frying, boiling;
An' tho' the gentry first are stechin,
Yet ev'n the ha' folk fill their pechan
Wi' sauce, ragouts, and siclike trashtrie,
That's little short o' downright wastrie.
Our Whipper-in, wee, blastit wonner,
Poor, worthless elf, it eats a dinner,
Better than ony tenant man
His Honour has in a' the lan':
An' what poor cot-folk pit their painch in,
I own it's past my comprehension.

LUATH

    Trowth, Caesar, whyles they're fash't enough;
A cotter howkin in a sheugh,
Wi' dirty stanes biggin a dyke,
Baring a quarry, and siclike,
Himsel, a wife, he thus sustains,
A smytrie o' wee duddie weans,
An' nought but his han' darg to keep
Them right an' tight in thack an' rape.

    An' when they meet wi' sair disasters,
Like loss o' health or want o' masters,
Ye maist wad think, a wee touch langer,
An' they maun starve o' cauld and hunger:
But how it comes, I never kend yet,

They're maistly wonderfu' contented;
An' buirdly chiels, an' clever hizzies,
Are bred in sic a way as this is.

CAESAR

But then to see how ye're negleckit,
How huff'd, and cuff'd, and disrespeckit!
Lord, man, our gentry care as little
For delvers, ditchers, an' sic cattle;
They gang as saucy by poor folk,
As I wad by a stinking brock.

I've notic'd, on our Laird's court-day,
An' mony a time my heart's been wae,
Poor tenant bodies, scant o' cash,
How they maun thole a factor's snash;
He'll stamp an' threaten, curse an' swear,
He'll apprehend them, poind their gear:
While they maun stan', wi' aspect humble,
An' hear it a', an' fear an' tremble!'

I see how folk live that hae riches;
But surely poor folk maun be wretches!

LUATH

They're nae sae wretched's ane wad think;
Tho' constantly on poortith's brink,
They're sae accustom'd wi' the sight,
The view o't gies them little fright.

Then chance an' fortune are sae guided,
They're ay in less or mair provided;
An' tho' fatigu'd wi' close employment,
A blink o' rest's a sweet enjoyment.

The dearest comfort o' their lives,
Their grushie weans an' faithfu' wives;
The prattling things are just their pride,
That sweetens a' their fire-side.

An' whyles twalpennie worth o' nappy
Can mak the bodies unco happy;
They lay aside their private cares,

To mind the Kirk and State affairs;
They'll talk o' patronage and priests,
Wi' kindling fury in their breasts,
Or tell what new taxation's comin,
An ferlie at the folk in Lon'on.

    As bleak-fac'd Hallowmass returns,
They get the jovial, ranting Kirns,
When rural life, o' ev'ry station,
Unite in common recreation;
Love blinks, Wit slaps, an' social Mirth
Forgets there's Care upo' the earth.

    That merry day the year begins,
They bar the door on frosty win's;
The nappy reeks wi' mantling ream,
An' sheds a heart-inspiring steam;
The luntin pipe, an' sneeshin mill,
Are handed round wi' right guid will;
The cantie, auld folks, crackin crouse,
The young anes ranting thro' the house—
My heart has been sae fain to see them,
That I for joy hae barkit wi' them.

    Still it's owre true that ye hae said,
Sic a game is now owre aften play'd;
There's monie a creditable stock
O' decent, honest fawsont folk,
Are riven out baith root and branch,
Some rascal's pridefu' greed to quench,
Wha thinks to knit himsel the faster
In favor wi' some gentle Master,
Wha ablins thrang a parliamentin
For Britain's guid his saul indentin—

CAESAR
    Haith, lad, ye little ken about it;
For Britain's guid! guid faith! I doubt it.
Say rather, gaun as Premiers lead him,
An' saying *aye* or *no's* they bid him:
At operas an' plays parading,
Mortgaging, gambling, masquerading:
Or maybe in a frolic daft,

To Hague or Calais taks a waft,
To mak' a tour, an' tak a whirl,
To learn *bon ton* an' see the worl'.

There, at Vienna or Versailles,
He rives his father's auld entails;
Or by Madrid he taks the rout,
To thrum guitars an' fecht wi' nowt;
Or down Italian vista startles,
Whore hunting amang groves o' myrtles:
Then bouses drumly German water,
To mak himsel look fair and fatter,
An' clear the consequential sorrows,
Love-gifts of Carnival Signoras.

For Britain's guid! for her destruction!
Wi' dissipation, feud an' faction.

LUATH
Hech man! dear sirs! is that the gate
They waste sae mony a braw estate!
Arc we sae foughten an' harass'd
For fear to gang that gate at last!

O would they stay aback frae courts,
An' please themsels wi' countra sports,
It wad for ev'ry ane be better,
The Laird, the Tenant, an' the Cotter!
For thae frank, rantin, ramblin billies,
Fient haet o' them's ill hearted fellows;
Except for breakin o' their timmer,
Or speakin lightly o' their Limmer,
Or shootin o' a hare or moorcock,
The ne'er-a-bit they're ill to poor folk.

But will ye tell me, master Caesar,
Sure great folk's life's a life o' pleasure?
Nae cauld nor hunger e'er can steer them,
The vera thought o't need na fear them.

CAESAR
Lord, man, were ye but whyles whare I am,
The gentles ye wad ne'er envy 'em.

It's true, they need na starve or sweat,
Thro' winter's cauld, or Simmer's heat;
They've nae sair wark to craze their banes,
An' fill auld age wi' grips an' granes;
But human bodies are sic fools,
For a' their colleges and schools,
That when nae real ills perplex them,
They mak enow themsels to vex them;
An' ay the less they hae to sturt them,
In like proportion, less will hurt them.
A country fellow at the pleugh,
His acre's till'd, he's right eneugh;
A country girl at her wheel,
Her dizzen's done, she's unco weel:
But Gentlemen, an' Ladies warst,
Wi' ev'n down want o' wark are curst.
They loiter, lounging, lank, an' lazy;
Tho' deil haet ails them, yet uneasy;
Their days, insipid, dull an' tasteless,
Their nights, unquiet, lang and restless,
An'ev'n their sports, their balls an' races,
Their galloping thro' public places,
There's sic parade, sic pomp an' art,
The joy can scarcely reach the heart.
The Men cast out in party matches,
Then sowther a' in deep debauches,
Ae night, they're mad wi' drink an' whoring,
Niest day their life is past enduring.
The Ladies arm-in-arm in clusters,
As great an' gracious a' as sisters;
But hear their absent thoughts o' ither,
They're a' run deils an jads thegither.
Whyles, owre the wee bit cup an' plaitie,
They sip the scandal potion pretty;
Or lee-lang nights, wi' crabbit leuks,
Pore owre the devil's pictur'd beuks;
Stake on a chance a farmer's stackyard,
An' cheat like ony unhang'd blackguard.

There's some exception, man an' woman;
But this is Gentry's life in common.

By this, the sun was out o' sight,
An' darker gloamin brought the night:
The bum-clock humm'd wi' lazy drone,
The kye stood rowtin i' the loan;
When up they gat an' shook their lugs,
Rejoic'd they were na *men*, but *dogs*;
An' each took aff his several way,
Resolv'd to meet some ither day.

ROBERT BURNS

45 (p 164) and 46   The Twa Dogs, from *The Entire Works of Burns*, edited by
James Currie.

DOGS AND WOLVES

Across eternity, across its snow,
   I see my unborn poems; the paw-marks breaking
The harsh white of the snow; fur starting,
Bloody-tongued lean dogs and wolves, mad chasing
   Across the dykes, mad racing
Beneath the wild tree shadows, parting
The pass of the narrow glens, taking
   The sweep and the gale-blow
Of the hills; their throaty howls rending
Across the stark bareness of this time,
   Their eternal baying in my ears,
   Their hot rush taking my bounds
   Of mind; a race of wolves and ghostly hounds,
Swift chase of the hunt through the tiers
Of words without turning, across the sheer climb
Of the tops of the mountains unbending;
   Mad gentle dogs of my songs, lean wolves in chase
   Of beauty, the beauty of soul, the beauty of face,
   White deer across hill and desolate space,
   Deer of gentle loved loveliness; and my songs wolves, wending
A chase without waiting, a chase without ending.

SORLEY MACLEAN (TR J M RUSSELL)

THE THREE TYKES

'I had three tykes, ' the silly old Man saith,
'called Discipline, Imagination, Faith.
They kept my soul and its bigging safe from skaith.

Ae night in the bygoing came a fellow fell
who's tongue gaed clatter like the College bell
that secret ferlies told and garred me tell.

As frae an ower-turned blanket sprint the bugs
sae crept his words intil my bizzing lugs
and syne the wight unchristened my three dugs.

The bulldog he called *Refrenatio*;
the whippet he called *Aberratio*;
the terrier, Faith, was *Cupida Ratio*.

The Latin words disjaskit me;
I hung the curs upon a tree,
and there they hung for a' to see.

Doon cam the riever lads frae the Hanging Shaw
and riped my biggings to the naked wa'
wi never a tyke to bark at them ava'.

JAMES BRIDIE (O H MAVOR)

47   Marquis the wolf with Lisa. Courtesy of David and Jess Stephen.

HOUNDS AND HORSEMEN

Those who have studied European balladry know that similar themes and situations occur in the folk-traditions of several countries. Here, we have an anonymous ghost dog from Albania, *a poem said to be by a Scots clergyman of about twenty-four years of age, published in London in 1737, only one copy of which survived to fall into the hands of Sir Walter Scott's friend, John Leyden.*

> Ere since of old the haughty thanes of Ross—
> So to the simple swain tradition tells—
> Were wont with clans and ready vassals thronged
> To wake the bounding stag or guilty wolf.
> There oft is heard at midnight, or at noon,
> Beginning faint, but rising still more loud
> And nearer, voices of hunters and of hounds
> And horns hoarse-winded, blowing far and keen.
> Forthwith the hubbub multiplies, the gale
> Labours with wilder shrieks and rifer din
> Of hot pursuit—the broken cry of deer
> Mangled by throttling dogs, the shouts of men,
> And hoofs thick beating on the hollow hill.
> Sudden the grazing heifer in the vale
> Starts at the noise, and both the herdsman's ears
> Tingle with inward dread. Aghast he eyes
> The mountain's height and all the ridges round;
> Yet not one trace of living wight discerns,
> Nor knows, o'erawed and trembling as he stands
> To what or whom he owes his idle fear—
> To ghost, to witch, to fairy, or to fiend;
> But wonders, and no end of wondering finds.

THE AUTHOR OF ALBANIA

THE WILD HUNTSMAN

Sir Walter Scott began his poetic career by translating German ballads. 'The Wild Huntsman', though quite long, presents so memorable an image of the ghostly hunter and his hounds that it seemed worth including in full. According to Scott, it is 'a translation, or rather an imitation of the Wilde Jäger *of the German poet Bürger'. The Waldegrave, or keeper of a royal forest, became so obsessed with hunting that he carried out his 'unhallowed amusement' on the Sabbath. As he was also 'profligate and cruel', uncouth sounds from the depths of the forest gave rise to the legend of the dreadful chase lasting 'till time itself shall have an end'. Scott notes the relationship between Bürger's ballad and the lines by the author of* Albania, *as well as to 'le Grand Veneur', who it seems haunts the forest of Fontainebleau.*

> The Wildgrave winds his bugle-horn,
>   To horse, to horse! halloo, halloo!
> His fiery courser snuffs the morn,
>   And thronging serfs their lord pursue.
>
> The eager pack, from couples freed,
>   Dash through the bush, the brier, the brake;
> While, answering hound, and horn, and steed,
>   The mountain echoes startling wake.
>
> The beams of God's own hallow'd day
>   Had painted yonder spire with gold,
> And, calling sinful men to pray,
>   Loud, long, and deep the bell had toll'd.
>
> But still the Wildgrave onward rides;
>   Halloo, halloo! and, hark again!
> When spurring from opposing sides,
>   Two Stranger Horsemen join the train.
>
> Who was each Stranger, left and right,
>   Well may I guess, but dare not tell;
> The right-hand steed was silver white,
>   The left, the swarthy hue of hell.

The right-hand Horseman, young and fair,
  His smile was like the morn of May;
The left, from eye of tawny glare,
  Shot midnight lightning's lurid ray.

He waved his huntsman's cap on high.
  Cried, 'Welcome, welcome, noble lord!
What sport can earth, or sea, or sky,
  to match the princely chase, afford?'

'Cease thy loud bugle's clanging knell,'
  Cried the fair youth, with silver voice;
'And for devotion's choral swell,
  Exchange the rude unhallow'd noise.

To-day, the ill-omen'd chase forbear,
  Yon bell yet summons to the fane;
To-day the Warning Spirit hear,
  To-morrow thou mayst mourn in vain.'

'Away, and sweep the glades along!'
  The Sable Hunter hoarse replies;
'To muttering monks leave matin-song,
  And bells, and books, and mysteries.'

The Wildgrave spurr'd his ardent steed,
  And, launching forward with a bound,
'Who, for thy drowsy priestlike rede,
  Would leave the jovial horn and hound?

Hence, if our manly sport offend!
  With pious fools go chant and pray;
Well hast thou spoke, my dark-brow'd friend:
  Halloo, halloo! and hark away!'

The Wildgrave spurr'd his courser light,
  O'er moss and moor, o'er holt and hill;
And on the left and on the right,
  Each Stranger Horseman follow'd still.

Upsprings, from yonder tangled thorn,
  A stag more white than mountain snow;
And louder rung the Widgrave's horn,
  'Hark forward, forward! holla, ho!'

A heedless wretch has cross'd the way;
   He gasps the thundering hoofs below;—
But, live who can, or die who may,
   Still, 'forward, forward!' on they go.

See, where yon simple fences meet,
   A field with Autumn's blessings crown'd:
See, prostrate at the Wildgrave's feet,
   A husbandman with toil embrown'd:

'O mercy, mercy, noble lord!
   Spare the poor's pittance,' was his cry,
'Earn'd by the sweat these brows have pour'd,
   In scorching hour of fierce July.'

Earnest the right-hand Stranger pleads,
   The left still cheering to the prey;
The impetuous Earl no warning heeds,
   But furious holds the onward way.

'Away, thou hound! so basely born,
   Or dread the scourge's echoing blow!'
Then loudly rung his bugle-horn,
   'Hark forward, forward! holla, ho!'

So said, so done: A single bound
   Clears the poor labourer's humble pale;
Wild follows man, and horse, and hound,
   Like dark December's stormy gale.

And man and horse, and hound and horn,
   Destructive sweep the field along;
While, joying o'er the wasted corn,
   Fell Famine marks the maddening throng.

Again uproused, the timorous prey
   Scours moss and moor, and holt and hill;
Hard run, he feels his strength decay,
   And trusts for life his simple skill.

Too dangerous solitude appear'd;
   He seeks the shelter of the crowd;
Amid the flock's domestic herd
   His harmless head he hopes to shroud.

O'er moss and moor, and holt and hill,
    His track the steady blood-hounds trace;
O'er moss and moor, unwearied still,
    The furious Earl pursues the chase.

Full lowly did the herdsman fall;
    'O spare, thou noble Baron, spare
These herds, a widow's little all;
    These flocks, an orphan's fleecy care!'

Earnest the right-hand Stranger pleads,
    The left still cheering to the prey;
The Earl nor prayer nor pity heeds,
    But furious keeps the onward way.

'Unmanner'd dog! To stop my sport
    Vain were thy cant and beggar whine,
Though human spirits, of thy sort,
    Were tenants of these carrion kine!'

Again he winds his bugle-horn,
    'Hark forward, forward! holla, ho!'
And through the herd, in ruthless scorn,
    He cheers his furious hounds to go.

In heaps the throttled victims fall;
    Down sinks their mangled herdsman near;
The murderous cries the stag appal.
    Again he starts, new-nerved by fear,

With blood besmear'd, and white with foam,
    While big the tears of anguish pour,
He seeks, amid the forest's gloom,
    The humble hermit's hallow'd bower.

But man and horse, and horn and hound,
    Fast rattling on his traces go;
The sacred chapel rung around
    With, 'Hark away! and, holla, ho!'

All mild, amid the rout profane,
    The holy hermit pour'd his prayer;
'Forbear with blood God's house to stain;
    Revere his altar, and forbear!

The meanest brute has rights to plead,
    Which, wrong'd by cruelty, or pride,
Draw vengeance on the ruthless head:
    Be warn'd at length, and turn aside.'

Still the Fair Horseman anxious pleads;
    The Black, wild whooping, points the prey:
Alas! the Earl no warning heeds,
    But frantic keeps the forward way.

'Holy or not, or right or wrong,
    Thy altar, and its rites, I spurn;
Not sainted martyrs' sacred song,
    Not God himself, shall make me turn!'

He spurs his horse, he winds his horn,
    'Hark forward, forward! holla, ho!'
But off, on whirlwind's pinions borne,
    The stag, the hut, the hermit, go.

And horse and man, and horn and hound,
    And clamour of the chase, was gone;
For hoofs, and howls, and bugle-sound,
    A deadly silence reign'd alone.

Wild gazed the affrighted Earl around;
    He strove in vain to wake his horn,
In vain to call: for not a sound
    Could from his anxious lips be borne.

He listens for his trusty hounds;
    No distant baying reach'd his ears:
His courser, rooted to the ground,
    The quickening spur unmindful bears.

Still dark and darker frown the shades,
    Dark as the darkness of the grave;
And not a sound the still invades,
    Save what a distant torrent gave.

High o'er the sinner's humble head
    At length the solemn silence broke;
And, from a cloud of swarthy red,
    the awful voice of thunder spoke.

Oppressor of creation fair!
　Apostate Spirits' harden'd tool!
Scorner of God! Scourge of the poor!
　The measure of thy cup is full.

Be chased for ever through the wood;
　For ever roam the affrighted wild;
And let thy fate instruct the proud,
　God's meanest creature is his child.'

'Twas hush'd: One flash, of sombre glare,
　With yellow tinged the forests brown;
Uprose the Wildgrave's bristling hair,
　And horror chill'd each nerve and bone.

Cold pour'd the sweat in freezing rill;
　A rising wind began to sing;
And louder, louder, louder still,
　Brought storm and tempest on its wing.

Earth heard the call; her entrails rend;
　From yawning rifts, with many a yell,
Mix'd with sulphureous flames, ascend
　The misbegotten dogs of hell.

What ghastly Huntsman next arose,
　Well may I guess, but dare not tell;
His eye like midnight lightning glows,
　His steed the swarthy hue of hell.

The Wildgrave flies o'er bush and thorn,
　With many a shriek of helpless woe;
Behind him hound, and horse, and horn,
　And 'Hark away!' and 'Holla, ho!'

With wild despair's reverted eye,
　Close, close behind, he marks the throng.
With bloody fangs and eager cry;
　In frantic fear he scours along.

Still, still shall last the dreadful chase,
　Till time itself shall have an end;
By day, they scour earth's cavern'd space,
　At midnight's witching hour, ascend.

This is the horn, and hound, and horse,
    That oft the lated peasant hears;
Appall'd, he signs the frequent cross,
    When the wild din invades his ears.

The wakeful priest oft drops a tear
    For human pride, for human woe,
When, at his midnight mass, he hears
    the infernal cry of 'Holla, ho!'

SIR WALTER SCOTT

48   Drumclog, by Sir George Harvey. Courtesy of Glasgow Art Gallery and Museum.

PROVERBIAL AND HERALDIC DOGS

Proverbs are meant to enshrine folk-wisdom in easily remembered phrases. Heraldry uses the emblems of everday mediaeval life to lend distinction to families or places in need of a continuing symbol. Dogs have featured in both. The earliest collection of Scottish Proverbs was that made by David Fergusson in 1641. This was reprinted by the Scottish Text Society in 1924, edited by Erskine Beveridge. Then followed James Kelly's *A Complete Collection of Scottish Proverbs Explained and made Intelligible to the English Reader*, published in 1721. The first fourteen proverbs in this section come from Fergusson's collection, the remainder from Kelly's book. The three heraldic drawings are taken from the now standard work on the subject, R M Urquhart's *Scottish County and Burgh Heraldry*. *The Law and Practice of Heraldry in Scotland* (1863) by George Seton explains the principles upon which crests are made up. Frequently, families would incorporate flowers or creatures that appeared to them to symbolise the qualities they possessed, or believed they possessed. Some years ago the then Lord Lyon King-at-Arms, Sir Thomas of Learney, was persuaded to demonstrate in front of the television cameras while I interviewed him, a possible coat of arms for me. It included some symbols associated with the Lindsay clan along with devices representing my interests, poetry, music and broadcasting. The whole thing was duly rehearsed and we left the studio to go to the make-up department. At the end of the broadcast, before I could thank Sir Thomas, he leant towards me and declared impromptu, in his high-pitched squeaky voice: 'And that will cost you fifty guineas!' In Scotland, when the Lord Lyon grants a coat-of-arms—and any honourable man, company or place is eligible provided he pays the fee—it is registered and held at Register House, Edinburgh.

PROVERBS

An old hound bytes sair.

At open doors dogs come in.

Follie is a bonnie dog.

A tuilzeling (quarrelsome) tyk comes ay tyrd home.

A houndless man comes to the best hunting.

An ill dog comes halting home.

Ding not the dog for the bitches fart.

Ane good dog never barked without ane bone.

Dogs will red (clear away) swine.

Fiddlers dogs and flies come to feasts uncalled.

He that has ane dog of his awin may go to the kirk with ane clean breast.

Twa dogs stryves for ane bone: in comes a third and taks it from them baith.

He can lie as well as a dog can lick a dish.

It is ill to wakin sleeping dogs.

from DAVID FERGUSSON

I'll gar you ken the dog from the door-bar.
  (I'll make you keep your distance.)

He that sleeps with dogs must rise with fleas.
  (If you keep company with base and unworthy fellows, you will get
  some ill by them.)

Like butter in the black dog's ha'se.
  (That is, past recovery.)

Better hald with the hound as run with the hare.
  (Better be able to grapple with difficulty than to have a probability to
  escape it.)

The foremost hound grips the hare.

A dog's life, mickle hunger, mickle ease.
  (Applied to careless, lazy lubbers who will not work, and therefore
  have many a hungry meal.)

We hounds slew the hare, quoth the messan (lapdog).
  (Spoken to insignificant persons when they attribute to themselves
  any part of a great achievement.)

Many a dog's dead since you were a whelp.

from JAMES KELLY

HERALDIC DOGS

Heraldry is popularly supposed to have had its origins in the shields of
knights, enabling them to be distinguishable in battle. The best description
of what heraldry is about is perhaps that by Sir Thomas Innes of Learney
(1893–1971), himself once Lord Lyon King-of-Arms. It comes from his
book *Scots Heraldry* (1978).

> It is now accepted by most historians that whilst conventional designs
> were used on shields prior to the eleventh century, heraldry in the sense
> of scientific armorial symbols had not then begun to exist. The designs
> which we can affirm to have subsequently become hereditary are found
> in the first half of the twelfth century—say 1138–57—and are repeated

in the following generation, so that by 1189 heraldry had automatically evolved, and by the end of the century was a recognised science of identification. The earliest known Scottish armorial bearings are those on the seals of Allan, High Steward of Scotland, about 1177, and Patrick, Earl of Dunbar, about 1182. Early armorial seals show the owner of the seal on horseback with the device by which he could be distinguished from other men emblazoned on his shield, surcoat and horse-trappings. There is, however, good reason to suppose that 'ensigns armorial' were first made on leaders' flags, from which the devices soon came to be repeated on their shields and surcoats. The idea of hereditary armorial symbols was conceived by kings and nobles, without any necessary connection with fighting, and the convenience experienced from the use of seals on deeds, charters and leases had more to do with the recognition of the advantages of armory, than the use to be made of it in war. Identification and therefore heraldry were for practical purposes necessary for prelates, military leaders, chiefs of clans, landowners and public officials, the categories who were, either by descent or from office, 'nobles'. Consequently, heraldry became necessarily an indication of nobility.

Nevertheless, the instant popularity of the new science came because it supplied the people of an illiterate age with a means for the immediate identification of local and national leaders. Heraldry is therefore not, as some people have supposed, an idle amusement, but is essentially a practical science for the service of the general public. Its use has been rendered even more popular by the artistic and architectural appreciation of its decorative advantages.

In these modern days when the public has no time to read more than headlines, as in the twelfth century when few people could read at all, heraldry remains *par excellence* the decorative shorthand for identification of our clan houses, national leaders and public institutions.

Here are two examples of the coats of arms of clan chiefs incorporating dogs. First, that of the Chief of the Innes of that Ilk (The Duke of Roxburghe), the arms show 'three stars azure', the crest, a boar's head, the supporters, two greyhounds wearing 'collars azure with the stars of the first'; the motto, 'be traist', be trustworthy.

The second is the arms of the Chief of the Forbes, Lord Forbes. For arms, it has 'three bears' heads couped argent, muzzled gules', for crest, 'a stag's head proper' and for supporters, 'two bloodhounds argent, collared gules'. The motto is 'Grace me guide'.

49 Coat of Arms of the Chief of the Innes of that Ilk (Duke of Roxburghe).
Courtesy of the Duke of Roxburghe.

50 Coat of Arms of Lord Forbes. Courtesy of Lord Forbes.

Now two examples of the use of dogs in burgh and county heraldry. first, the former Royal Burgh of Cullen. Cullen was made a Royal Burgh between 1189 and 1198 by William the Lyon. The original old town around the parish church was virtually demolished about 1820, because it interfered with extension plans for Cullen House, and a new town was built nearer to the sea. The arms are a minor rearrangement of the device on the Burgh seal. The coat of arms is well described in *Scottish Burgh and County Heraldry* (1973).

The black and silver colours allude to Sinclair of Deskford, the early adjacent family. The Virgin and Child recall that the thirteenth-century parish church is dedicated to St Mary, while the gold and red colours in the faldstool refer to the Burgh's long-standing connection with the Ogilvy family, now represented by the Earl of Seafield, whose seat was Cullen House. The reason for the dog or whelp in base is not certain but it is commonly thought to be a play on the word 'Cullen' as the Gaelic 'cuilean' means 'whelp'. The Latin motto—'For ever and ever'—was a local choice. The arms were registered in connection with the presentation of a Chain-of-Office for the Provost by Mrs Emily Wood in memory of her grandfather, William Duffus, Provost of Cullen, 1881–86.

51   Coat of Arms of the former Royal Burgh of Cullen, from *Scottish Burgh and County Heraldry*, by R M Urquhart; London: Heraldry Today 1973.

The arms of Helensburgh, also a variation on the device of the original Burgh seal, fulfil the wishes of Sir James Colquhoun that it should include some reference to the Colquhoun arms, and to those of his mother, a daughter of Lord Strathnaver and Master of Sutherland. So the upper part of the shield shows the black engraved Saltire of the Colquhouns on its silver field, and the lower part, the three golden stars of Sutherland of their red fields. The red stag's head crest and the greyhound supporter recall similar features in the Colquhoun arms and the savage, the almost identical supporter in the Sutherland arms. The French motto 'If I can' is that of the Colquhouns, while the Gaelic one, 'The Willow Hill', is the Colquhoun war-cry.

52   Coat of Arms of the Burgh of Helensburgh, from *Scottish Burgh and County Heraldry*, by R M Urquhart; London: Heraldry Today 1973.

WALLY DUGS

Scottish pottery was established after the discovery of suitable clay in 1767 at Portobello, near Edinburgh. Bricks and tiles, pipes and chimney cowls were made from this clay. The firm of Rathbone and Company were well-known for their range of figures based on local characters such as fishwives and highlanders, but as the nineteenth century wore on, it was animal figures which had the greatest appeal to the Victorian householder, particularly pairs of spaniels which were seated facing each other on the mantelpiece. These wally dugs, as they were known in Scotland, were made cheaply and in great numbers. Poodles and greyhounds were also favourites. Other potteries making wally dugs were located at Pollokshaws, near Glasgow, and at Prestonpans, near Edinburgh.

53 and 54 Wally Dugs. Photographs by Peter Davenport.

LITERARY DOGS

Dogs have often been the companions of authors. The greatest Scottish author who was also a dog-lover was Sir Walter Scott. As Burns (whose relationship with dogs was that of a working farmer), largely saved Scots poetry and 'the guid Scots tongue' from succumbing to the late eighteenth century cult of North British anglicisation, so Scott through the greatest of his Waverley Novels, revived an awareness of Scotland's sense of nationhood by making available to ordinary people, the history of her past in the guise of popular fiction. James Hogg's relationship with dogs was that of a working shepherd, Thomas Carlyle's, that of an indulgent husband. Robert Louis Stevenson, on the other hand, viewed dogs in a more objective literary manner.

55   Hamish, the Skye Terrier. Drawing by Morven Cameron.

SIR WALTER SCOTT

No author was more devoted to his dogs than Scott. They were silent companions in his study while he wrote and they accompanied him when his legal work took him over a wide stretch of the country, picking up legends and ballads wherever he travelled. 'A man who is so hearty with dogs,' said one old Borderer, 'is one a farmer can understand and talk to himself.'

Next to the children (says John Buchan in his *Life of Sir Walter Scott*) in the family circle came the dogs. 'There were a couple of greyhounds, Douglas and Percy, who leapt in and out of the open study window, and were noted performers on the hill. Especially, there was Camp, the bull-terrier, to whom Scott always spoke as he would to a man, a wise old fellow as compared to the lighthearted grews. Camp began to fail in 1808, and could no longer accompany his master's pony, but waited on the hearth-rug to greet his home-coming. The old dog died in Edinburgh in the beginning of the following year and was buried in the little garden behind the house in Castle Street, while the whole family stood in tears round the grave.'

The degree to which dozens of dogs bark, gambol and fight in the pages of the anonymous Waverley Novels is said to have provided a clue to the identity of their authorship—the publishers were under a bond of two thousand pounds not to divulge it—since the writer was clearly not only a Scot, man of law, an antiquary, a bibliomaniac, a poet and a lover of outdoor sport, but also a passionate lover of dogs.

The dogs were even more in evidence at Abbotsford than in Edinburgh or Scott's first Border home, Ashestiel. At Abbotsford, 'the breakfast-room, like the library, was encumbered with dogs—Maida, the deerhound; Hamlet, the black greyhound; Finette, Lady Scott's spaniel; Ourisque, a Highland terrier from Kintail; a motley of Dandies named after the cruet-stand—Pepper, Mustard, Ketchup and so forth; as well as the cat Hinse of Hinsfeldt' (Buchan: Ibid).

The most celebrated of them all, however, was Maida, whose arrival was announced in a letter to his friend Miss Clephane (in January or February 1816). 'I have got a deer-hound, or blood-hound, or wolf-hound that is the most magnificent creature for height and strength. All Edinburgh is agape at him. I got him from Glengarry. He is descended of the Blue Spanish wolf-dog, and the real deer greyhound, and might have followed Johnnie Armstrong for size and dignity.' In April 1816,

Joanna Baillie was told of 'a most romantic addition to my family, a large bloodhound allowed to be the finest dog of the kind in Scotland, perfectly gentle, affectionate and good-natured and the darling of all the children. . . . He is between the deer greyhound and mastiff with a shaggy mane like a lion, and always sits beside me at dinner—his head is as high as the back of my chair.' For *Albyn's Anthology*, a miscellany to which he contributed he tells Lady Campbell (30 May 1816), he made 'a present of the frontispiece which represents my large grey wolfhound with a slaughtered deer, a harp, a bugle horn, with other emblems of Highland spirit and song. This wolfhound is a most splendid animal and the admiration of the populace of Edinburgh, who crowd round him whenever he trots out along with me or with the carriage.'

Maida was one of the two dogs who appeared with Sir Walter in the picture of him by Sir John Watson Gordon, as he told Lady Abercorn (2 August 1820).

> The dog which I am represented as holding in my arms is a highland terrier from Kintail of a breed very sensible, very faithful and very ill-natured. It sometimes tires, or pretends to do so, when I am on horseback and whines to be taken up, when it sits before me like a child without any assistance. I have a very large wolfhound I think the finest dog I ever saw, but he has sat to so many artists that whenever he sees brushes and a pallet, he gets up and leaves the room, being sufficiently tired of the constraint.

When the King commanded Scott to sit for Sir Thomas Lawrence, Scott told William Laidlaw (22 February 1821) that he 'wanted to have in Maida that there may be one handsome fellow in the party'. Maida 'sat for Mr Naysmyth as a figure for the foreground of a landscape (letter to Terry, December 1916) and was again painted, much to Scott's satisfaction, by Sir David Wilkie the following year.

> There is an old proverb which saith Love me love my dog and I feel much flattered indeed to judge of your regard by the honour which you have done Maida. The picture is most beautiful and expresses the form and character of the animal perfectly.

'I have sometimes thought of the final cause of dogs having such short lives,' Scott wrote to the Irish novelist, Maria Edgeworth (1767–1849), 'and I am quite satisfied it is in compassion to the human race; for, if we suffer so in losing a dog after an acquaintance of ten or twelve years, what would it be if they were to live double that time?'

At last Maida died, 'quietly on his straw . . . after a grand supper', Scott wrote to his son Charles (22 October 1821). Maida was buried below a monument in the form of a mounting stone Scott had had made by his

56   Sir Walter Scott with his deerhound Maida, by Sir John Watson Gordon.

master-mason the year before, and which stood by the gate. Moved now
to the entrance to the house, it bore an epitaph in what Buchan calls
'doubtful Latinity', which Scott translated:

> Beneath the sculptured form which late you wore
> Sleep soundly Maida at the master's door

In 1817, the American writer Washington Irving visited Abbotsford.
He left a vivid account of Scott and his dogs, quoted at some length in
J G Lockhart's *Memoirs of the Life of Sir Walter Scott Bart.*

> The noise of my arrival disturbed the quiet of the establishment. Out sailed
> the warden of the castle, a black greyhound, and leaping on one of the
> blocks of stone began a furious barking. This alarm brought out the whole
> garrison of dogs, all open-mouthed and vociferous. In a little while the
> Lord of the Castle made his appearance . . . by his side jogged along a large
> iron-grey staghound of the most grave demeanour who took no part in the
> clamour of the canine rabble but seemed to consider himself bound, for the
> dignity of the house, to give me a courteous reception.

Scott and Irving went for a walk.

> As we sallied forth every dog in the establishment turned out to attend us.
> There was the old staghound Maida, that I have already mentioned, a
> noble animal, and Hamlet, the black greyhound, a wild thoughtless
> youngster not yet arrived at years of discretion, and Finette, a beautiful
> setter, with soft silken hair, long pendant ears and a mild eye—the parlour
> favourite.
>
> When in front of the house we were joined by a superannuated
> greyhound, who came from the kitchen wagging his tail, and was cheered
> by Scott as an old friend and comrade.
>
> In our walk he would frequently pause in conversation to notice his dogs
> and speak to them as if they were rational companions, and indeed there
> appears to be a vast deal of rationality in these faithful attendants on man
> derived from their close intimacy with him.
>
> Maida deports herself with a gravity becoming his age and size, and
> seemed to consider himself called upon to preserve a great deal of dignity
> and decorum in our society. As he jogged along a little distance ahead of
> us the young dogs would gambol about him, leap upon his neck, worry at
> his ears and endeavour to tease him into a gambol. The old dog would keep
> on for a long time with imperturbable solemnity, now and then seeming
> to rebuke the levity of his companions. At length he would make a sudden
> turn, seize one of them and tumble him into the dust, then, giving a glance
> at us, as much as to say: 'You see, gentlemen, I can't help giving way to
> this nonsense,' would resume his gravity and jog on as before.

Scott amused himself with these peculiarities. 'I make no doubt,' he said, 'when Maida is alone with these young dogs, he throws gravity to the winds and plays the boy as much as any one of them; but he is ashamed to do so in our company, and seems to say: "Ha' done with your nonsense, youngsters. What will the laird and that other gentleman think of me if I give way to such foolery?"'

Another of the dogs was a little shamefaced terrier with large glassy eyes, one of the most sensitive little bodies to insult and indignity in the world, according to Scott. If ever he whipped him, the little fellow would sneak off and hide himself from the light of day in a lumber garret, whence there was no drawing him forth but by the sound of the chopping knife as if chopping up his victuals, when he would steal out with humiliated and downcast look, but would skulk away again if any one looked at him.

While we were discussing the characteristics of our canine companions some object provoked their spleen and produced a sharp and petulant barking from the smaller fry, but it was some time before Maida was sufficiently aroused to ramp forward two or three bounds and join in the chorus with a deep-mouthed bow-wow. This was but a transient outbreak, and he returned instantly, wagging his tail and looking up dubiously into his master's face, uncertain whether he would receive censure or applause.

'Ay, ay, old boy,' cried Scott. 'You have done wonders, you hae shaken the Eildon Hills with your roaring; you may now lay aside your artillery for the rest of the day . . . Maida,' continued he, 'is like the great gun at Constantinople. It takes so long to get it ready that the smaller guns can fire off a dozen times first, but when it does go off it plays the very devil.'

Maida was the prototype of two of Scott's fictional dogs; Bevis, the 'wolf dog in strength . . . mastiff in form, and in fleetness almost a greyhound' who defended the cavalier Sir Henry Ditchley and his daughter, Alice, in *Woodstock* and Roswal, in *The Talisman*, who defends the honour of his master Kenneth, Prince Royal of Scotland, while he is crusading in the Holy Land.

Few of the novels are without a dog. In *The Heart of Midlothian*, a dog lies under the chair of the Laird of Dumbiedykes. In *Waverley*, Captain Waverley first meets Fergus MacIvor, MacIvor is attended by his hounds, led by Bran—the name also given by Scott to a deerhound he received from Macpherson of Cluny and who lay yawning at his master's feet while he was working on *Count Robert of Paris*. Guy Mannering has Wasp—Scott's Spice was perhaps his prototype—the rough-haired terrier who accompanied Harry Bertram, then disguised as Vanbeest Brown, tramping the Cumberland Fells, where he meets up with Mr Dandie Dinmont, the owner of a famous breed.

'A bonny terrier that, sir, and a fell chield at the vermin, I warrant him,

57   Sir Walter Scott with Spice, his rough-haired terrier, cut by August Edouart in 1831, from *Sir Walter's Dogs*, E Thornton, published by Grant & Murray, 1931.

that, if he's been weel entered, for it lies in that,' says Dinmont, examining Wasp.

'Really sir,' answers Vanbeest Brown, 'his education has been somewhat neglected and his chief property is being a pleasant companion.'

'Ay, sir? That's a pity, begging your pardon—it's a great pity that: beast or body, education should aye be minded. I have six terriers at hame, forbye twa couples of slow hounds, five grews and a wheen other dogs. There's auld Pepper and auld Mustard, and young Pepper and young Mustard, and little Pepper and little Mustard—I had them a' regularly entered, first wi otter then wi' stots or weasels, and then wi' the tods and brocks: and now they fear naething that ever came wi' a hairy skin on it.'

'I have no doubt, sir, they are thoroughbred, but to have so many dogs you seem to have a very limited variety of names for them?'

'Oh, that's a fancy of my ain, to mark the breed, sir.'

Hector McIntyre's dog, Juno in *The Antiquary*, 'makes havoc of the antiquary's treasures', while scheming to steal a pat of butter from the sideboard.

The bloodhound, Wolf-fanger, appears in *Anne of Geiersten*; hounds in *The Bride of Lammermoor*; the Newfoundland, Neptune and Thetis in *Redgauntlet*; a terrier and a cocker spaniel in *Old Mortality* and dogs, too, in the long early poems, *The Lady of the Lake*, *Marmion* and *The Lay of the Last Minstrel*. Here are two scenes from the poems. First, from *Marmion*, a shepherd and his dog, Yarrow, brave a November storm in Ettrick.

> When red hath set the beamless sun,
> Through heavy vapours dark and dun;
> Where the tir'd ploughman, dry and warm,
> Hears, half asleep, the rising storm
> Hurling the hail, and sleeted rain,

58   Dandie Dinmont. Drawing by Colin Gibson.

Against the casement's tinkling pane;
The sounds that drive wild deer, and fox,
To shelter in the brake and rocks,
Are warnings which the shepherd ask
To dismal and to dangerous task.
Oft he looks forth, and hopes, in vain,
The blast may sink in mellowing rain;
Till, dark above, and white below,
Decided drives the flaky snow,
And forth the hardy swain must go.
Long, with dejected look and whine,
To leave the hearth his dogs repine;
Whistling and cheering them to aid,
Around his back he wreaths the plaid;
His flock he gathers, and he guides,
To open downs, and mountain-sides,
Where fiercest though the tempest blow,
Least deeply lies the drift below.
The blast, that whistles o'er the fells,
Stiffens his locks to icicles;
Oft he looks back, while, streaming far,
His cottage window seems a star,—
Loses its feeble gleam,—and then
Turns patient to the blast again,
And, facing to the tempest's sweep,
Drives through the gloom his lagging sheep.
If fails his heart, if his limbs fail,
Benumbing death is in the gale:

His paths, his landmarks, all unknown,
Close to the hut, no more his own,
Close to the aid he sought in vain,
The morn may find the stiffen'd swain;
The widow sees, at dawning pale,
His orphans raise their feeble wail;
And, close beside him, in the snow,
Poor Yarrow, partner of their woe,
Couches upon his master's breast,
And licks his cheek to break his rest.

Second, the famous hunting scene from *The Lady of the Lake*.

I

The stag at eve had drunk his fill,
Where danced the moon on Monan's rill,
And deep his midnight lair had made
In lone Glenartney's hazel shade;
But, when the sun his beacon red
Had kindled on Benvoirlich's head,
The deep-mouth'd bloodhound's heavy bay
Resounded up the rocky way,
And faint, from farther distance borne,
Were heard the clanging hoof and horn.

II

As chief, who hears his warder call,
'To arms! the foemen storm the wall,'
The antler'd monarch of the waste
Sprung from his heathery couch in haste.
But, ere his fleet career he took,
The dew-drops from his flanks he shook;
Like crested leader proud and high,
Toss'd his beam'd frontlet to the sky;
A moment gazed adown the dale,
A moment snuff'd the tainted gale,
A moment listen'd to the cry,
That thicken'd as the chase drew nigh;
Then, as the headmost foes appear'd,
With one brave bound the copse he clear'd,
And, stretching forward free and far,
Sought the wild heaths of Uam-Var.

III

Yell'd on the view the opening pack;
Rock, glen, and cavern, paid them back;

59 The Alarm. Drawing by Edwin Landseer, from *The Works of Sir Edwin Landseer, RA*, published by Cosmo Monkhouse Virtue & Co, London.

To many a mingled sound at once
The awaken'd mountain gave response.
A hundred dogs bay'd deep and strong,
Clatter'd a hundred steeds along,
Their peal the merry horns rung out,
A hundred voices join'd the shout;
With hark and whoop and wild halloo,
No rest Benvoirlich's echoes knew.
Far from the tumult fled the roe,
Close in her covert cower'd the doe;
The falcon, from her cairn on high,
Cast on the rout a wondering eye,
Till far beyond her piercing ken
The hurricane had swept the glen.
Faint and more faint, its failing din
Return'd from cavern, cliff, and linn,
And silence settled, wide and still,
On the lone wood and mighty hill.

IV

Less loud the sounds of silvan war
Disturb'd the heights of Uam-Var,
And roused the cavern, where, 'tis told,
A giant made his den of old;
For ere that steep ascent was won,
High in his pathway hung the sun,
And many a gallant, stay'd perforce,
Was fain to breathe his faltering horse,
And of the trackers of the deer,
Scarce half the lessening pack was near;
So shrewdly on the mountain side
Had the bold burst their mettle tried.

V

The noble stag was pausing now
Upon the mountain's southern brow,
Where broad extended, far beneath,
The varied realms of fair Menteith.
With anxious eye he wander'd o'er
Mountain and meadow, moss and moor,
And ponder'd refuge from his toil
By far Lochard or Aberfoyle.
But nearer was the copsewood grey,
That waved and wept on Loch-Achray,

And mingled with the pine-trees blue
On the bold cliffs of Benvenue.
Fresh vigour with the hope return'd
With flying foot the heath he spurn'd,
Held westward with unwearied race,
And left behind the panting chase.

VI

'Twere long to tell what steeds gave o'er,
As swept the hunt through Cambusmore:
What reins were tighten'd in despair,
When rose Benledi's ridge in air;
Who flagg'd upon Bochastle's heath,
Who shunn'd to stem the flooded Teith,—
For twice that day, from shore to shore,
The gallant stag swam stoutly o'er.
Few were the stragglers, following far,
That reach'd the lake of Vennachar;
And when the Brigg of Turk was won,
The headmost horseman rode alone.

VII

Alone, but with unbated zeal,
That horseman plied the scourge and steel;
For jaded now, and spent with toil,
Emboss'd with foam, and dark with soil,
While every gasp with sobs he drew,
The labouring stag strain'd full in view.
Two dogs of black Saint Hubert's breed,
Unmatch'd for courage, breath, and speed,
Fast on his flying traces came,
And all but won that desperate game;
For, scarce a spear's length from his haunch,
Vindictive toil'd the bloodhounds stanch;
Nor nearer might the dogs attain,
Nor farther might the quarry strain.
Thus up the margin of the lake,
Between the precipice and brake,
O'er stock and rock their race they take.

VIII

The Hunter mark'd that mountain high,
The lone lake's western boundary,
And deem'd the stag must turn to bay,
Where that huge rampart barr'd the way;
Already glorying in the prize,
Measured his antlers with his eyes;
For the death-wound and death-halloo,

Muster'd his breath, his whinyard drew;—
But thundering as he came prepared,
With ready arm and weapon bared,
The wily quarry shunn'd the shock,
And turn'd him from the opposing rock;
Then, dashing down a darksome glen,
Soon lost to hound and hunter's ken,
In the deep Trosachs' wildest nook
His solitary refuge took.
There, while close couch'd, the thicket shed
Cold dews and wild-flowers on his head,
He heard the baffled dogs in vain
Rave through the hollow pass amain,
Chiding the rocks that yell'd again.

When financial ruin overtook Scott, after his children his thoughts turned to his dogs. He confided to his *Journal*: 'My dogs will wait for me in vain. It is foolish but the thought of parting from these dumb animals has moved me more than any of the painful recollections I have put down . . . Poor things, I must get them kind masters; there may yet be those who, loving me may love my dog because it had been mine . . .'

Fortunately, things did not come to such a pass, and the dogs were with him during the final years when he strove to pay off his debts. 'Be careful of my dogs!', he enjoined his staff before setting out on his last visit abroad in a vain search for health. When he returned to Abbotsford to die, his dogs greeted him, and they were near him when the end came.

JAMES HOGG, THE ETTRICK SHEPHERD

In the issue of Blackwood's Magazine *for January, 1818 an anonymous contributor had a piece on 'The Sagacity of a Shepherd's Dog', provoked by an article that had appeared in the October 1817 issue 'On the Depravity of Animals'. The defender of animal intelligence instanced an affair during 'the tyrannical reign of James, Duke of York, as they still call him' (James VII and II), when Covenanters and Cameronians had to worship in secret. One old shepherd had such an intelligent dog that the animal could be left to round up the sheep on his own while his master obeyed the call of his God and went off to worship at a secret Conventicle. This story drew from Hogg a long and lively letter, dated 22 February 1818, written from 'Eltrieve Lake', as he called his Altrive farm, about his own sheepdog, Sirrah.*

I was a shepherd for ten years on the same farm, where I had always about 700 lambs put under my charge every year at weaning-time. As they were of the *short*, or *black-faced* breed, the breaking of them was a very ticklish and difficult task. I was obliged to watch them night and day for the first four days, during which time I had always a person to assist me. It happened one year, that just about midnight the lambs broke and came up the moor upon us, making a noise with their running louder than thunder. We got up and waved our plaids, and shouted, in hopes to turn them, but we only made matters worse, for in a moment they were all round us, and by our exertions we cut them into three divisions; one of these ran north, another south, and those that came up between us straight up the moor to the westward. I called out, 'Sirrah, my man, they're away'; the word, of all others, that set him most upon the alert, but owing to the darkness of the night, and the blackness of the moor, I never saw him at all. As the division of the lambs that ran southward were going straight towards the fold, where they had been that day taken from their dams, I was afraid they would go there, and again mix with them; so I threw off part of my clothes, and pursued them, and by great personal exertion, and the help of another old dog that I had beside Sirrah, I turned them, but in a few minutes afterward lost them altogether. I ran here and there, not knowing what to do, but always at intervals, gave a loud whistle to Sirrah, to let him know that I was depending on him. By that whistling, the lad who was assisting found me out, but he likewise had lost all traces of the lambs whatsoever. I asked if he had never seen Sirrah? He said, he had not; but that after

60   James Hogg, from the statue by A Currie at St Mary's Loch.

I left him a wing of the lambs had come round him with a swirl, and that he supposed Sirrah had then given them a turn, though he could not see him for the darkness. We both concluded, that whatever way the lambs ran at first, they would finally land at the fold where they left their mothers, and without delay we bent our course towards that; but when we came there, we found nothing of them, nor was there any kind of bleating to be heard, and discovered with vexation that we had come on a wrong track.

My companion then bent his course towards the farm of Glen on the north, and I ran away westward for several miles, along the wild track where the lambs had grazed while following their dams. We met after it was day, far up in a place called the Black Cleuch, but neither of us had been able to discover our lambs, nor any traces of them. It was the most extraordinary circumstance that had ever occurred in the annals of pastoral life! We had nothing for it but to return to our master, and inform him that we had lost his whole flock of lambs to him, and knew not what was become of one of them.

On our way home, however, we discovered a body of lambs at the bottom of a deep ravine, called the Flesh Cleuch, and the indefatigable Sirrah standing in front of them, looking all around for some relief, but still standing true to his charge. The sun was then up; and when we first came in view of them, we concluded that it was one of the divisions of the lambs, which Sirrah had been unable to manage until he came to that commanding situation, for it was about a mile and a half distant from the place where they first broke and scattered. But what was our astonishment, when we discoverd by degrees that not one lamb of the whole flock was wanting! How had he got all the divisions collected in the dark is beyond my comprehension. The charge was left entirely to himself from midnight until the rising of the sun; and if all the shepherds in the Forest had been there to have assisted him, they could not have effected it with greater propriety. All that I can say farther is, that I never felt so grateful to any creature below the sun as I did to my honest Sirrah that morning.

I remember another achievement of his which I admired still more, but which I cannot make an Edinburgh man so thoroughly to understand. I was sent to a place in Tweeddale, called Stanhope, to bring home a wild ewe that had strayed from home. The place lay at the distance of about fifteen miles, and my way to it was over steep hills, and athwart deep glens;—there was no path, and neither Sirrah nor I had ever travelled the road before. The ewe was brought in and put into a barn overnight; and, after being frightened in this way, was set out to me in the morning to drive home by herself. She was as wild as a roe, and bounded away to the side of the mountains like one. I sent Sirrah on a circular route

wide before her, and let him know that he had the charge of her. When
I left the people at the house, Mr Tweedie, the farmer, said to me, 'Do you
really suppose that you will drive that sheep over these hills, and out
through the midst of all the sheep in the country?' I said I would try to
do it. 'Then, let me tell you,' said he, 'that you may as well try to travel
to yon sun.' The man did not know that I was destined to do both the
one and the other. Our way, as I said, lay all over wild hills, and through
the middle of flocks of sheep. I seldom got a sight of the ewe, for she was
sometimes a mile before me, sometimes two; but Sirrah kept her in
command the whole way—never suffered her to mix with other sheep—
nor, as far as I coud judge, ever to deviate twenty yards from the track
by which he and I went the day before. When we came over the great
height towards Manor Water, Sirrah and his charge happened to cross
it a little before me, and our way lying down hill for several miles, I lost
all trace of them, but still held on my track. I came to two shepherds'
houses, and asked if they had seen anything of a black dog, with a
branded face and a long tail, driving a sheep? No; they had seen no such
thing; and, besides, all their sheep, both above and below the houses,
seemed to be unmoved. I had nothing for it but to hold on my way
homeward; and at length, on the corner of a hill at the side of the water,
I dscovered my trusty coal-black friend sitting with his eye fixed intently
on the burn below him, and sometimes giving a casual glance behind
to see if I was coming:—he had the ewe standing there safe and unhurt.

When I got her home, and set her at liberty among our own sheep, he
took it highly amiss. I could scarcely prevail with him to let her go; and
so dreadfully was he affronted that she should have been let go free after
all his toil and trouble, that he would not come near me all the way to
the house, nor yet taste any supper when we got there. I believe he
wanted me to take her home and kill her.

He had one very laughable peculiarity, which often created disturbance
about the house,—it was an outrageous ear for music. He never heard
music, but he drew towards it; and he never drew towards it, but he
joined in it with all his vigour. Many a good psalm, song, and tune, was
he the cause of being spoiled; for when he set fairly to, at which he was
not slack, the voices of all his coadjutors had no chance with his. It was
customary with the worthy old farmer with whom I resided, to perform
family worship evening and morning; and before he began, it was
always necessary to drive Sirrah to the fields, and close the door. If this
was at any time forgot or neglected, the moment that the psalm was
raised, he joined in with all his zeal, and at such a rate, that he drowned
the voices of the family before three lines could be sung. Nothing farther
could be done till Sirrah was expelled. But then! when he got to the peat-
stack knowe before the door, especially if he got a blow in going out, he

61   Altrive—the residence of the Ettrick Shepherd, from *The Works of the Ettrick Shepherd, Poems and Ballads, 1869.*

did give his powers of voice full scope without mitigation, and even at that distance he was often a hard match for us all.

Some imagined that it was from a painful sensation that he did this. No such thing. Music was his delight: it always drew him towards it like a charm. I slept in the byre-loft—Sirrah in the hay-nook in a corner below. When sore fatigued, I sometimes retired to my bed before the hour of family worship. In such cases, whenever the psalm was raised in the kitchen, which was but a short distance, Sirrah left his lair; and laying his ear close to the bottom of the door to hear more distinctly, he growled a low note in accompaniment, till the sound expired; and then rose, shook his lugs, and returned to his hay-nook. Sacred music affected him most; but in either that or any slow tune, when the tones dwelt upon the key-note, they put him quite beside himself; his eyes had the gleam of madness in them; and he sometimes quitted singing, and literally fell to barking. All his race have the same qualities of voice and ear in a less or greater degree.

In 1824, when Hogg published The Shepherd's Calendar, *he paid tribute to Sirrah's son, Hector (and, incidentally, to Sirrah's grandson, Lion). The account of Hector is a lively piece of dog-portraiture.*

There being no adage more generally established, or better founded, than that the principal conversation of shepherds meeting on the hills is either about DOGS or LASSES, I shall make each of these important topics a head, or rather a *snag*, in my Pastoral Calendar, whereon to hang a few amusing anecdotes; the one of these forming the chief support, and the other the chief temporal delight, of the shepherd's solitary and harmless life.

Though it may appear a singular perversion of the order of nature to put the dogs before the lasses, I shall nevertheless begin with the former . . .

A shepherd may be a very able, trusty, and good shepherd, without a sweetheart—better, perhaps, than with one. But what is he without his dog? . . .

Without the shepherd's dog, the whole of the open mountainous land in Scotland would not be worth a sixpence. It would require more hands to manage a stock of sheep, gather them from the hills, force them into houses and folds, and drive them to markets, than the profits of the whole stock were capable of maintaining. Well may the shepherd feel an interest in his dog; he is indeed the fellow that earns the family's bread, of which he is himself content with the smallest morsel; always grateful, and always ready to exert his utmost abilities in his master's interest. Neither hunger, fatigue, nor the worst of treatment, will drive him from his side; he will follow him through fire and water, as the saying is, and through every hardship, without murmur or repining, till he literally fall down dead at his foot. If one of them is obliged to change masters, it is sometimes long before he will acknowledge the new one, or condescend to work for him with the same avidity as he did for his former lord; but if he once acknowledges him, he continues attached to him till death; and though naturally proud and high-spirited, in as far as relates to his master, these qualities (or rather failings) are kept so much in subordination, that he has not a will of his own. Of such grateful, useful, and disinterested animal, I could write volumes . . .

I must give you some account of my own renowned Hector . . . He was the son and immediate successor of the faithful old Sirrah; and though not nearly so valuable a dog as his father, he was a far more interesting one. He had three times more humour and whim about him; and though exceedingly docile, his bravest acts were mostly tincture with a grain of stupidity, which shewed his reasoning faculty to be laughably obtuse.

I shall mention a striking instance of it. I was once at the farm of Shorthope, on Ettrick head, receiving some lambs that I had bought, and was going to take to the market, with some more, the next day. Owing to some accidental delay I did not get final delivery of the lambs till it was growing late; and being obliged to be at my own house that night, I was not a little dismayed lest I should scatter and lose my lambs, if darkness overtook me. Darkness did overtake me by the time I got half way, and no ordinary darkness for an August evening. The lambs having been weaned that day, and of the wild black-faced breed, became exceedingly unruly, and for a good while I lost hopes of mastering them. Hector managed the point, and we got them safe home; but both he and his master were alike sore forefoughten. It had become so dark, that we were obliged to fold them with candles; and after closing them safely up, I went home with my father and the rest to supper. When Hector's supper was set down, behold he was wanting! and as I knew we had him at the fold, which was within call of the house, I went out, and called and whistled on him for a good while, but he did not make his appearance. I was distressed about this; for having to take away the lambs next morning, I knew I could not drive them a mile without my dog, if it had been to save me the whole drove.

The next morning, as soon as it was day, I arose and inquired if Hector had come home. No; he had not been seen. I knew not what to do; but my father proposed that he would take out the lambs and herd them, and let them get some meat to fit them for the road; and that I should ride with all speed to Shorthope, to see if my dog had gone back there. Accordingly, we went together to the fold to turn out the lambs, and there was poor Hector sitting trembling in the very middle of the fold door, on the inside of the flake that closed it, with his eyes still steadfastly fixed on the lambs. He had been so hardly set with them after it grew dark, that he durst not for his life leave them, although hungry, fatigued, and cold; for the night had turned out a deluge of rain. He had never so much as lain down, for only the small spot that he sat on was dry, and there had he kept watch the whole night. Almost any other colley would have discerned that the lambs were safe enough in the fold, but honest Hector had not been able to see through this. He even refused to take my word for it, for he durst not quit his watch though he heard me calling both at night and morning.

Another peculiarity of his was, that he had a mortal antipathy at the family mouser, which was ingrained in his nature from very puppyhood; yet so perfectly absurd was he, that no impertinence on her side, and no baiting on, could ever induce him to lay his mouth on her, or injure her in the slightest degree. There was not a day, and scarcely an hour passed over, that the family did not get some amusement with these two animals. Whenever he was within doors, his whole occupation was watching and pointing the cat from morning to night. When she flitted from one place to another, so did he in a moment; and then squatting down, he kept his point sedulously, till he was either called off or fell asleep.

He was an exceedingly poor taker of meat, was always to press to it, and always lean; and often he would not taste it till we were obliged to bring in the cat. The malicious looks that he cast at her from under his eyebrows on such occasions, were exceedingly ludicrous, considering his utter incapability of wronging her. Whenever he saw her, he drew near his bicker, and looked angry, but still he would not taste till she was brought to it; and then he cocked his tail, set up his birses, and began a lapping furiously, in utter desperation. His good nature was so immovable, that he would never refuse her a share of what he got; he even lapped close to the one side of the dish, and left her room—but mercy as he did ply!

It will appear strange to you to hear a dog's *reasoning faculty* mentioned, as I have done; but I declare, I have hardly ever seen a shepherd's dog do anything without perceiving his reasons for it. I have often amused myself in calculating what his motives were for such and such things, and I generally found them very cogent ones. But Hector had a droll stupidity about him, and took up forms and rules of his own, for which I could never perceive any motive that was not even farther out of the way than the action itself. He had one uniform practice, and a very bad one it was, during the time of family worship, and just three or four seconds before the conclusion of the prayer, he started to his feet, and ran barking round the apartment like a crazed beast. My father was so much amused with this, that he would never suffer me to correct him for it, and I scarcely ever saw the old man rise from the prayer without his endeavouring to suppress a smile at the extravagance of Hector. None of us ever could find out how he knew that the prayer was near done, for my father was not formal in his prayers; but certes he did know,—of that we had nightly evidence. There never was anything for which I was so puzzled to discover a motive as this; but, from accident, I did discover it, and, however ludicrous it may appear, I am certain I was correct. It was much in character with many of Hector's feats, and rather, I think, the most *outré* of any principle he ever acted on. As I said, his great daily occupation was pointing the cat. Now, when he saw us kneel all down in a circle, with our faces couched on our paws, in the same posture with himself, it struck his absurd head, that we were all engaged in pointing the cat. He lay on tenters all the time, but the acuteness of his ear enabling him, through time, to ascertain the very moment when we would all spring to our feet, he thought to himself, 'I shall be first after her for you all.'

He inherited his dad's unfortunate ear for music, not perhaps in so extravagant a degree, but he ever took care to exhibit on the most untimely and ill-judged occasions. Owing to some misunderstanding between the minister of the parish and the session clerk, the precenting in church devolved to my father, who was the senior elder. Now, my father could have sung several of the old church tunes middling well, in his own family circle; but it so happened, that, when mounted in the desk, he never could command the starting notes of any but one (St Paul's), which were always in undue readiness at the root of his tongue, to the exclusion of every other semibreve in the whole range of sacred melody. The minister, giving out psalms four times in the course of every day's service, consequently, the congregation were treated with St Paul's, in the morning, at great length, twice in the course of the service, and then once again at the close. Nothing but St Paul's. And, it being of itself a monotonous tune, nothing could exceed the monotony that prevailed in the primitive church of Ettrick. Out of pure sympathy for my father alone, I was compelled to take the precentorship in hand; and, having plenty of tunes, for a good while I came on as well as could be *expected*, as men say of their wives. But, unfortunately for me, Hector found out that I attended church every Sunday, and though I had him always closed up carefully at home, he rarely failed in making his appearance in church at some time of the day. Whenever I saw him a tremor came over my spirits, for I well knew what the issue would be. The moment that he heard my voice strike up the psalm, 'with might and majesty', then did he fall in with such overpowering vehemence, that he and I seldom got any to join in the music but our two selves. The shepherds hid their heads, and laid them down on the backs of the seats rowed in their plaids, and the lasses looked down to the ground and laughed till their faces grew red. I despised to stick the tune, and therefore was obliged to carry on in spite of the obstreperous accompaniment; but I was, time after time, so completely put out of all countenance with the brute, that I was obliged to give up my office in disgust, and leave the parish once more to their old friend, St Paul.

Hector was quite incapable of performing the same feats among sheep that his father did; but, as far as his judgement served him, he was a docile and obliging creature. He had one singular quality, of keeping true to the charge to which he was set. If we had been shearing, or sorting sheep in any way, when a division was turned out, and Hector got the word to attend to them, he would have done it pleasantly, for a whole day, without the least symptom of weariness. No noise or hurry about the fold, which brings every dog from his business, had the least effect on Hector, save that it made him a little troublesome on his own charge, and set him a running round and round them, turning them in at corners, out of a sort of impatience to be employed as well as his baying neighbours at the fold. Whenever old Sirrah found himself hard set, in commanding wild sheep on steep ground, where they are worst to manage, he never failed, without any hint to the purpose, to throw himself wide in below them, and lay their faces to the hill, by which means he got the command of them in a minute. I could never make Hector comprehend this advantage, with all my art, although his father found it out entirely of himself. The former would turn or wear sheep no other way, but on the hill above them; and though very good at it, he gave both them and himself double the trouble and fatigue.

It cannot be supposed that he could understand all that was passing in the little family circle, but he certainly comprehended a good part of it. In particular, it was very easy to discover that he rarely missed aught that was said about himself, the sheep, the cat, or of a hunt. When aught of that nature came to be discussed, Hector's attention and impatience soon became manifest. There was one winter evening, I said to my mother that I was going to Bowerhope for a fortnight, for that I had more conveniency for writing with Alexander Laidlaw, than at home; and I added, 'But I will not take Hector with me, for he is constantly quarrelling with the rest of the dogs, singing music, or breeding some uproar.'— 'Na, na,' quoth she, 'leave Hector with me; I like aye best to have him at hame, poor fellow.'

These were all the words that passed. The next morning the waters were in great flood, and I did not go away till after breakfast; but when the time came for tying up Hector he was wanting.—'The d——'s in that beast,' said I, 'I will wager that he heard what we were saying yesternight, and has gone off for Bowerhope as soon as the door was opened this morning.'

'If that should really be the case, I'll think the beast no canny,' said my mother.

The Yarrow was so large as to be quite impassable, so that I had to go up by St Mary's Loch, and go across by the boat; and, on drawing near to Bowerhope, I soon perceived that matters had gone precisely as I suspected. Large as the Yarrow was, and it appeared impassable by any living creature, Hector had made his escape early in the morning, had swum the river, and was sitting, 'Like a drookit hen,' on a knoll at the east end of the house, awaiting my arrival with great impatience. I had a great attachment to this animal, who, with a good deal of absurdity, joined all the amiable qualities of his species. He was rather of a small size, very rough and shagged, and not far from the colour of a fox.

Hector was also celebrated in verse in 'The Author's Address to his Auld Dog Hector', which Hogg published in his collection, The Mountain Bard *(1807).*

> Come, my auld, towzy trusty friend;
>   What gaurs ye look sae douth an' wae?
> D'ye think my favour's at an end,
>   Because thy head is turnin' gray?
>
> Although thy feet begin to fail,
>   Their best were spent in serving me;
> An' can I grudge thy wee bit meal,
>   Some comfort in thy age to gi'e?
>
> For mony a day, frae sun to sun,
>   We've toil'd an' helpit ane anither;
> An' mony a thousand mile thou'st run,
>   To keep my thraward flocks thegither.
>
> To nae thrawn boy, nor scawghin wife,
>   Shall thy auld banes become a drudge;
> At cats an' callans, a' thy life,
>   Thou ever bore a mortal grudge.
>
> An' whiles thy surly looks declared,
>   Thou lo'ed the women warst of a';
> 'Cause aft they my affection shared,
>   Which thou couldst never bruik ata'.

When sitting with my bonny Meg,
    Mair happy than a prince could be,
Thou plac'd thee by her other leg,
    An' watched her wi' a jealous ee.

An' then, at ony start or steer,
    Thou wad ha'e worried furiouslye;
While I was forc'd to curse and swear,
    Afore thou wad forbidden be,

Yet wad she clasp thy towzy paw;
    Thy greesome grips were never skaithly;
An' thou than her hast been mair true!
    An' truer than the friend that ga'e thee!

Ah, me! of fashion, health, an' pride,
    The world has read me sic a lecture!
But yet it's a' in part repaid
    By thee, my faithful, grateful Hector!

O'er past imprudence, oft alane
    I've shed the saut an' silent tear;
Then, sharing ay my grief an' pain,
    My poor auld friend came snoovin' near.

For a' the days we've sojourned here,
    An' they've been neither fine nor few,
That thought possest thee year to year,
    That a' my griefs arase frae you.

Wi' waesome face, and hingin' head,
    Thou wad ha'e press'd thee to my knee;
While I thy looks as weel could read,
    As thou hadst said in words to me,—

'O my dear master, dinna greet;
    What ha'e I ever done to vex ye?
See here I'm cowrin' at your feet;
    Just take my life if I perplex ye.

For a' my toil, my wee drap meat
    Is a' the wage I ask of thee;
For whilk I'm oft oblig'd to wait
    Wi' hungry wame, an' patient ee.

Whatever wayward course ye steer;
    Whatever sad mischance o'ertake ye;
Man, here is ane will hald ye dear!
    Man, here's a friend will ne'er forsake ye!'

Yes, my puir beast! though friends me scorn,
    Whom mair than life I valued dear;
An' throw me out to fight forlorn,
    Wi' ills my heart dow hardly bear,

While I have thee to bear a part—
    My plaid, my health, an' heezle rung—
I'll scorn the silly haughty heart,
    The saucy look, and slanderous tongue.

Sure friends by pop'lar envy sway'd,
    Are ten times waur than ony fae!
My heart was theirs, an' to them laid
    As open as the light o' day.

I fear'd my ain; but never dredd
    That I for loss o' theirs should mourn;
Or that, when luck or favour fled,
    Their friendship wad injurious turn.

But He, who feeds the ravens young,
    Lets naething pass unheeded bye;
He'll sometimes judge of right an' wrong,
    An' ay provide for you and I.

And hear me, Hector: thee I'll trust,
    As far as thou hast wit an' skill;
Sae will I ae sweet lovely breast,
    To me a balm for every ill.

To these my faith shall ever run,
    While I have reason truth to scan;
But ne'er, beyond my mother's son,
    To aught that bears the shape of man.—

I ne'er could thole thy cravin' face,
    Nor when ye pattit on my knee;
Though in a far an' unco place,
    I've whiles been forc'd to beg for thee.

Even now I'm in my master's power,
    Where my regard may scarce be shown;
But ere I'm forced to gi'e thee o'er,
    When thou art auld an' useless grown,

I'll get a cottage o' my ain,
    Some wee bit cannie, lonely biel',
Where thy auld heart shall rest fu' fain,
    An' share with me my humble meal.

Thy post shall be to guard the door,
    An' bark at pethers, boys, an' whips;
Of cats an' hens to clear the floor,
    An' bite the flaes that vex thy hips.

When my last bannock's on the hearth,
    Of that thou sanna want thy share;
While I have house or hald on earth,
    My Hector, shall ha'e shelter there.

An' should grim death thy noddle save,
    Till he has made an end of me;
Ye'll lye a wee while on the grave
    Of ane wha ay was kind to thee.

There's nane alive will miss me mair;
    An' though in words thou canst not wail,
On a' the claes thy master ware,
    Thou'lt smell, and fawn, an' wag thy tail.

An' if I'm forc'd with thee to part,
    Which will be sair against my will,
I'll sometimes mind thy honest heart,
    As lang as I can climb a hill.

Come my auld, touzy, trusty tike,
    Let's speel to Queensb'ry's lofty brow;
There greedy midges never fike;
    There care an' envy never grow.

While gazing down the fertile dales,
    Content an' peace shall ay be by;
An' muses leave their native vales.
    To rove at large wi' you and I.

THOMAS AND JANE CARLYLE'S DOG, NERO

Thomas Carlyle liked cats, but his wife, Jane Welsh Carlyle, preferred lapdogs and canaries. Columbine was the cat at Cheyne Row when Nero, the dog that played the most significant role in their lives, arrived. He was given to Jane in 1849 by Stauros Dilberglue, a Greek whom she had met in Manchester. Telling him of her sadness at the recent loss of a previous cat, she remarked that she thought a dog would be better company, recalling her mother's little dog, Shandy. To her surprise, Dilberglue took her seriously and, soon after, wrote to tell her that a dog was on its way to Cheyne Row.

Not surprisingly, she was nervous about the reception it would get from her husband. 'My dear,' she told him, 'it's borne upon my mind that I am to have a dog.' A railway guard delivered him to the Carlyle's door. He turned out to be a cross between a Maltese terrier and a mongrel, a small black and white dog 'about the size of Shandy', but with 'long white silky hair lying all about him—and over his eyes which are very large and black'. In *The Carlyle's at Home*, a study of their domestic life, Thea Holme describes how Nero settles in. Said Jane:

'I was afraid Mr Carlyle would have found him a plague and ordered him about his business—and so he would if the dog had been noisy—but he is as good as dumb—*never* barks unless I make him do it in play—and then when Mr C comes in in bad humour the little beast never troubles its head but dances round him on its hind legs—till he comes *to* and feels quite grateful for his confidence in his good will. So he gives it raisins, of which it is very fond, one by one, and blows tobacco smoke in its face which it does not like so well—and calls it "you little villain" in a tone of great kindness.'

Jane was immensely relieved. Her delight in owning Nero had to be shared with all her friends.

'Oh, Lord! I forgot to tell you I have got a little dog,' she told Forster, 'and Mr C has accepted it with an amiability! To be sure, when he comes down gloomy in the morning, or comes in wearied from his walk, the infatuated little beast dances round him on its hind legs as I ought to do and can't; and he feels flattered and surprised by such unwonted capers to his honour and glory.'

And to her sympathetic friend Mary Russell she confided:

'*The* pleasantest fact of my life for a good while is, that I have got a beautiful little dog.' She hopes that she will not make a fool of herself with the creature, and repeats firmly that 'he is not of course, either so pretty or so clever as Shandy'. But 'I like him better,' she admits, 'than I should choose to show publicly.'

Nero's conquest of Carlyle pleased her: 'Not only has Mr C no temptation to "kick his foot thro' it", but seems getting quite fond of it and looks flattered when it musters the hardihood to leap on *his* knee.'

'My fear now,' she continues, 'is not that Mr C will put it away, but that I shall become the envy of surrounding dog-stealers! . . . Well! I can but get a chain, to fasten it to my arm, and keep a sharp look out.'

Although soon after Nero disappeared—a habit he repeated several times in his life, causing his mistress considerable anguish—he was discovered on this occasion being led by a man who claimed to have found him. Jane did not believe the story, but gave the man twopence to get him back. Nero settled in again, sleeping at the foot of her bed and following her like a shadow.

In January 1850, when Carlyle was away from home, visiting his friends the Ashburtons, he received a letter from Nero written in two parts during one day and finished the next day.

Dear Master,—I take the liberty to write to you myself (my mistress being out of the way of writing to you she says) that you may know Columbine and I are quite well, and play about as usual. There was no dinner yesterday to speak of; I had for my share only a piece of biscuit that might have been round the world; and if Columbine got anything at all, I didn't see it. I made a grab at one or two of the "small beings" on my mistress's plate; she called them "heralds of the morn", but my mistress said, "Don't you wish you may get it?" and boxed my ears. I wasn't taken to walk on account of its being wet. And nobody came, but a man for "burial rate"; and my mistress gave him a rowing because she wasn't going to be buried here at all. Columbine and I don't mind where we are buried.

Dear Master,—My mistress brought my chain, and said "come along with me, while it shined and I could finish after". But she kept me so long in the London Library and other places, that I had to miss the post. An old gentleman in the omnibus took such notice of me! He looked at me a long time, and then turned to my mistress and said "Sharp, isn't he?" and my mistress was so good as to say "Oh Yes!" And the old gentleman said again, "I knew it; easy to see that!" And he put his hand in his hind-pocket, and took out a whole biscuit, a sweet one, and gave it me in bits. I was quite sorry to part from him, he was such a good judge of dogs.

I left off last night, dear master, to be washed. This morning I have seen a note from you, which says you will come to-morrow. Columbine and I are extremely happy to hear it; for then there will be some dinner to come and go on. Being to see you so soon, no more at present from your

Obedient little dog,
Nero.

Various minor vicissitudes befell Nero and Jane always hated having to leave him. Thea Holme again.

In the summer of 1857 she went to Scotland, leaving Nero at Cheyne Row with his master. Her letters contain messages to him—'a kiss to Nero'; 'Be kind to Nero'; and when she announced the time of her return, 'Tell Nero'. But when she arrived, 'I am shocked', she wrote, 'to have to confess that Nero was far from showing the enthusiasm "England expected" of him! He knew me quite well, but took me very coolly indeed. Ann said he had just been sleeping. Let us hope he was in a state of indigestion, in which dogs are not capable of being more amiable than their owners.'

In a household where indigestion was synonymous with bad temper it was natural that Nero's 'interior' should be thought to influence his state of mind. Jane watched over his health with as much care as if he were a child. Just as she raged at Carlyle for eating crystallised greengages at Lady Ashburton's she inveighed against 'everyone stuffing (Nero) with dainties, out of kindness'.

'When I say I am well, it means also Nero is well; he is part and parcel of myself', she wrote. He was her constant companion—'the chief comfort of my life—night and day he never leaves me, and it is something, I can tell you, to have such a bit of live cheerfulness always beside one'.

She flattered herself that Nero returned her affection.

'Going down into the kitchen the morning after my return from Sherborne, I spoke to the white cat, in common politeness, and even stroked her', she wrote to Carlyle in 1852; 'whereupon the jealousy of Nero rose to a pitch. He snapped and barked at me, then flew at the cat quite savage. I "felt it my duty" to box his ears. He stood a moment as if taking his resolution; then rushed up the kitchen stairs; and; as it afterward appeared, out of the house! For, in ten minutes or so, a woman came to the front door with master Nero in her arms; and said she had met him running up Cook's grounds, and was afraid he "would go and lose himself!" He would take no notice of *me* for several hours after!' 'And yet', she added, 'he had never read "George-Sand Novels", that dog, or any sort of Novels!'

To Jane this display of jealousy was entrancing; often she was to write of Nero as if he were human.

'The clock struck twelve', she wrote to Carlyle, 'and Nero with his usual good sense, insisted on my going to bed; he had gone half an hour before by himself, and established himself under the bedclothes; but he returned at twelve and jumped till I rose and followed him.'

'I could stand the creature's loss now less than ever', she wrote in 1852, after Nero had disappeared while his mistress was in the nursery-man's buying plants. 'After looking all about for him, I hurried back home and when the door was opened he bounded into my arms. Ann said "he got a lady to knock at the door for him!" 'The half-hour's fright', she added, 'had given me what Ann called "quite a turn".'

In 1859, Nero was run over by a butcher's cart 'driving furiously round a sharp corner,' and suffered severely, being run over on the throat. As the year wore to its close, he was clearly not his old self. Frequently, he was 'arrested by a paroxysm of coughing' while running up the kitchen stairs to greet his mistress, and 'the more he tried to show his joy the more he could not do it'.

Carlyle thought he ought to be put down with 'a little prussic acid'. Jane could not face this prospect. But Nero grew worse, and on 1 February 1860, weeping profusely, she called in her own doctor and asked him to end her companion's sufferings.

Carlyle was in tears, though he soon recovered himself. Jane, however, felt the loss more deeply. 'What is become of that little, beautiful, graceful *Life*,' she mourned, 'so full of love and loyalty and sense of duty, up to the last minute that it animated the body of that little dog?' Her aunt, Grace Walsh, comforted her with 'a reference in certain verses of *Romans* which seemed to warrant my belief in the immortality of animal life as well as human. . . . One thing is sure, however; my little dog is buried at the top of our garden; and I grieve for him as if he had been my little human child.'

ROBERT LOUIS STEVENSON

Robert Louis Stevenson was rather more critical of dogs than Sir Walter Scott; but in Memories and Portraits, *Stevenson revealed considerable insight into 'The Character of Dogs', a character he believed to have been altered through their long association with men.*

The civilisation, the manners, and the morals of dog-kind are to a great extent subordinated to those of his ancestral master, man. This animal, in many ways so superior, has accepted a position of inferiority, shares the domestic life, and humours the caprices of the tyrant. But the potentate, like the British in India, pays small regard to the character of his willing client, judges him with listless glances, and condemns him in a byword. Listless have been the looks of his admirers, who have exhausted idle terms of praise, and buried the poor soul below exaggerations. And yet more idle and, if possible, more unintelligent has been the attitude of his express detractors; those who are very fond of dogs 'but in their proper place'; who say 'poo' fellow, poo' fellow,' and are themselves far poorer; who whet the knife of the vivisectionist or heat his oven; who are not ashamed to admire 'the creature's instinct'; and flying far beyond folly, have dared to resuscitate the theory of animal machines. The 'dog's instinct' and the 'automaton-dog', in this age of psychology and science, sound like strange anachronisms. An automaton he certainly is; a machine working independently of his control, the heart like the mill-wheel, keeping all in motion, and the consciousness, like a person shut in the mill garret, enjoying the view out of the window and shaken by the thunder of the stones; an automaton in one corner of which a living spirit is confined: an automaton like man. Instinct again he certainly possesses. Inherited aptitudes are his, inherited frailities. Some things he at once views and understands, as though he were awakened from a sleep, as though he came 'trailing clouds of glory'. But within him, as with man, the field of instinct is limited; its utterances are obscure and occasional; and about the far larger part of life both the dog and his master must conduct their steps by deduction and observation.

The leading distinction between dog and man, after and perhaps before the different duration of their lives, is that the one can speak and that the other cannot. The absence of the power of speech confines the dog in the development of his intellect. It hinders him from many speculations, for words are the beginning of metaphysic. At the same blow it saves him from many superstitions, and his silence has won for him a higher name for virtue than his conduct justifies. The faults of the dog are many. He is vainer than man, singularly greedy of notice, singularly intolerant of ridicule, suspicious like the deaf, jealous to the degree of frenzy, and radically devoid of truth. The day of an intelligent small dog is passed in the manufacture and the laborious communication of falsehood; he lies with his tail, he lies with his eye, he lies with his protesting paw; and when he rattles his dish or scratches at the door his purpose is other than appears. But he has some apology to offer for the vice. Many of the signs which form his dialect have come to bear an aribtrary meaning, clearly understood both by his master and himself; yet when a new want arises he must either invent a new vehicle of meaning or wrest an old one to a different purpose; and this necessity frequently recurring must tend to lessen his idea of the sanctity of symbols. Meanwhile the dog is clear in his own conscience, and draws, with a human nicety, the distinction between formal and essential truth. Of his punning perversions, his legitimate dexterity with symbols, he is even vain; but when he has told and been detected in a lie, there is not a hair upon his body but confesses guilt. To a dog of gentlemanly feeling theft and falsehood are disgraceful vices. The canine, like the human, gentleman demands in his misdemeanours Montaigne's *je ne sais quoi de généreux*. He is never more than half-ashamed of having barked and bitten; and for those faults into which he has been led by the desire to shine before a lady of his race, he retains, even under physical correction, a share of pride. But to be caught lying, if he understands it, instantly uncurls his fleece.

Just as among dull observers he preserves a name for truth, the dog has been credited with modesty. It is amazing how the use of language blunts the faculties of man—that because vainglory finds no vent in words, creatures supplied with eyes have been unable to detect a fault so gross and obvious. If a small spoiled dog were suddenly to be endowed with speech, he would prate interminably, and still about himself; when we had friends, we should be forced to lock him in a garret; and what with his whining jealousies and his foible for falsehood, in a year's time he would have gone far to weary out our love. I was about to compare him to Sir Willoughby Patterne, but the Patternes have a manlier sense of their own merits; and the parallel, besides is ready. Hans Christian Andersen, as we behold him in his startling memoirs, thrilling from top to toe with an excruciating vanity, and scouting even along the street for shadows of offence—here was the talking dog.

It is just this rage for consideration that has betrayed the dog into his satellite position as the friend of man. The cat, an animal of franker appetites, preserves his independence. But the dog, with one eye ever on the audience, has been wheedled into slavery, and praised and patted into the renunciation of his nature. Once he ceased hunting and became a man's plate-licker, the Rubicon was crossed. Thenceforth he was a gentleman of leisure; and except the few whom we keep working, the whole race grew more and more self-conscious, mannered and affected. The number of things that a small dog does naturally is strangely small. Enjoying better spirits and not crushed under material cares, he is far more theatrical than average man. His whole life, if he be a dog of any pretension to gallantry, is spent in vain show, and in the hot pursuit of admiration. Take out your puppy for a walk, and you will find the little ball of fur clumsy, stupid, bewildered, but natural. Let but a few months pass, and when you repeat the process you will find nature buried in convention. He will do nothing plainly; but the simplest processes of our material life will all be bent into the forms of an elaborate and mysterious etiquette. Instinct, says the fool, has awakened. But it is not so. Some dogs—some, at the very least—if they be kept separate from others, remain quite natural; and these, when at length they meet with a companion of experience, and have the game explained to them, distinguish themselves by the severity of their devotion to its rules. I wish I were allowed to tell a story which would radiantly illuminate the point; but men, like dogs, have an elaborate and mysterious etiquette. It is their bond of sympathy that both are the children of convention.

The person, man or dog, who has a conscience is eternally condemned to some degree of humbug; the sense of the law in their members fatally precipitates either towards a frozen and affected bearing. And the converse is true; and in the elaborate and conscious manners of the dog, moral opinions and the love of the ideal stand confessed. To follow for ten minutes in the street some swaggering, canine cavalier, is to receive a lesson in dramatic art and the cultured conduct of the body; in every act and gesture you see him true to a refined conception; and the dullest cur, beholding him, pricks up his ear and proceeds to imitate and parody that charming ease. For to be a high-mannered and high-minded gentleman, careless, affable, and gay, is the inborn pretension of the dog. The large dog, so much lazier, so much more weighed upon with matter, so majestic in repose, so beautiful in effort, is born with the dramatic means to wholly represent the part. And it is more pathetic and perhaps more instructive to consider the small dog in his conscientious and imperfect efforts to outdo Sir Philip Sidney. For the ideal of the dog is feudal and religious; the ever-present polytheism, the whip-bearing Olympus of mankind, rules them on the one hand; of the other, their singular difference of size and strength among themselves effectually prevents the appearance of the democratic notion. Or we might more exactly compare their society to the curious spectacle presented by a school—ushers, monitors, and big and little boys— qualified by one circumstance, the introduction of the other sex. In each, we should observe a somewhat similar tension of manner, and somewhat similar points of honour. In each the larger animal keeps a contemptuous good humour; in each the smaller annoys him with a wasp-like impudence, certain of practical immunity; in each we shall find a double life producing double characters, and an excursive and noisy heroism combined with a fair amount of practical timidity. I have known dogs, and I have known school heroes that, set aside the fur, could hardly have been told apart; and if we desire to understand the chivalry of old, we must turn to the school playfields or the dungheap where the dogs are trooping.

Woman, with the dog, has been long enfranchised. Incessant massacre of female innocents has changed the proportion of the sexes and perverted their relations. Thus, when we regard the manners of the dog, we see a romantic and monogamous animal, once perhaps as delicate as the cat, at war with impossible conditions. Man has much to answer for; and the part he plays is yet more damnable and parlous than Corin's in the eyes of Touchstone. But his intervention has at least created an imperial situation for the rare surviving ladies. In that society they reign without a rival: conscious queens; and in the only instance of a canine wife-beater that has ever fallen under my notice, the criminal was somewhat excused by the circumstances of his story. He is a little, very alert, well-bred, intelligent Skye, as black as a hat, with a wet bramble for a nose and two cairngorms for eyes. To the human observer, he is decidedly well-looking; but to the ladies of his race he seems abhorrent. A thorough elaborate gentleman, of the plume and sword-knot order, he was born with a nice sense of gallantry to women. He took at their hands the most outrageous treatment; I have heard him bleating like a sheep, I have seen him streaming blood, and his ear tattered like a regimental banner; and yet he would scorn to make reprisals. Nay more, when a human lady upraised the contumelious whip against the very dame who had been so cruelly misusing him, my little great-heart gave but one hoarse cry and fell upon the tyrant tooth and nail. This is the tale of a soul's tragedy. After three years of unavailing chivalry, he suddenly changed in one hour, threw off the yoke of obligation; had he been Shakespeare he would then have written *Troilus and Cressida* to brand the offending sex; but being only a little dog, he began to bite them. The surprise of the ladies whom he attacked indicated the monstrosity of his offence; but he had fairly beaten off his better angel, fairly committed moral suicide; for almost in the same hour, throwing aside the last rags of decency, he proceeded to attack the aged also. The fact is worth remark, showing, as it does, that ethical laws are common both to dogs and men; and that with both a single deliberate violation of the conscience loosens all. 'But while the lamp holds on to burn,' says the paraphrase, 'the greatest sinner may return.' I have been cheered to see symptoms of effectual penitence in my sweet ruffian; and by the handling that he accepted uncomplainingly the other day from an indignant fair one, I begin to hope the period of *Sturm und Drang* is closed.

All these little gentlemen are subtle casuists. The duty to the female dog is plain; but where competing duties rise, down they will sit and study them out, like Jesuit confessors. I knew another little Skye, somewhat plain in manner and appearance, but a creature compact of amiability and solid wisdom. His family going abroad for a winter, he was received for that period by an uncle in the same city. The winter over, his own family home again, and his own house (of which he was very proud) reopened, he found himself in a dilemma between two conflicting duties of loyalty and gratitude. His old friends were not to be neglected, but it seemed hardly decent to desert the new. This was how he solved the problem. Every morning, as soon as the door was opened, off posted Coolin to his uncle's, visited the children in the nursery, saluted the whole family, and was back at home in time for breakfast and his bit of fish. Nor was this done without a sacrifice on his part, sharply felt; for he had to forego the particular honour and jewel of his day—his morning's walk with my father. And, perhaps from this cause, he gradually wearied of and relaxed the practice, and at length returned entirely to his ancient habits. But the same decision served him in another and more distressing case of divided duty, which happened not long after. He was not at all a kitchen dog, but the cook had nursed him with unusual kindness during the distemper; and though he did not adore her as he adored my father—although (born snob) he was critically conscious of her position as 'only a servant'—he still cherished for her a special gratitude. Well, the cook left, and retired some streets away to lodgings of her own; and there was Coolin in precisely the same situation with any young gentleman who has had the inestimable benefit of a faithful nurse. The canine conscience did not solve the problem with a pound of tea at Christmas. No longer content to pay a flying visit, it was the whole forenoon that he dedicated to his solitary friend. And so, day by day, he continued to comfort her solitude until (for some reason which I could never understand and cannot approve) he was kept locked up to break him of the graceful habit. Here, it is not the similarity, it is the difference, that is worthy of remark; the clearly marked degrees of gratitude and the proportional duration of his visits. Anything further removed from instinct it were hard to fancy; and one is even stirred to a certain impatience with a character so destitute of spontaneity, so passionless in justice, and so priggishly obedient to the voice of reason.

There are not many dogs like this good Coolin, and not many people. But the type is one well marked, both in the human and canine family. Gallantry was not his aim, but a solid and somewhat oppressive respectability. He was a sworn foe to the unusual and the conspicuous, a praiser of the golden mean, a kind of city uncle modified by Cheeryble. And as he was precise and conscientious in all the steps of his own blameless course, he looked for the same precision and an even gravity in the bearing of his deity, my father. It was no sinecure to be Coolin's idol: he was exacting like a rigid parent; and at every sign of levity in the man whom he respected, he announced loudly the death of virtue and the proximate fall of the pillars of the earth.

I have called him a snob; but all dogs are so, though in varying degrees. It is hard to follow their snobbery among themselves; for though I think we can perceive distinctions of rank, we cannot grasp what is the criterion. Thus in Edinburgh, in a good part of the town, there were several distinct societies or clubs that met in the morning to—the phrase is technical—to 'rake the backets' in a troop. A friend of mine, the master of three dogs, was one day surprised to observe that they had left one club and joined another; but whether it was a rise or a fall, and the result of an invitation or an expulsion, was more than he could guess. And this illustrated pointedly our ignorance of the real life of dogs, their social ambitions and their social hierarchies. At least, in their dealings with men they are not only conscious of sex, but of the difference of station. And that in the most snobbish manner; for the poor man's dog is not offended by the notice of the rich, and keeps all his ugly feeling for those poorer or more ragged than his master. And again, for every station they have an ideal of behaviour, to which the master, under pain of derogation, will do wisely to conform. How often has not a cold glance of an eye informed me that my dog was disappointed; and how much more gladly would he not have taken a beating than to be thus wounded in the seat of piety! . . .

Dogs live with man as courtiers round a monarch, steeped in the flattery of his notice and enriched with sinecures. To push their favour in this world of pickings and caresses is, perhaps, the business of their lives; and the joys may lie outside. I am in despair at our persistent ignorance. I read in the lives of our companions the same processes of reason, the same antique and fatal conflicts of the right against the wrong, and of unbitted nature with too rigid custom; I see them with our weakness, vain, false, inconstant against appetite, and with our one stalk of virtue, devoted to the dream of an ideal; and yet, as they hurry

62   Henry, 3rd Duke of Buccleuch by Thomas Gainsborough. Courtesy of the
     Duke of Buccleuch and Queensberry, KT.

by me on the street with tail in air, or come singly to solicit my regard, I must own the secret purport of their lives is still inscrutable to man. Is man the friend, or is he the patron only? Have they indeed forgotten nature's voice? or are those moments snatched from courtiership when they touch noses with the tinker's mongrel, the brief reward and pleasure of their artificial lives? Doubtless, when man shares with his dog the toils of a profession and the pleasures of an art, as with the shepherd or the poacher, the affection warms and strengthens till it fills the soul. But doubtless, also, the masters are, in many cases, the object of a merely interested cultus, sitting aloft like Louis Quatorze, giving and receiving flattery and favour; and the dogs, like the majority of men, have but foregone their true existence and become the dupes of their ambition.

DUSTY

Wars have to be paid for. Pitt had to finance the war with France at the end of the eighteenth century. He introduced Income Tax in 1797, having already taxed light in his Window Tax, which affected houses with more than five windows. One result was that some people blocked some of their windows. Continuing his policy of taxing supposed luxuries, on 5 July 1796 he introduced 'An Act for granting to His Majesty certain duties on Dogs'. The tax amounted to five shillings for owners with sporting dogs or with more than one dog of any kind, three shillings for people who owned a non-sporting dog or fifteen pounds for people with several dogs. In 1797, these charges were increased by 10 per cent. As with windows, people got rid of their dogs. James Hogg sold his dog Sirrah—whose merits are described under Literary Dogs— because of the Dog Tax, and greatly regretted the transaction. Some dogs were shot to avoid the tax. The unfortunate Dusty, whose end is described in Hogg's early poem, 'Dusty, or Watie an' Geordie's Review of Politics', was subjected to a bungled hanging. The poem, from Hogg's first collection, Scottish Pastorals (1801), was couched in a form that was already outmoded by the time the book appeared. Watie is, on the whole, pro-Government, Geordie highly critical of taxes on 'Our hats, our claes, our drink, our meat / Our snuff, our baca, shoon o'ur feet, / Our candles, watches, horses, even / The very blessed light of heaven;/dogs . . .' Watie offers to treat Geordie to a toast to the Government Ministers 'in acquavitty'. Geordie turns his offer down, with . . .

Geordie

I canna do't, their names disgust me,
An' gar me mind my heartsome Dusty;
Yet their defence I'll gladly hear,
Wad they mak peace within a year,
An' mak the taxes somewhat leucher,
I'd rather see't than farm the Deuchar.

Watie

I wish as much for peace as ye do,
Tho' little ill the war I see do;
In gen'ral ilka thrifty man
Is richer than when it began.
Wi' faes we ne'er had sic a tilt,
In which less British blude was spilt;
Quite masters o' the sea they find us,
An' heavy neibers i' the Indies.

But man 'tis queer to mak sic fike
About an useless gauffin tike;
That ne'er cude gie a decent turn
At sheddin', fauldin', bought, nor burn;
But ran wi' inconsid'rate force,
An' bate their heels as they'd been horse.
I never thought, for a' your ruse,
That e'er he was for muckle use,
Except for drivin' nout to fairs,
Or rinnin' whinkin' after hares.
But if ye saw that ye wad need him,
Five shillins yearly wad hae freed him.

Geordie

I never saw a finer beast,
Sin' I cou'd ken the west frae east;
But yet a crown was unco sair
On ane that cou'd sae little spare;
For a' the wages e'er I won
Can scarcely keep my head aboon:
But I bude either flit or slay him,
For nae man off my hand wid hae him;
I didna like to flit, for fear

I might have idle lien a year;
My friends war poor, an' had nae need
That I sude hang on them for bread;
Sae was I forc'd, tho' vext and anger'd,
To gie consent to hae him hanged,
He had some prospects o' the deed,
For back he drew, and wadna lead.
His looks to me, I'll ne'er forget them,
Nae doubt he lookit for protection;
While I, unfeeling as the tree,
Stood still, an' saw him hung on hie.
At first he spurr'd, an' fell a bocking,
Then gollar'd, pisht, an just was choaking:
Deil tak the King, an' burn his crown,
Quoth I, an' ran to cut him down;
When poor, unlucky, senseless brute!
(Afore I never saw him do't)
He bate me till the blude did spring;
Confus'd an' hurt, I loot him hing
Owr lang for life; for on the green
He sprawl'd to death before my een.
I really felt extrodner pain;
I kend we ne'er wad meet again.
I grat for grief, his death to see
Whae aft had ventur'd life for me:
For ay when wi' ane I had grips,
He ran an' bit ther heels or hips;
An' when I warstled wi' the women,
He tugg'd their tails, an' held them screamin'.

    Last year he play'd a desp'rate prank,
When gaun wi' me to Staggshaw-bank:
I wi' a man, that houn'd our hogs,
Koostout an' feught, sae did our dogs;
I own I was but roughly guidit,
Nor was the quarrel weel decidet;
But ere we ceas'd frae rough contention,
The Saxon's dog was past redemption.

    When weazels snirtit frae the dykes,
Or fumerts frae the braes o' sykes,
He cock'd his tail, an' geed his head,
O' scores o' them he was the dead.

Nae beast on yirth cude hae defy'd him;
If I had said the word, he try'd him.

But yet for a' his gruesome dealin's,
He was a dog o' tender feelin's;
When I lay sick an' like to die,
He watch'd me wi' a constant eye;
An' then when e'er I spak' or sturr'd,
He wagg'd his tail, an' whing'd, and nurr'd.
When samms were sung at any meetin'
He yowl'd, an' thought the fock war greetin'.

For wearin' corn of hens an' cocks,
For huntin' o' the hare or fox,
For chasin' cats, an' craws, an' hoodies,
An' chackin mice an' howkin moudics,
An' settin moorfowl, snipes, an' petrics,
His match was never made for thae tricks.
But now, poor beast, he's dead an' rotten,
An' his good deeds are a' forgotten.

Watie

I ken what grief I felt mysel'
In partin' wi' my auld Springkell;
I wadna been as muckle troubl'd
For a' his value ten times doubl'd.

Geordie

But my night draws on, and I'm to meet
My Nelly up on Annan's treat.
Be o' our cracks a wee discreeter,
For HOGG pits a' we say to meter.
Fare-weel; I hope ere lang to see thee:—

Watie

Fare-weel; success an' joy gang wi' thee.

JAMES HOGG

DOGS REMEMBERED

When the moment of parting comes, whether through accident or as a result of 'the last sad one-way journey to the vet', the memories live on. In this final section we have brought together a selection of epitaphs and elegies, culminating in Byron's savagely-powerful lines inscribed on the monument to his Newfoundland dog.

63   Lindy. Drawing by Morven Cameron.

EPITAPH ON A DOG

The great Marquis of Montrose was born in 1612. At first indignant at Charles I's attempts to impose the Episcopalian liturgy in Scotland, he signed the National Covenant. When the Covenanting party in Scotland assumed a more sinister aspect, however, Montrose, who withheld his signature from the more aggressive Solemn League and Covenant of 1638, became a royalist. His victories at Tippermuir and Kilsyth made him master of Scotland. He was horrified at the execution of the king, an event which gave rise to his most famous poem. In 1650, he landed at Caithness to begin another campaign in the royalist cause, but was betrayed by Macleod of Assynt, taken ignominiously to Edinburgh and in May of that year, barbarously executed. His early 'Epitaph on a Dog' has a certain pathos, in the light of the betrayal, so to say, on a second front which led to his downfall. The dog, which belonged to the Marquis of Newcastle, was 'killed in anger' by the Duke of Hamilton while engaged in fighting another dog.

> Here lies a dog whose quality did plead
> Such fatal end from a renownèd blade:
> And blame him not that he succumbèd now,
> E'en Hercules could not combat against two.
> For while he on his foe revenge did take
> He manfully was killed behind his back.
> Then say, to eternise the cur that's gone,
> He fleshed the maiden sword of Hamilton.

THE MARQUIS OF MONTROSE

ELEGY ON A DOG THAT WENT THROUGH THE ICE

The Gaelic poet Duncan Ban Macintyre (1724–1812) was non-literate, his poems being taken down by a friendly minister. They were first published in 1768. For much of his life, Macintyre was employed by the Campbell aristocracy, but he settled in Edinburgh in 1767, became a member of the City Guard and in later life served in the Breadalbane Fencibles. Iain Crichton Smith, who writes in Gaelic as well as English, made this translation of Macintyre's Elegy specially for this anthology.

One day when Patrick was hunting
over the sloping moor
he visited Glen Artney
and the forest of the deer:
he let his dog go coursing—
a beast that was ardent and strong,
matchless within the country
but for legendary Bran.

A deer hound, rough and bristly,
hardy and furious-eyed,
shapely in form and in figure
and vicious in the fight.
He'd fetch the deer from the hill-top
and the roebuck from the brush
and his journey was never fruitless
in his usual moorland parish.

Unequalled at felling the stags
on the top of mounds and of hills:
scourge of the otter and fox:
the badger too he would kill.
The crosswise hare in his mouth,
together they fell in the pit,
cheek by jowl they were drowned—
how great my sorrow tonight.

IAIN CRICHTON SMITH

LISA

On 1 November 1980, in *The Scotsman*, I quoted my postman as saying: 'I wish all the houses I delivered to had dogs that gave me such a welcome . . .'

Three days later he was a welcome short, and a considerable chunk of what makes me tick went into the ground to stay there.

For Lisa, the *schwerpunkt* of his welcome, was dead: my timber-wolf-size Lisa, my gentlest of the gentle, charismatic German Shepherd, was in the past tense.

For nearly eleven years she was my shadow, my adjutant, my rearer-of-all-things, my carer-for-all-things, the mother-figure, lover of children, favourite of the handicapped, who only twice in her life used her weaponry, and that at my express command.

We knew near the end that she was ailing, and probably beginning to feel pain. So we let her go for surgery, and she came back in the past tense. I keep thinking now that I should, myself, have taken her trusting, gentle life. With that compassionate treason I could have felt more like the person she thought I was. Instead I let her die, distressed, alone, in the clinical hands of strangers.

They keep telling me it was all done for the best. But one of us knows better. The other, had she been capable of thought, would have known too. In the end I failed her.

Looking at the empty cavern in the kitchen corner that her giant frame used to fill we are all agreed that she will be remembered best, by most, as a mother-figure, for although she never had a family of her own she treated every young thing in fur or feather as her own puppy, and that includes the Labrador and the Jack Russell who are no longer puppies.

As a puppy herself she took charge of the Siamese cat Skipper, and as she grew up she became his hatchet woman, ready to take a door down to get to him if he squalled outside. Skipper is now fifteen years old, and that relationship remained unshakeable until the day she died.

Then she had to put up with the weasels, Tammas and Teen, running over her like ants or slyly nibbling her nails. The most they ever got from her was a gentle *woof* of reproach. She was the same with the wild kittens, Teuchter and Pibroch. They liked the warmth of her. They also liked to tread on her belly with their hindfeet, and sometimes they pricked her enough to draw blood. The most they ever got for that was to be pinned down with a monstrous paw until they behaved.

She fostered the fox cubs, Glen and Fiddich, who slept, ate and played with her. She was their vixen, and she was vixen to them. A few years later she played wolf to the wolf cubs Marquis and Magda. For four months of their lives they slept with her, roistered with her, ate with her and obeyed her. I think her wolf days were among the happiest of her life.

When I was bottle-rearing my roe fawns, Bounce and Sanshach, Lisa took charge of them in the garden. She played with them, mothered them in sleep against her ample flank, and protected them with a consuming jealousy. When they went into their two-acre enclosure she played with them there. When Sanshach had her first two fawns, twins, she allowed Lisa to lick them over without the slightest expression of alarm or distrust.

One of the funniest things I remember was the day she met her first wild roe deer: truly wild but with a growing tolerance of people because they were never under pressure. They ran about fifty yards, then stopped and looked back. Lisa trotted out towards them, and they ran another fifty yards and stopped. She tried again, and they ran again. She came back to me with a look on her face that was asking: 'Why are they running from me?' I knew how she felt. She could never understand why wild roe deer and foxes ran away from her.

My badger cubs Spick and Span were probably her roughest assignment. Badger cubs play exceedingly boisterously. She accepted all the gurrying, all the bear-claw grapples and brulzie, with tolerant dignity that was never ruffled. When it went too far she used the mighty paw to pin them down. Never did she utter a growl or flash brief ivory.

Once, when my terrier growled at Marquis (understandably because the horsing around was getting a bit much for her) Lisa rushed from her basket and dunted her aside. From that day my wife called her the referee. She would not stand for any aggressive display, any grumping or moaning or girning. She waded in and showed the iron fist inside the velvet glove. Her motto might well have been: if you can't stand the heat stay out of the kitchen.

She was well aware of her size, her weight and her fist-feet, and it was something to see her trying to cat-foot across the floor avoiding leverets, rabbits, polecat kits, blackbirds, owlets, goslings or whatever, while the Siamese cat, on top of the heater, looked down at her as though saying (which he wasn't): 'For a disgustingly big dog you might yet graduate to becoming a cat.' If Siamese cats could speak that's probably the way they would speak,

Little William, the wild goat kid, she loved, and he followed her

64 Lisa with fox cubs. Courtesy of David and Jess Stephen.

around like her shadow. Cassius, my big dog polecat, she loved, and if she wanted him in her basket he had to go, by the scruff of the neck if need be. And Polar, the greylag goose, she loved, and would try to make room for him in her basket, even when he was fully grown and flying free.

My wife always addressed her as The Greatest, and Lisa could never resist the rhetorical question: 'Who's the Greatest?' That always fetched her for due commendation. She was the greatest, and she knew it. We did too.

Now she's dead. So what the hell? After all, she was only a dog.

DAVID STEPHEN

65   Lisa with young hare. Courtesy of David and Jess Stephen.

PRAISE OF A COLLIE

She was a small dog, neat and fluid—
Even her conversation was tiny:
She greeted you with *bow*, never *bow-wow*.

Her sons stood monumentally over her
But did what she told them. Each grew grizzled
Till it seemed he was his own mother's grandfather.

Once, gathering sheep on a showery day,
I remarked how dry she was. Pollóchan said, 'Ah,
It would take a very accurate drop to hit Lassie.'

She sailed in the dinghy like a proper sea-dog.
Where's a burn?—she's first on the other side.
She flowed through fences like a piece of black wind.

But suddenly she was old and sick and crippled . . .

I grieved for Pollóchan when he took her for a stroll
And put his gun to the back of her head.

NORMAN MACCAIG

ANGUS'S DOG

Black collie, do you remember yourself?

Do you remember your name was Mephistopheles,
though (as if you were only a little devil)
everyone called you Meph?

You'd chase everything—sea gulls, motor cars,
jet planes. (It's said you once set off
after a lightning flash.) Half over a rock,
you followed the salmon fly arcing
through the bronze water. You loved everything.

except rabbits—though
you grinned away under the bed
when your master came home
drink taken. How you'd lay your head
on a visitor's knee and look up, so soulfully,
like George Eliot playing Sarah Bernhardt.

. . . Black Meph, how can you remember yourself
in that blank no-time, no-place where
you can't even greet your master
though he's there too?

NORMAN MACCAIG

MONGREL

There was a hi-jack, and a pop-star died
of self-indulgence. Politicians lied
to an investigating jury. Good and bad
men everywhere got murdered. The usual sad
day, should you be rash enough to think
of it. Except that from a swirling chink
of Glasgow fog, a black dog padded through
abandoned isolation. *Yes, you'll do, . . .*
his questioning tail and panting tongue proclaimed.
Woozy, this wag of energy was named.

He cut a dash of eager agitation
in search of dumb uncoloured information
about the human world he breathily loved,
wriggling affection till he was approved.
Wherever water gathered, he would swim,
his fur a forest shadow, nose a skim
of movement. Tracing miles of hidden scent,
he'd keep unearthing primitive content,
beyond the reach of our bewilderment.

As men are dropped from life before their time,
this dog was clawed by cancer in its prime;
and on the day it slipped to whence it came,
six terrorists crept out to kill or maim;
a child of five drowned in a shallow pool,
held under as it made its way from school;
while holy men ran up their prayers again
to shake the silent God of human shame.

A dog was dead, an ordinary day
compost upon the heap of history.

MAURICE LINDSAY

AN ELEGY FOR LEON, THE BRINDLED BOUVIER
(age 3½, dead of a heart attack)

Last thing at night I opened the front door;
dazily from his human fireside doze
my dog leapt out and rushed off to explore
the ancient world he brushed with his black nose;

a map of sniffs and scents beneath the ground—
signals, faint shuffles that I couldn't hear—
while I, supposedly the more profound,
gazed upwards at a sky filled far and near

with burnt-out proclamations of infinity.
Doubting his local darkness, green eyes stared
for reassurance, while this dog's divinity
pondered the *why* of breath we briefly shared.

MAURICE LINDSAY

66 Leon. Drawing by Morven Cameron.

LOST
Black Labrador Retriever
Answers to the name of Swimmer

Over the wall the leap was difficult,
awkward, more a scramble, managed
with the soft belly moulding to the stone.
Left by his master with a friend,
after much travel away from earth's smells,
from cabbage, rhubarb, decaying fungus at the gate,
leather, horse-dung, peat moor, whiff of gunshot,
brown burn, springy heather underfoot, from
sweet green grass, the wide strath, river, loch,
locked in a walled yard smelling of fish,
his kennel once a kiln for smoking haddock.
He barked till dark. At night the foghorn
boomed from the cliff. He howled back. Morning.
Down through the steep, twisting street he ran.
There was no doubting the way to the water.
'Fa echts ee?' asked Jeems, the fisherman,
baiting the great lines for his motor-boat;
'Thon's a richt blackie', as the dog hurried by,
slipping soft-footed over the moist pebbles,
then on with a bound to the launching pier,
and raced to a halt at the end. Gulls flew up
in a flurry about him. He sniffed the sea air.
It told tales unheard by him, but known
from his unknown past in traces of the brain,
buried memories waiting on the place, time,
the event, for transmission to nerves, to muscle, to act.
The acts in Labrador were for survival. In winter
the ground is iron. Along the irregular
coast-line serrated skerries, towering cliffs
threatened the small craft of the fishermen,
colonists of the indented bays. In summer cod
and haddock soused in brine, hung on frames
in the open air to dry to be held for winter.
Survival required co-operation. To the North
Eskimoes made huskies their agents for transport.
Fishermen on the Atlantic's face found allies

in dogs, strong and sinuous swimmers,
accurate, gentle-mouthed they took back
to the boats cod and haddock, even sea-trout
unmarked, through the wash and buffet of water.
They took the name of their place abroad—Labrador.
A boy with all the force he could, from the pier,
threw a stick out to sea. 'Get it! Go! Get it!'
Dog launched himself. The swell was slow, easy.
He was part of the heaving mass, yielding to it,
it yielding to him, salt sea lifted him up, buoyant.
Once, long time back, a child, girl, Morag.
slipped from the river bank to the Spey.
In a moment he was at her, held her clothes,
bunched, face above water, just, with difficulty,
pushed hard against the stream to outstretched hands.
'Swimmer,' she called him. So baptised the name stuck.
The stick offered itself to his jaws. But deep beneath
over the rocky sea-floor a shadow, a swift shape
that carried a command. Here was fish.
The stick floated free. He dived.
In Labrador the sea men knew the flow
and drag of currents, the force of seas
in narrow rents the boats must risk
to win the open sea, knew when to, when
not to, crew boats, men and dogs to hunt.
Boys on the shores of Scottish waters dive
into the breaking wave, giving their bodies
to the undertow, hold breath till sudden
the dynamic fails. Freed they burst surface
into generous air. They know where force
is spent, know too that the calm surface far out
does not disclose below the penetrating race that
holds and brings all caught to the blind depths.
From the pier he saw dog seize the stick,
saw it float free. No more.

Spiered the man: 'Fa echts ee?' "Nae man has me.
But the shavie watters o the cauld North Sea'.

GEORGE BRUCE

ZELDA
(for Doug and Deirdre Eadie)
'The yellow sun of the afternoon poured a warm
vanilla sauce in the window.'
Zelda Fitgerald, *Save Me the Waltz*

Cultural animal-owners
Make a song and dance,
Or a painting or a poem,
Of the naming of pets.
I knew a painter who called her cat
Heironymus
Though it came from Kensington
Not Hertogenbosch
And seemed content,
Not tormented by infernal visions.
A poet I knew
Called his goldfish
Ezra, after Pound, But the fish
Caused no commotion
And had no cantos to croon
As it opened and closed
Its golden mouth.
But the filmmaker friend
Who called his Labrador bitch
Zelda
Got nearer the mark.
Like her eccentric namesake,
Zelda was a character.
She would bark
And growl at strangers
Who knocked on the door
But once they entered,
Even unintroduced,
She would lavish love on them,
Lick their hands,
And nuzzle her head
Against their knees.
Like her celebrated namesake,
Zelda was a survivor.

Knocked down by a car,
In Kinlochewe,
She was pronounced
Unfit to live
By a vet
Who shook his head
Over her injuries.
But Zelda's humans
Refused to confirm
The death sentence
And gave Zelda another chance.
Her legs mended,
She bounced back,
She barked at strangers,
And loved them,
Even unintroduced.
I recall,
One fuzzy afternoon,
Going to see my filmmaker friend
At Cupar.
I knew, by the absence of the car,
Doug and Deirdre were away shopping.
Still, I knocked at the door,
And the barking started:
A barrage of barking,
A racket of snapping and snarling,
An outburst of canine abuse.
I pushed the door
And it opened
And Zelda licked my hand
And nuzzled against my knees.
When Doug returned and found me in
He asked, 'Who let you in?'
And I answered 'Zelda let me in.'
She lay doggo on the carpet but,
At the sound of her name,
One ear uplifted
And one eye scrutinised her humans.
Deirdre threw a rubber bone
To Zelda who chewed it
Dutifully.
That was Zelda.
I knew she was dead

When I knocked on the door one day
And heard no bark,
No scraping of paws,
Only the human footsteps.
The door opened
And closed
After a handshake,
Warm to the touch.
I said nothing
About the missing bitch.

ALAN BOLD

INSCRIPTION ON THE MONUMENT OF A NEWFOUNDLAND DOG

When some proud son of man returns to earth,
Unknown to glory, but upheld by birth,
The sculptor's art exhausts the pomp of woe,
And storied urns record who rest below:
When all is done, upon the tomb is seen,
Not what he was, but what he should have been:
But the poor dog, in life the firmest friend,
The first to welcome, foremost to defend,
Whose honest heart is still his master's own,
Who labours, fights, lives, breathes for him alone,
Unhonour'd falls, unnoticed all his worth,
Denied in heaven the soul he held on earth:
While man, vain insect! hopes to be forgiven,
And claims himself a sole exclusive heaven,
O man! thou feeble tenant of an hour,
Debased by slavery, or corrupt by power,
Who knows thee well must quit thee with disgust,
Degraded mass of animated dust!
Thy love is lust, thy friendship all a cheat,
Thy smiles hypocrisy, thy words deceit!
By nature vile, ennobled but by name,
Each kindred brute might bid thee blush for shame.
Ye! who perchance behold this simple urn,
Pass on—it honours none you wish to mourn:
To mark a friend's remains these stones arise;
I never knew but one,—and here he lies.

Newstead Abbey
30 November 1808.

LORD BYRON

67   The Black and White of it. Drawing by Morven Cameron.

GLOSSARY

Aa aa
Abeen above
Ablins perhaps
Aboon above
Ae one only
Ahint behind
Aiblins perhaps, possibly
Amangst among
Ance once
Ane one
Arase arose
Arn elder
Auld old
Ava at all
Awfae awful
Ay always

Bane bone
Bannock a thick, flat cake generally made of oatmeal
Bap a small breakfast roll
Baring clearing
Barra barrow
Bate bit
Bauld bold
Bawsant streaked white on the face
Beddy quick at hunter's cry
Beseekand beseeching
Beuk book
Bicker bowl, properly of wood
Bide stay
Biel house, shelter
Bigging house, building
Billie young fellow
Birses, set up his put himself in a rage
Blink moment
Blude blood
Bocking retching
Bonnie good-looking, handsome, fine
Bothie cottage in common

Bought sheep pen
Boune extent, width, land contained within certain boundaries
Bowes booze
Brae hill
Brak broke
Braw beautiful
Breechin breeches, the strap passed round the breech of a shaft horse to let it push forwards
Breenge move impetuously
Breid bread
Breith breath
Brocht brought
Brock badger
Broon brown
Bruik brook, bear
Brulzie to fight; disturbance
Bubblyjock turkey
Bude must
Buirdly stalwart
Bumclock humming, flying beetle
Buns hind quarters
Bure bore
By going passing by

Callan stripling, lad
Cannie comfortable, safe
Cannie unnatural
Cantie, cantry lively, cheerful
Cantrip trick
Carle man
Chackin biting
Chalmers rooms
Chiel man
Claes clothes
Clap shut
Cleuch precipice
Clink stroke of a bell

253

Close enclosed land, alley; tenement building
Clout blow
Coortin courting
Cosh neat, snug
Court-day rent day
Cowp overturn
Crabbet cross
Crack gossip
Craig crag, rocky place
Cratur creature
Crouse brisk, cheerful, lively
Cude could

Dae do
Daffin dallying
Dairk dark
Daur'd dared
Dee die
Deil devil
Deil-haet nothing at all
Denty large, plump, comely
Devil's pictur'd books playing cards
Dicht wipe
Dike wall of stone or turf
Disjaskit dejected
Dir do
Dizzen dozen; as much yarn as a woman might spin in a day
Doag dog
Doggis dogs
Doited stupid, confused
Doon down
Doot doubt
Dour sullen
Douth snug, comfortable
Dow to be able to
Dred feared
Drookit drenched
Drugg drag
Drumlie turbid, muddy
Duddie ragged
Dunt knock
Duntin knocking
Durst dared
Dyke wall of stone or turf

Ee, een eye, eyes
Eejit idiot
Eident industrious, diligent
Eild old

Embdy anybody
Eneugh enough
Esil vinegar
Ev'n down utter
Everilt every kind of

Fa echts ee? who owns you?
Fae foe; from
Fae's from us
Fain eager, fond, affectionate
Fairm farm
Fang catch
Fank an enclosure; a sheep cot
Fash bother, trouble
Fauld dike the wall of a sheep fold
Fauldin putting sheep in a pen or fold
Fawsont honest, seemly
Fechtin fighting
Feint not a one
Fell strange; eager, keen
Felny packy pash cruel, familiar head
Ferlie strange wonder
Fienta not a jot
Fike fidget
Fit foot
Flae flee
Flake hurdle
Flee in yir lug flea in your ear
Fleggit frightened
Flerr floor
Fike fuss
Flit move house or job
Flyte argue
Focht fought
Fock people, folk
Foo lang? how long?
Forbye besides
Forefoughten exhausted
Forrit forward
Fouchten worn out
Foumart an offensive person
Frier friar
Frog, fut syd wide sleeved garment reaching to the feet
Fu full
Fule fool
Fumart pole-cat
Furr for
Furth out
Fyke fidget
Fyle condemn; soil

Gaed went
Gallous gallows
Gang walk
Gar make, cause
Gart me caused me
Gash wise, sagacious
Gate way
Gauffin foolish, thoughtless
Gaun going
Gawsie plump, ample
Gear to gang wealth to go
Geed moved to one side, tilted
Gein giving
Geordie guinea
Gi', gied give, gave
Gin if
Girn snarl, complain
Girnel meal chest
Gloamin twilight
Goat got
Gollar'd growled, barked violently
Goun gown
Gowl howl, yell, growl
Granes groans
Grat cried, wept
Gree to agree, come to terms, be friends
Greesome gruesome
Greet cry
Grem, gram very eager; overjoyed, fervour; grandma
Grew greyhound
Grips gripes
Grushie thriving
Gurrin growling

Haddie haddock
Haet not a, damn all, devil a thing
Ha'folk servants
Haik hawk
Haith exclamation, such as Faith!
Hald hold
Hale whole
Han darg, daurk toil by hand
Haud hold;—*yer wheesht* be quiet
Hauds oot sets out
Haur cold, easterly wind bringing mist
Heck exclamation of surprise, contempt
Heid head
Heezle wheezle
Hie high
Hiest gree highest degree

Hing hang
Hizzie young woman
Hoggie young sheep
Hoodie hooded or carrion crow
Houn'd chased, pursued
Howcket dug out
Howe hollow
Howckan digging out
Hull hill
Hurdies buttocks, hips
Hurled threw
Huv have

Ilka every
Ill-fauredness ugliness
Ingle fire

Jad jade
Jalouse guess
Jink dodge, swerve quickly aside

Kane rent in kind
Keek peep
Ken, Kent know, knew
Kep keep
Kinuffa kind of a
Kirk church
Kirns harvest feasts
Knawin known
Knowe little hill, knoll
Koost cast, threw
Kye cows

Laid water course leading to a mill
Lang long
Lang syne long ago
Lap jumped
Lauchin' laughing
Laun land
Leal loyal
Leddy lady
Leear liar
Lee-lang live long
Leuchar lower
Leuks looks
Licht light
Lickit licked
Lien lane
Limmer mistress, woman
Loan lane, pasture
Loot let, allowed

Loun   rascal
Loup   jump
Lowp't   leapt
Lowse   loose
Lugs   ears
Luntan   smoking

Main,-e   complaint
Mair   more
Marra   match, equal
Maukin   hare
Mawkit   maggot infested
Me down thring   throw me down
Meikle   large
Merr   more
Messan,-in   lap-dog, tinker's cur
Micht   might
Midden   dunghill
Mind   remember
Mirk   darkness, night
Modewurks   moles
Moose   mouse
Mou   mouth
Moudies   moles
Muckle   much
Mune   moon
Murn   mourn

Na   not
Nane   none
Nappy   strong ale
Neibers   neighbours
Nevoy   nephew
Noddle   head
Nout   sheep
Nurr'd   growled, snarled

Oan   on
Oaxter   armpit
Or   before
Orra   odd
Ower, owre   too, over, too often

Painch   paunch
Palmie   blow on the palm of the hand
Parliamentin   Member of Parliament
Pass off the town   leave town
Pattit   patted
Pauted   pawed
Pechan   stomach
Pechin'   puffing

Peewee   lap-wing
Peghan   stomach
Perquier   accurately
Pethers   pedlars
Pettricks   partridges
Pish't   urinated
Pit   put
Pit aboot   disconcerted
Plaid   an outer loose weave of tartan worn
   by Highlanders
Pleugh   plough
Ploy   amusement
Poind   seize
Poke   bag
Poortith   poverty
Pucklie   a small quantity
Puir   poor
Put me furth   turn me out

Quaich   a two-eared drinking cup

Racked   wrenched
Ranting   romping, roistering, rollicking
Rashes   rushes
Ream   froth
Redd   settled
Reek   smoke
Remeed   remedy, relief
Repair   turn
Rerr   rare
Richts   rights
Riever   robber
Rigg   ridge
Ripe   search thoroughly
Rive   tear
Roon   round
Rottens   rats
Rowed   rolled
Rowtan   lowing, bellowing
Rue the race   circumstance
Rug   unfair advantage; tug, pull
Run-deil   thorough, downright devil
Rung   staff
Ruse   complaints, regrets

Saam   psalm
Sair   greatly
Sair-wark   heavy work
Sang   song
Sanna   shall not
Saut   salt

Schaw   show
Schuil   school
Scour, scour'd   scamper,-ed
Scrawghin   shrieking
Scrog   stunted bush, shrub, branch
Sen syne   long ago since
Sery   cunning, wise
Shair's   sure as
Shank   leg
Shavie   deceitful
Shaws   stalks
Sheddin'   dividing stock into different pens
Sheenin'   shining
Sheugh   ditch, drain
Shoon   shoes
Sib   related to
Skailed   scattered
Skaith   damage, injury
Skaithly   injurious, hurtful
Skelpit   ran, dashed
Skite   blow, clip
Slaps   glances
Slaverin   slobbering
Slee   sly
Slochk   gully
Sma   small
Smeddum   spirit, force of character
Smiddie   forge, smithy
Smytrie   a collection of small (children), swarm
Snag   a branch broken from a tree
Snash   abuse
Sneck   cupboard latch
Sneeshin-mull   snuff-mill
Snirtit   snorted
Snook't   scented (as a dog does)
Snoovin   sneaking
Snowk   sniffle, snuffle
Sonsie   cheerful, good tempered, pleasant
Sooth   facts
Soudan   southern
Souple   supple
Sowther   to solder
Spaul   shoulder, forequarter
Speel   climb
Speir at   ask
Speug   sparrow
Spiered   asked
Sprint   sprang, leapt
Spurr'd   scratched
Stane   stone

Stan't   stand
Stechin   stuffing
Steek   stitch; burr; shut
Steer   disturb
Steghan   stuffing with food
Stent   rents in kind, taxes
Stirk   steer
Stoiter   stagger, stumble, totter
Stot   young bull or ox
Stoot   stout
Stroan't   urinate
Stude   stood
Sturt   trouble, annoy
Suner   sooner
Suppie   little mouthful
Syke   small rill, stream, water course often in boggy ground which dries up in summer
Syne   then

Tae   to
Tae win doon   to get down to
Tattie scone   potato scone
Tawtied   matted, shaggy
Teug   tug
Thack an' raep   thatch and rope; home comforts
Thae   those
Thick thegither   friendly
Thocht   thought
Thole   bear, endure
Thrang   busy
Thrangity   bustle
Thraw   throw
Thrawn   obstinate
Thraward   perverse
Throch the scrog   right through the shrubs
Throple   windpipe, throat
Throw   through
Tike   tyke, cur
Till   to
Tilt   trouble
Timmer   timber, wood
Tip   tup, ram
Tither   other
Tod   fox
Tooly   broil, fight
Toom   empty
Torve   trouble
Tousled   ruffled
Touzie, -y   rough, shaggy

Towsy rough, shaggy
Traiv'lin travelling
Treid tread
Tulzeour bully
Tummle tumble

Unco unknown, strange
Unco sair very hard
Ur or

Vier compete with

Wad would
Wadna would not
Wae, waesome sad, sorrowful
Wait nocht whare do not know where to turn
Wally porcelain, china, glazed earthenware
Wame stomach
Wan one
Wark work
Warst worst
Warstled wrestled, tussled
War wrangit was wronged
Waur worse
Wean child
Wearin' guarding
Wedder whether
Weel well
Weil-bieldit well protected
Weepies turnips, potatoes; common ragwort
Weet wet

Whalpet whelped
Whame to whom
Whaup curlew
Whaur where
Wheen a lot of, number, quantity
Wheesht quiet
Whiffle drive before the wind
Whiles sometimes
Whill till
Whilk which
Whin gorse-bush
Whing'd whined, whimpered
Whinkin' barking or yapping in a suppressed way
Whummeled became upset
Whustlin' whistling
Whuttled whittled
Wight fellow
Wirriand worrying
Wisnae wasn't
Wonner wonder
Worl' world
Wouched barked
Wrang wrong; hurt, injure
Wrocht wrought
Wull will

Yalla yellow
Yett gate
Yirth earth
Yowe ewe
Yowling yelp, howl
Y'urnie you are not

INDEX OF LITERARY SOURCES

The editors and publishers are grateful to all authors, publishers and other copyright holders who have given permission for us to print copyright material, and for permission to use copyright visual material. Every effort has been made to trace copyright holders. Where this has proved impossible, we offer our apologies and hope that our use of the material will nevertheless prove welcome.

Authors whose work is included in this anthology are indexed in alphabetical order, together with the title of the source from which they were taken.

ANNAND, J K: 'Dog Show' (*Thrice to Show Ye*, Macdonald, 1979)

ANONYMOUS Author of *Albania*: 'Hounds and Horsemen' (*Albania: A Poem*, 1737)

ANON: 'The Chip Shop' (*The Singing Kettle*, ed Cilla Fisher and Art Trezise, Lynn Breeze, Gary Coupland, Kettle Records, 1985)
     'Dog in the Midden' (*Scottish Nursery Rhymes*, ed T Ritchie, 1964)
     'Ma Bonnie Doggie' (*Scottish Nursery Rhymes*, ed T Ritchie, 1964)
     'I Had a Wee Dog' (*Sandy Candy and Other Scottish Nursery Rhymes*, ed Norah and William Montgomerie, Hogarth, 1948)
     'Tailpiece' (*Scottish Nursery Rhymes*, ed T Ritchie, 1964)

BECKWITH, Lilian: 'The Spuddy' (*The Spuddy*, Hutchinson and Co, 1974)

BOLD, Alan: 'Cat and Dog' and 'Zelda' (The Author)

BENDON, Chris: 'If Life Has Any Meaning' (*Lines Review*, Macdonald, 1988)

BRIDIE, James: 'The Three Tykes' (*Tedious and Brief*, Constable, 1944)

BROWN, George Mackay: 'Wolf' (*A Scottish Bestiary*, The Author)

BROWN, Dr John: 'Dry Humour', 'Toby', 'Bob', 'Peter', 'Plea for an Edinburgh Dog Home' and 'A Dog Fight' (*Horae Subsecivae*, 1858–1882)

BROWN, Hilton: 'Glen, a Sheepdog' (*Punch*, 1937)

BRUCE, George: 'The Life and Death of Spicey' and 'Lost' (The Author)

BURNS, Robert: 'The Twa Dogs' (*Poems and Songs*, ed J Kingsley, 1969)

BURNSIDE, John: 'Tundra's Edge' (*The Hoop*, Carcanet Press, 1988)

BYRON, Lord: 'Inscription on the Monument of a Newfoundland Dog' (*Poetical Works*, ed J L Robertson, 1894)

CAMPBELL, Donald: 'Donald Fraser's Dog' (The Author)

CARLYLE, Jane and Thomas: 'Literary Dogs' (*Letters* and *The Carlyles at Home*, The Holme, Oxford University Press, 1965)

CARMICHAEL, Alexander: 'The Dog' (*Carmina Gadelica*, I C Smith translation, Ward Lock Educational Co Ltd, 1982)

COCKER, W D: 'Wee Freenly Doug', 'The Lost Collie' and 'Dandie' (*Further Poems in Scots and English*, 1935 and *Random Rhymes*, 1935 Brown Son and Fergusson Ltd)

DAVIDSON, John: 'Two Dogs' (*The Poems of John Davidson*, ed A Turnbull, Scottish Academic Press, 1973)

DUNBAR, William: 'Of James Dog' (Poems of William Dunbar, ed Mackay Mackenzie, 1932)

FERGUSSON, David: *Scottish Proverbs* (ed E Beveridge, Scottish Text Society, Blackwood, 1916)

FIDLER, Kathleen: 'Flash's Training Begins' (*Flash the Sheepdog* Canongate, 1984)

GARIOCH, Robert: 'Nemo Canem Impune Lacessit' and 'The Dog' (*Collected Poems*, Macdonald, 1983)

GILLIES, Valerie: 'The Greyhound' and 'Deerhounds' (*Each Bright Eye*, Canongate, 1977); 'Hounds Leaping' (*Bed of Stone* Canongate, 1984)

HAMILTON, William of Gilbertfield: 'The Last Dying Words of Bonnie Heck' (*Scottish Poetry of the Eighteenth Century*, ed George Eyre Todd, 1896)

HOGG, James: 'Sirrah' and 'Hector' (*Blackwood's Magazine*, 1818); 'The Author's Address to his Auld Dog Hector' (*The Mountain Bard*, 1807) and 'Dusty' (*Scottish Pastorals*, ed E Paine, Stirling University Press, 1988)

JACOB, Violet: 'The Yellow Dog' (*The Lum Hat and Other Stories*, ed R Garden, Aberdeen University Press, 1982)

KEYS, Bill: 'A Doug' (The Author)

LAUDER, Sir Thomas Dick: 'Collies', 'The Last Wolf' (*Scottish Rivers*, 1847);

LINDSAY, Maurice: 'The Ballad of the Hare and the Bassethound' (*The French Mosquitoes' Woman*, Hale, 1985); 'Mongrel', (*Collected Poems*, ed A Scott, Paul Harris 1979); 'Childless' (*Requiem for a Sexual Athlete*, Hale, 1988); 'Celia, the Wife of the Laird' (The Author); 'Elegy for a Brindled Bouvier' (The Author)

LOCKHART, John Gibson: 'Washington Irving Visits Abbotsford' (*Life of Scott*, 1838)

LOCHHEAD, Liz: 'It's a Dog's Life' and 'Midsummer Night's Dog' (*True Confessions*, Polygon Books, 1985)

MACBETH, George: 'At Cruft's' (*Poems 1958-1969*, Macmillan, 1970)

MACCAIG, Norman: 'Praise of a Collie' and 'Angus's Dog' (*Collected Poems*, Chatto and Windus, 1985)

MACGREGOR, Forbes: 'Greyfriars Bobby' (*The Scots Magazine*, 1988)

MACINTYRE, Duncan Ban: 'Elegy on a dog that went through the Ice' 'Latho do Phàdraig a' Sealg' (from *The Songs of Duncan Bàn Macintyre*, ed Angus Macleod, Scottish Gaelic Text Society, 1952)

MACLEAN, Sorley: 'Dogs and Wolves' (*Scottish Verse*, ed D Young, Nelson, 1952)

MONTGOMERIE, Norah and William: 'Finn and the Grey Dog' (*The Well at the World's End*, Canongate, 1985)

MONTROSE, Marquis of: 'Epitaph on a Dog' (*Scottish Poetry of the Seventeenth Century*, ed Eyre Todd, 1896)

MORGAN, Edwin: 'An Addition to the Family', 'Trio' (*Poems of Thirty Years*, Carcanet Press, 1982)

OUTRAM, George: 'What Will I do Gin My Doggie Dee?' (*Lyrics Legal and Miscellaneous*, 1874)

RAMSAY, Allan: 'The Broad Hint' and 'The Tykes Tooly' (*Poems*, Scottish Text Society, 1972)

ROBERTSON, Bell: 'My Dog and I' (*Greig-Duncan Folksong Collection*, Vol 2, Aberdeen University Press, 1984)

RUSSELL, J: 'Dogs and Wolves' (translated from the Gaelic, of Sorley Maclean)

SCOTT, Sir Walter: 'The Wild Huntsman', extracts from 'Guy Mannering', and 'The Lady of the Lake' (*Poems; Letters*, ed Grierson, 1932. Notes Corson, 1979)

SMITH, Alexander: 'Otter Hunt' (*A Summer in Skye*, 1857)

SMITH, Iain Crichton: 'Elegy on a Dog that went through the Ice' (translated from the Gaelic of Duncan Bàn Macintyre); 'The dog runs away' (The Village and Other Poems, Carcanet, 1989)

SOUTAR, William: 'Paiks for A' and 'Roon, Roon, Roon' (*Poems of William Soutar*, ed W Aitken, Scottish Academic Press, 1988)

STEPHEN, David: 'Not the Word for It'. 'The Cleverest—and Laziest—of Dogs', 'Lisa' (*The World Outside*, Gordon Wright, 1983)

STEVENSON, Robert Louis: 'The Oldest Herd in the Pentlands' (*Memories and Portraits*, Tusitala Edition Vol xxiv, 1924) and 'The Character of Dogs' (Longman's Magazine, 1893)

TANNAHILL, Robert: 'Towser' (*The Poems and Songs* of Robert Tannahill, ed David Semple, 1875)

TANNER Manuscript: 'Faithful to the End' (*MS 78 F 129*, The Bodleian Library, Oxford)

TAYLOR, John: 'Hunting in the Highlands' (*The Penniless Pilgrim*, 1618)

THOMSON, Derrick: 'The Black Dog' (from *Leabhar na Feinne*, tr The Author)

THOMSON, James: 'Against and For Hunting' (Autumn, *The Seasons*, 1730)

TRANTER, Nigel: 'Lost and Found Dog' (*Tinker Tess*, Dobson, 1967)

URQUHART, Fred: 'The Wedding' (*Palace of Green Days*, 1979) abridged by the author